Introduction to

Personal Financial Planning

A Practical Approach

Second Edition

Alexander G. Kondeas, PhD, MA, MBA, CFP®
Associate Professor of Financial Planning
Winston-Salem State University

David B. Stewart, PhD, MBA, MS
Associate Professor of Finance
Winston-Salem State University

Nicholas A. Daves, MBA
Director, Center of Excellence in Financial Services
Instructor of Finance
Winston-Salem State University

Cover image © Shutterstock, Inc.

Kendall Hunt
publishing company

www.kendallhunt.com
Send all inquiries to:
4050 Westmark Drive
Dubuque, IA 52004-1840

ISBN 978-1-4652-3137-6

Printed in the United States of America
10 9 8 7 6 5 4 3 2 1

Contents

About the Authors

Alexander G. Kondeas, PhD, MA, MBA, CFP®
Associate Professor of Financial Planning
Winston-Salem State University

Alexander Kondeas holds a PhD in Economics with a Finance concentration from Auburn University, an MA in Economics and an MBA with a Finance concentration from the University of South Florida, and an undergraduate degree in Accounting from the Technological Educational Institute of Larissa, Greece. He has taught at Auburn University, Greensboro College, Guilford College, and Winston-Salem State University. His research interests include Financial Planning, International Finance, and Macroeconomics. His research is published in the International Journal of Business and Social Science, Real World Economic Review, Academy of Business Journal, Journal of Business and Behavioral Sciences, and Applied Financial Economics Letters. He is a Certified Financial Planner™.

David B. Stewart, PhD, MBA, MS
Associate Professor of Finance
Winston-Salem State University

David Stewart holds a PhD in Finance from the University of Tennessee, an MBA with a Finance concentration from Indiana University, and an MS and BS in Statistics from Purdue University. As the former Chair of the Department of Economics and Finance, he led Winston-Salem State University to register the Personal Finance Degree Program with the Certified Financial Planner Board of Standards, Inc. His research interests include Financial Planning, Market Efficiency, and International Finance. His research is published in the International Journal of Finance, American Economist, and Economic System, among others.

Nicholas A. Daves, MBA
Director, Center of Excellence in Financial Services
Instructor of Finance
Winston-Salem State University

Nicholas Daves holds an MBA from the University of North Carolina at Chapel Hill, and a BA in History with a minor in Economics from Davidson College. He has more than forty years experience in commercial banking with North Carolina National Bank (now part of Bank of America), Northwestern Bank (now part of Wells Fargo), and as the founding president and CEO of Enterprise National Bank in Winston-Salem, North Carolina, which later merged with Lexington State Bank. Following his retirement from Lexington State Bank in 2007, Daves joined the faculty of the School of Business and Economics at Winston-Salem State University. He is the Program Director for the university's undergraduate Personal Finance Degree Program, which is registered with the Certified Financial Planner Board of Standards, Inc. In addition, he is the Director of the Center of Excellence in Financial Services.

Preface

We decided to write this book for use in our Personal Financial Planning course, which serves as the introductory course to the Personal Finance Degree Program at Winston-Salem State University. We aimed for it to be concise, rigorous, yet exciting to students exposed to finance and personal finance material for the first time. It has to be rigorous to serve the needs of students who will follow through the program to seek careers as financial planners or advisors. It has to be concise to offer a real alternative to the 700-page financial textbooks, that instructors cannot teach and students cannot complete in a semester. Equally important, the book has to be exciting to read and make economics and finance material relevant to readers' lives. To this end, every topic of the book is infused with real life examples and practical applications, allowing students to realize how they can personally benefit from the material they study. Furthermore, throughout the chapters the book follows a typical family, the "Milfords," showing how each topic addresses a different aspect or need in their financial life. The Milfords Practical Applications leave students with a lasting impression of the integrating approach of the financial planning process.

The textbook is suitable for both Personal Finance and Personal Financial Planning courses. Instructors can easily adjust the rigor of the material to suit the needs of their audience. For courses that are part of a Financial Planning Curriculum however, instructors may want to cover all the Practical Applications and end of chapter Review Questions, to further raise their students' skill level. Instructors have access to the Instructor Manual with solutions to chapter Review Questions, the PowerPoint slides which follow the material in the chapters, and the Test Bank with questions and problems similar to the end of chapter Review Questions.

The second edition updates chapters, PowerPoint slides and Instructor Manual to the latest income tax, Retirement, and estate tax changes.

We would like to thank the extremely capable and patient people at Kendall Hunt for putting this project together. Specifically, we would like to thank Nick Beitzel, for convincing us to write this book, Lacey Reynolds and Abby Davis for putting everything together for us, Natalie White for her encouragement and support throughout the process.

CHAPTER ONE

Personal Financial Planning

1.1 Introduction

Personal financial planning is the process of gathering and analyzing financial data to develop a set of strategies that form an integrated plan to help people achieve their financial goals. The focus of the process is in defining the individual's goals, and then putting together a plan that includes all aspects of one's financial life in an integrated way. While the plan may consist of strategies addressing specific areas of personal finance, like the budget, investments, taxes, insurance, retirement or estate matters, each strategy is carefully evaluated for its side effects to all other areas of the person's finances.

For example, recommending to a client to purchase disability insurance will consume cash flows which otherwise would have been invested in a tax favored retirement account. As a result, not only will she be saving less for her retirement, but she will also be facing higher income taxes, which could further reduce her savings.

It is precisely this spillover effect of financial decisions to other areas of personal finance that complicates matters, and prompts people to seek the advice of a financial planner.

1.1.1 The Financial Planning Profession

Personal financial planning as a distinct profession is relatively new. Until the late 1960s a financial planner was someone who sold insurance, annuities, securities or tax shelters. Consequently, stock brokers, insurance agents, accountants and even lawyers could all claim to be financial advisors. Their limited area of expertise, however, did not allow for an integrated approach to financial planning. Thus there was no single source to coordinate and address all aspects of an individual's financial needs. Moreover, there were no industry standards for education, professionalism or ethics.

In the early 1970s, the Society for Financial Counseling Ethics was established in Colorado to recognize professionalism and provide education beyond what life insurance and mutual fund companies provided to their employees and agents. The College for Financial Planning was established in Denver to offer self-study courses on client needs and objectives, fee-based financial advice and a planning process. Sections of the original curriculum covered fundamentals, money management, financial media, investment models, effective planning considerations and counseling/consumer behavior. At the completion of the courses, students who successfully passed an examination earned the title "Certified Financial Planner™." The title was first awarded in 1973.

Both the National Association of Securities Dealers (NASD) and the Securities and Exchange Commission (SEC) cautioned that the planner designation implied a degree of expertise that many broker-dealers did not possess, and for them the title "representative" was preferable. The NASD and SEC agreed that the CFP® designation could only be used by someone certified by the College for Financial Planning.

Meanwhile, the terrible stock market of the early 1970s, and the adoption of individual retirement accounts in 1974 and 401(k) accounts in 1981, changed the way people were investing and planning for their retirement. More people realized they need professional help with their financial affairs.

By 1985 the College for Financial Planning had thousands of students, and various universities began to offer CFP courses for academic credit. In the early 1990s, the Certified Financial Planner™ Board of Standards was established in Denver. Subsequently, the organization moved its headquarters to Washington, D.C., its current location, in order to have a closer relationship with federal financial industry regulators.

Today the CFP Board of Standards has over 300 registered programs at colleges and universities across the country, and there are over 65,000 CFP® certificants, who practice according to the CFP Code of Ethics and Professional Responsibility, Rules of Conduct, and Financial Planning Practice Standards.

Compensation

With the advent of the term Certified Financial Planner™, emphasis was placed on the planning process in addition to the sale of financial products. The process is a comprehensive engagement between a planner and a client which may or may not include the sale of financial products by the planner. If no products are sold, the planner is designated as a "fee only" planner, and compensation is based on the scope and complexity of the plan. However, some planners may receive their compensation from commissions on products sold and from plan development. Full disclosure of a planner's compensation is covered in the initial step of a planning engagement. The following table shows the 2011 Financial Planning Association fees-survey results.

Fee Charged per Type of Compensation	Mean	Median
Typical hourly rate	$192.70	$180
Typical annual retainer fee amount	$4,998.85	$2,500
Typical fee for a comprehensive plan	$2,876.32	$2,000
Typical fee for a subject specific plan	$990.51	$750

2011, FPA Research Center, Financial Planning Association

The Fiduciary Standard

All individuals who have earned the Certified Financial Planner™ designation are committed to place the interests of their clients first, which is referred to as the fiduciary standard. This means that in choosing between two financial products, one of which better meets the client's needs, but offers lower compensation to the planner, and another financial product which is suitable (but not the best available), but which offers higher compensation to the planner, the choice is the better product. In the long run, placing the client's interest first will solidify the client-planner relationship, and any loss of current income will be more than made up by future sales opportunities and referrals of others by a satisfied client. The CFP Board Code of Ethics and the fiduciary standard are established for the ultimate protection of clients. It is therefore to the best interest of clients to seek financial advisors who are committed to this standard.

1.2 The Financial Planning Process

The process of financial planning consists of six distinct steps, which are described below. Financial planning touches all financial aspects of an individual's life including budgeting, insurance, investments, retirement, borrowing money, income tax planning and estate planning. Frequently individuals begin the planning process with a focus on saving for retirement, but in most instances, the other topics are so closely interrelated that they are drawn into a comprehensive plan. Let's look at each of the six steps in more detail.

Step One: The Initial Meeting—Establishing the Advisor-Client Relationship

The CFP Board of Standards has established a Code of Ethics and Professional Responsibility, which details required disclosures by the planner in this meeting. The planning process begins when a planner and the potential client meet to discuss the client's needs and financial goals. A major goal of this meeting is for the parties to establish a bond of trust. The planner should listen carefully to the potential client's comments and begin to establish the framework of the relationship. The planner should provide the client with an explanation of all the steps in the planning process, including the needed documents from the client, how the planner will use the information, the range of services provided and the estimated time for completing the plan.

In addition, during the initial meeting the planner must discuss his or her background and educational qualifications, as well as the method of compensation for the services provided. If the planner anticipates the need to bring in specialists, the projected costs should also be disclosed. At the conclusion of this first step, the planner (or advisor) will prepare a letter agreement outlining the expectations of both parties to the relationship, and submit it for the client's approval along with a compensation disclosure document like the SEC Form ADV Part 2.

Step Two: Setting Goals and Gathering Data

This step may actually begin at the conclusion of step one, assuming that the advisor-client relationship is clearly defined. Few people bring specific financial goals to the table at the beginning of this step. It is the duty of the advisor to ask the client about existing goals and to inquire as to other related topics. For example, a client may have a general goal of having enough assets to retire early. The goal to retire early is vague, and the advisor should ask questions to sharpen the goal to retiring at a specific age and with a specific post-retirement standard of living comparable to pre-retirement. The vague goal should evolve into narrow objectives involving appropriate investments, education funding, income tax planning, individual and company-provided retirement plans, life, disability and long-term care insurance.

Once the client's goals have been defined, the advisor will ask for comprehensive and specific financial information using a multipage fact finder form. See the Appendix at the end of this chapter for an abbreviated fact finder form. The information requested should have a direct relationship to the goals to be included in the plan. Some of this information will be highly confidential, and this is where the trust established in the first step becomes important. The client will be asked to provide at minimum the following:

- Family relationships (children, spouse, parents, special needs children and adults)
- Bank and brokerage account statements
- Evidences of ownership such as deeds and vehicle titles
- Recent statements from creditors
- Insurance policies (life, disability, property and long-term care)
- Estate planning documents such as wills, powers of attorney, powers of appointment, health care powers of attorney, living wills and DNR orders

- Separation and divorce documents
- Employee benefits statements

This is no small task to accomplish as some potential clients may be either reluctant to submit all necessary documents (perhaps concerned about privacy issues), or may not be well organized to have these documents readily available. In the case where a client does not provide the planner with a number of the necessary documents, the planner has two choices. If the planner feels the missing documents are an indication of a lack of trust from the client side, the planner can release the client from their agreement and refer him/her to another financial planner. If the planner feels the missing documentation is due to the client's poor organizational skills, the planner can proceed with the analysis of the incomplete set of information, but inform the client of potential revisions and amendments to the plan once the missing documentation is submitted.

Another responsibility of the advisor in step two is to determine the client's risk tolerance. This can be accomplished by asking the client to complete a survey, which the advisor will use to detect the client's true risk preferences. This way the planner can recommend appropriate financial products, while avoiding those which will expose the client to an uncomfortable level of risk. Risk is discussed in the next section, and more thoroughly in Chapter 7.

Step Three: Analyzing and Evaluating the Data Collected

Logically, in the next step the advisor uses the information gathered to develop a complete picture of the client's current financial situation. This includes assets and liabilities, income and cash flow, gaps in insurance coverage, participation in employer-provided retirement plans and the adequacy of estate planning. Strengths and weaknesses observed from the data are to be evaluated in preparation for the advisor's recommendations on how to achieve the goals agreed upon in step two. For example, the net worth statement analysis could reveal lack of liquidity, excessive concentration of assets in one asset category or improperly structured debt. The income statement analysis may reveal unstable sources of income and disproportioned increases over time in some expense categories. Debt payments can be evaluated and possible alternatives to structure the debt may be identified.

It is entirely possible that the advisor will come to the conclusion that the client's current goals cannot be achieved therefore both goals and objectives may have to be changed. For example, if the achievement of an early retirement goal is unrealistic, the advisor may have to counsel the client for a delayed retirement, major changes in savings and investment strategies, or a downgrade of the expected standard of living at retirement.

Step Four: Developing and Presenting the Plan

In this step the advisor will use all of the information gathered and the analysis performed to develop a realistic plan of action for the client. Even with the educational requirements to become and remain a CFP®, few advisors will have the expertise needed to cover all aspects of a plan. It may be necessary to involve attorneys, accountants, insurance agents and other specialists, as was mentioned in step one.

Presenting the plan to the client is a critical step in the process. The advisor should explain all aspects of the plan and how each goal and objective will be handled. Importantly, the client must adopt the plan and agree to implement it!

If the advisor offers financial products which meet the fiduciary standard of care and help the client achieve agreed-upon objectives, the advisor will propose that the client purchase these products. A fee only advisor will just recommend trusted sources for acquisition of the necessary products by the client.

Step Five: Implementing the Plan

A plan is useless unless it is acted upon. The advisor's responsibility is to develop action steps, a timeline for completion and specific responsibilities. For example, a recommendation might be for the client to change the way an asset is owned to make transfer of the asset at the client's death easier. Another recommendation could be for the client to transfer ownership of a life insurance policy to a trust or to another person. Restructuring debt for lower payments and better income tax treatment of interest could mean that the client should refinance a home loan. A client without a current valid will and other estate planning documents would be directed to prepare and execute these documents in consultation with an estate planning attorney. Identified gaps in insurance coverage would be closed with modified or new policies. Once the duties have been completed, the advisor would make a final check to be sure everything is in order. The initial phase of the planning process will then be complete.

Step Six: Periodic Review of the Plan

If the recommended actions have been implemented, the client should begin to make progress toward the goals in the plan. If the relationship with the advisor is on-going, the advisor will revisit the plan from time to time to determine its effectiveness. If the plan is working satisfactorily and both advisor and client agree on this, no changes will be necessary. Otherwise, goals and strategies will need to be revised.

Major life events such as marriage, divorce, births and deaths of family members, serious illness, job loss or retirement call for a serious review of the plan. Unforeseen circumstances can mean major goal changes and revisions, and the process will begin again at step one. Obviously, the time and effort required for revisions will be much less than in the initial process.

1.2.1 Client and Planner Attitudes, Values and Behaviors

Client Risk Tolerance

Are you a risk taker or a risk avoider? Your answer will influence which strategies an advisor will choose to achieve your financial objectives. Initially, you might think risk in personal financial planning mainly applies to the likelihood of having a loss of principal in an investment. Your choice to take or avoid risk covers investments, but it also involves ownership of property, potential liability if you cause injury to another person or its property, exposure to health care costs, loss of income due to disability or premature death and the effects of inflation, interest rates and economic conditions.

Your choices regarding risk are influenced by your estimate of potential gain or loss and the likelihood and magnitude of both. Your estimate of your tolerance for risk may be rational and supported by quantitative evidence. On the other hand, you may think that certain risks only apply to others and not to you. This behavior simply indicates denial. You may be fearful of risks because of circumstances in your life where you have taken losses or observed others taking losses. Or you may be a "thrill seeker," willing to accept risks in nearly all aspects of your life. Day trading in the stock market is an example of thrill seeking behavior, in which gains and losses accompany a high level of both risk and volatility.

Major factors which influence your risk tolerance are age, gender, marital status, occupation (particularly your method of compensation, i.e. salary or commission), wealth, education and your birth order among siblings. Typically, older persons, females, married individuals, less educated individuals, salaried earners and firstborn children tend to exhibit lower risk tolerances. Wealth is not a very reliable predictor of risk tolerance, because risk exposure is meaningful when measured not in absolute dollars at risk, but as a percentage of assets at risk to total assets owned by a person. In other words, you and Tiger Woods are betting $1,000 each on the outcome of a football game. You cannot afford to lose this amount, while it is a rounding error to Tiger's fortune. Who is the bigger risk taker between the two of you?

Obviously, your tolerance for risk depends on many factors. One of the most important and difficult tasks facing a financial advisor is to assess a client's appetite for risk. An accurate estimate of client risk tolerance will influence the advisor's recommendations in all aspects of a comprehensive financial plan. Recall that in step four of the financial planning process the advisor must present a realistic, custom-designed plan to the client that reflects the client's true risk tolerance.

The risk assessment process consists of more than just one measurement. The advisor should carefully observe the client in unstructured conversations, noticing both verbal and nonverbal behaviors. Verbal characteristics such as talking too much or too little can indicate client fear and uncertainty. Straightforward comments can indicate confidence and risk awareness. Nonverbal behaviors include tone of voice and body language, both of which should be incorporated into the verbal aspect of risk assessment. The advisor should look for inconsistencies between verbal and nonverbal behaviors. This part of the assessment process is qualitative, not based on numerical scoring.

A second aspect of client risk assessment is quantitative which involves questionnaires (see Chapter 7). A client may be asked to rank the importance of investment goals such as safety of principal, liquidity, current income, growth or income tax efficiency. Another question may ask for a client's reaction to a risk such as making a high risk but potentially rewarding investment. The range of responses could run from "no anxiety" to "unable to sleep at night." A properly constructed and scored questionnaire will help the advisor in putting together a plan that the client understands and accepts.

Effective Advisor-Client Communication

An effective advisor must have good listening skills, which involve paying close attention to what the client says and does, making sure that all communication is clearly understood. The advisor must use appropriate questioning techniques. An advisor's question which can be answered "yes" or "no" will not bring forth much information. An open ended question, however, will invite the client to open up and share a wide range of attitudes and information. Look for example at the following questions:

Do you plan to retire at age 65? (Yes or No type of question)
How do you plan to spend your time when you retire? (Open ended type of question)

An advisor may encounter resistance from clients on some particularly sensitive topics, such as illness and dying, marital stress and relationship problems with children. When this happens, it is important for the advisor to be nonjudgmental, concerned and able to explain the importance of addressing these topics in the financial plan. The bond of trust between a client and advisor must be established early in the planning process and maintained throughout the entire period of the relationship. A financial advisor must have good interviewing, counseling and advising skills to enable a potential client to develop and maintain this high level of confidence.

"Interviewing" is an information gathering process involving asking and answering specific questions. This is the basic technique used in steps one and two of the planning process. The fact finder form in step two may be completed only by the client, but most often it is completed when the advisor and the client are meeting face-to-face and the advisor asks the client a series of questions.

"Counseling" is the process of addressing the client's concerns and questions in a way that builds the bond of trust. Constructive feedback by the advisor will help the client understand his or her current situation, and how realistic his or her stated goals are. One of the great benefits for a client working with a financial planner is that the client receives an objective expert third party opinion about his or her financial situation and future prospects.

"Advising" is the other kind of communication between an advisor and client. This involves specific recommendations and strategies the advisor offers to the client. For example, an advisor may advocate and explain the need for the client to purchase additional insurance or to shift an investment choice to a better alternative in order to achieve the objectives of the plan.

1.3 The CFP Board of Standards Code of Ethics and Professional Responsibility

Earning the right to claim the designation Certified Financial Planner™ requires the certificant to (1) possess a bachelor's degree from an accredited institution, (2) complete the necessary courses in personal financial planning from a program registered with the CFP Board, (3) complete three years of practical experience in the personal financial planning field, and (4) agree to abide by the Code of Ethics and Professional Responsibility adopted by the CFP Board.

There are seven principles which are the foundations for a certificant's relationship with the public, clients, colleagues and employers:

1. Integrity: Certificants are placed in a position of trust by clients, and they must be honest and candid. The interests of the client must always come first. This is the fiduciary standard.
2. Objectivity: The certificant must be honest and impartial in all dealings. Decisions must not be subordinated to the opinions of others.
3. Competence: This means reaching and maintaining sufficient levels of knowledge and skills to provide financial services to clients. It also requires the certificant to have the wisdom to consult other professionals when necessary. Continuing education and professional development are requirements for on-going certification.
4. Fairness: This requires impartiality, intellectual honesty and disclosure of all sources of compensation, as well as all material conflicts of interest.
5. Confidentiality: Client information is provided for a specific purpose, and it should be available only on a need to know basis, or to comply with a legal process.
6. Professionalism: A certificant is required to be courteous and respectful in all dealings with clients, other professionals and the business community. The certificant is also responsible for using the CFP® and Certified Financial Planner™ appropriately.
7. Diligence: Services are to be well prepared and delivered promptly. Investment recommendations need to be adequately investigated. All subordinates are to be properly supervised. Actions should exceed the client's expectations.

1.3.1 The CFP Board of Standards Rules of Conduct

These rules govern all individuals who have been granted the right to use the CFP marks, without regard to whether or not the marks are actually used. Violation of the rules may subject a certificant or registrant to discipline. There are six broadly worded rules:

1. Defining the Relationship with the Prospective Client or Client
   The parties should reach a written agreement on responsibilities of each in the six steps of the financial planning process. Compensation to be paid to any party to the agreement should be specified, along with the terms of engaging other parties (e.g., accountants or attorneys). If the certificant intends to offer any proprietary products, the client must be notified.
2. Information Disclosed to Prospective Clients and Clients
   The certificant must disclose an accurate and understandable summary of costs to the client including any compensation to the certificant's employer. Any likely conflicts of interest between the client and certificant and the certificant's employer must be disclosed. If the services include financial planning or the financial planning process, this must also be disclosed.
3. Prospective Client and Client Information and Property
   Information provided to the certificant must be confidential except as required by a proper legal process. The certificant must take prudent steps to secure information and property. If necessary client information is not available or not provided, the certificant must notify the prospective client or client. Any assets over which the certificant takes custody, exercises investment discretion or supervises must be identified, and complete records of these assets must be maintained. Certificants should not borrow from or lend money to a client. The client's property should not be commingled with the certificant's property, the certificant's employer's property or with the property of other clients without specific written authorization. Lastly, the certificant must return a client's property to the client as requested within a reasonable period of time.
4. Obligations to Prospective Clients and Clients
   A certificant shall only offer advice in areas where he or she is competent. A certificant must be in compliance with all regulatory and licensing requirements, and any suspension or revocation from the CFP Board must be disclosed. A certificant is expected to use reasonable and prudent professional judgment in providing services.
5. Obligations to Employers
   A certificant who is an employee/agent will provide services in accordance with the employer's objectives and in compliance with the CFP Board's Code of Ethics. The employer will also be notified by the certificant of any suspension or revocation received from the CFP Board.
6. Obligations to CFP Board
   A certificant must adhere to the terms of all agreements with CFP Board. To retain the right to use the CFP marks, the certificant must meet continuing education requirements as specified by CFP Board. Contact changes such as phone number, email address and physical address must be provided to CFP Board within 45 days, and certificants must notify CFP Board within 10 days in writing of any convictions of crimes (other than misdemeanors or traffic violations, unless the offense involved the use of alcohol or drugs). Professional suspensions or revocations must also be promptly reported.

1.3.2 The CFP Board of Standards Financial Planning Practice Standards

The CFP Board has established a framework for the practice of financial planning which parallels the six steps in the financial planning process. The standards are intended to advance professionalism and enhance the value of the planning process.

Practice Standards 100 Series (Relates to Step One: Defining the scope of the engagement)

- Planner and client must agree on what topics and activities will be undertaken.
- Conflicts of interest, compensation, specific responsibilities of each party and the length of the engagement must be disclosed.
- Some disclosures may have to be in writing.

Practice Standards 200 Series (Relates to Step Two: Determining a client's personal and financial goals, needs and priorities)

- Prior to making any recommendations to a client, the planner must determine the client's values, attitudes, expectations and time horizons as they relate to the client's goals, needs and priorities.
- The role of the planner is to facilitate the goal-setting process. This includes agreeing on realistic goals in light of the client's situation and obtaining from the client a commitment to accomplish the goals.
- The planner must obtain adequate information from the client before making any recommendations.

Practice Standards 300 Series (Relates to Step Three: Analyzing and evaluating the client's Information)

- The planner must analyze the client's information to determine the feasibility of attaining the agreed-upon goals. Personal assumptions such as the time of retirement, life expectancy, income needs, risk factors, time horizon and special needs are included. In addition, the planner will utilize economic assumptions such as inflation, tax rates and investment returns.

Practice Standards 400 Series (Relates to Step Four: Developing and presenting the financial planning recommendations)

- Several tasks are part of this critical step. The tasks can be described with three questions: What is possible? What is recommended? How is it presented? The first two tasks require creativity, thought and judgment on the part of the planner, and these tasks are usually completed outside the presence of the client. Among the alternatives available, the planner then selects to recommend the ones that better serve the needs of the client, and communicates them to the client.
- In presenting the recommendations to the client, the planner should help the client understand the assumptions, advantages and disadvantages, risks and time frames used. At the conclusion of the presentation, the planner should obtain a commitment from the client to accept the recommendations.

Practice Standards 500 Series (Relates to Step Five: Implementing the financial planning recommendations)

- The planner and client should agree on implementation responsibilities to carry out the recommendations in step four.

- Specific activities must be identified and assigned. This may include selection of and involvement of other professionals such as accountants, insurance agents, attorneys and investment specialists. The client must give permission for any personal information in the plan to be shared with others.

Practice Standards 600 Series (Relates to Step Six: Monitoring)

- The client and financial planner should agree on responsibilities for monitoring the effectiveness of the plan. Some client engagements may not include on-going monitoring duties by the financial planner.
- If the financial planner is engaged to provide monitoring services, the scope, frequency and communication of progress must be defined.

1.3.3 Disciplinary Rules and Procedures

The CFP Board of Standards has the ability to enforce the Rules of Conduct and Practice Standards referred to earlier and to impose sanctions against offenders. A Disciplinary and Ethics Commission has been formed and given the responsibility of investigating, reviewing and taking action on alleged violations. Grounds for discipline include, among others, violations of the Rules of Conduct and Practice Standards, criminal convictions, failure to respond to the commission's requests for information and providing false or misleading information to the CFP Board. Discipline actions include private censure, a public letter of admonition, suspension of rights to use the CFP marks for up to five years or permanent revocation.

1.4 Practical Application: Meet the Milfords

Throughout the chapters of this book, you will be able to experience first hand the real life application of the material through the eyes of a typical American family, the Milfords. Ric Milford, age 42, earns $80,000 a year selling medical equipment. He has the potential to earn up to 25% of his salary as an annual bonus depending on his sales. Ric's wife, Vanessa, is 39 years old and earns $50,000 per year as a school teacher. Ric and Vanessa have two daughters: Samantha, 10 years old, and Cassandra, 7 years old. Ric also has a 15-year old son, Michael, from his first marriage.

In many special sections titled "Practical Application," you follow the Milfords as they face all kinds of financial situations that are typical in the life of a household. The Milfords often are assisted in their financial decision making process by the expert analysis and recommendations of a Certified Financial Planner™. These sections provide you with an opportunity to really connect with the material, to experience financial planning for all aspects of family finances and to practice being a financial planner. What would you advise the Milfords to do in each of these situations?

Summary

Personal financial planning is both a science and an art. The regulatory environment in which a financial planner works is extensive and constantly changing. Many aspects of planning are numbers driven, requiring major fact gathering, meaningful analysis and quantification of goals and objectives. On the other hand, a financial planner must be a good listener and a trusted advisor to develop and maintain a mutually beneficial relationship with each individual client. Competent financial planners, who maintain their skills through continuing education and practice at the fiduciary level of care, offer a great value to individuals who are willing to follow their leadership through the financial planning process.

The chapters that follow will introduce the major personal financial planning topics: budgeting, insurance and risk management, investments, education funding, income taxes, retirement planning and estate planning. Regulations, laws and rules pertaining to financial planning and each of these topics will also be introduced.

Review Questions

1. Describe the fiduciary standard.

2. What functions does a "fee only" financial planner provide?

3. What are some of the major life events that would call for a review of a financial plan?

4. What are the four requirements for an individual to become a certified financial planner?

5. In the financial planning process, why is it important that the planner and the client have a written agreement?

6. One of your clients is really annoying to you. He is rude, disrespectful and seems to be in your office all the time. You would prefer if he stopped using you as his financial planner. Should you start providing him with bad advice so he can look for another advisor?

7. What can the CFP Board do to a certificant who violates the Code of Ethics and/or the Rules of Conduct?

8. On the fact finder form, why does the client have to go to the trouble of providing statements on deposit and brokerage accounts and debts?

9. For what purpose would a financial planner use the information about how the client's assets are owned?

10. Should everyone in a financial planner's firm have access to the information on a fact finder form or to the planner's notes from meetings with a client?

Appendix

Abbreviated Fact Finder Form

Section One – Personal Information

Full Name

Gender

Date of Birth

Home Address

Telephone Numbers

Email Address

Social Security Number

Occupation

Employer

Length of Employment

Address of Employer

Marital Status (spouse's name)

Dependents (child/grandchild/other family members)

Section Two – Assets and Liabilities

Deposit Accounts (type of account, owner, method of ownership, current balance)

Marketable Stocks and Bonds (name of issuer, owner—if in a brokerage account, give specific details, current market value, cost basis)

Stock Options/Restricted Stock (issuers, type of grant, vesting, expiration dates, shares covered and strike prices)

Retirement Accounts (IRAs, employer-sponsored plans, annuities)

Notes Receivable (include copies of all documents)

Personal Property (vehicles, boats, equipment and machinery, furniture, art, jewelry)

Real Estate Owned (Primary residence, vacation houses, business property)

Personal Liabilities (credit cards, charge accounts, margin accounts, vehicle secured loans, real estate secured loans, student loans, other liabilities)

Section Three – Insurance

Life Insurance (details on all policies including issuer, owner, type of policy, death benefit, cash value, names of beneficiaries)

Disability Insurance (details on all policies)

Property and Casualty Insurance (details on all policies: homeowners, vehicle, umbrella coverage, personal articles floater coverage, worker's compensation for domestic workers, flood)

Long-Term Care Insurance (details on all policies)

Medical Insurance (sources of coverage, policy limits, deductibles, co-pays, premiums)

Section Four – Income and Expenses

Income (salaries, bonuses, commissions, interest, dividends, rental, alimony, child support, Social Security, retirement)

Expenses (loan payments, utilities, property taxes, food, entertainment, dues, vehicle related, clothing, home maintenance, transportation, child support, alimony, charitable gifts)

Taxation of Income (copies of federal, state and local tax returns for last three years, estimated tax payments, audits of tax returns)

Section Five – Retirement Plans

Retirement Goals (age, income needed, location changes, medical insurance coverage, asset retention goals–deplete or retain)

Section Six – Estate Planning

Status of Documents (copy of will, living will, powers of attorney, powers of appointment, health care power of attorney, DNR orders)

Trusts (copy of all whether grantor, trustee or beneficiary)

Charitable Giving (history and lifetime intentions; intended legacy gifts)

Inheritances (do you anticipate receiving any?)

Goals for Asset Distribution from Your Estate (individuals, charities)

Section Seven – Business Ownerships

Closely Held Businesses (name, address, type of business, percentage ownership, income tax status, key employees, cost basis, value of the business and how determined, buy-sell agreements, goals for the business, plans to transfer your interest at retirement or death)

Professional Practices (name, address, type of business, percentage ownership, income tax status, other owners/principals, buy-sell agreements, transfer agreements, key employees)

Section Eight – Education Objectives

Family Members (Would you like to provide funds for children, grandchildren or others for undergraduate or graduate school expenses?)

Education Accounts (provide details on 529 or pre-paid tuition plans, education trusts, UGMA/UTMA accounts)

CHAPTER TWO

Time Value of Money: Loan and Investment Calculations

2.1 Introduction

Of all the techniques used in finance, none is more important than the discounted cash flow analysis, which is often called time value of money (TVM). Financial managers deal with TVM calculations when they make investment decisions or establish the terms of a loan. You may be familiar already with student loans, and your future may also involve car loans, credit cards loans and home mortgages. You will also become increasingly familiar with investments and saving for retirement. This chapter addresses the mathematics behind the TVM calculations.

The main idea behind the TVM analysis is that "a dollar on hand today is worth more than a dollar to be received in the future," because if you had it today, you could invest it, earn a return, and end up with more than one dollar in the future.

2.1.1 Future Value of a Sum

Suppose you had a $1,000 which you choose not to spend for immediate consumption, but to save for deferred consumption at a future time when a need arises. You deposit the money into a bank savings account offering you 6% annually as compensation for using your money. We define as:

Present Value	PV = $1,000	the principal or beginning balance
Interest Rate	i = 6%	the percentage return or yield
Interest Amount	I = PV*i = $1,000*0.06 = $60	the dollar return
Number of Periods	N = 1 year	# of periods the transaction will last
Future Value	FV = PV+I = $1,000+$60 = $1,060	the ending balance or accumulation

So at the end of year-1, your ending account balance (FV) should equal your beginning balance (PV) plus the interest amount (I) earned during the year. Recall I = PV*i, therefore

$$FV = PV + I = PV + (PV * i) = PV * (1 + i) = \$1,000 * (1 + 0.06) = \$1,000 + (1.06) = \$1,060$$

So for a transaction that will last only one period: FV = PV * (1 + i) is a useful way to express the future value (FV) of a sum. What if, however, the transaction was to last for more periods? The following table shows the future value (FV) and earned interest (I) calculations for a transaction lasting N = 3 years.

Future Value of a $1,000 over 3 Years at 6%

N	PV	* (1 + i)	FV = PV * (1 +i)	I = PV * i
1	$1,000	* (1.06)	$1,060.00 = $1,000*1.06	$60
2	$1,060	* (1.06)	$1,123.60 = $1,000*1.06*1.06 = $1,000*1.06^2	$63.60
3	$1,123.60	* (1.06)	$1,191.016 = $1,000*1.06*1.06*1.06 = $1,000*1.06^3	$67.4160

Notice, that although the first year you lend your $1,000 to the bank you earn I = $60 in interest, the second year you earn I = $63.60, because you earn i = 6% on both the original principal $1,000 and on the $60 interest earned during the first year. So as long as you don't withdraw your earned dollar interest return at the end of each year, each additional year you maintain the deposit with the same terms you earn higher dollar interest returns. This is called compound interest and it is a powerful concept to grasp. Compound interest can be a great ally if you harness its power to build wealth (when you are the saver), but can also be a formidable foe if you find yourself on the wrong side of the transaction (when you are the borrower).

Also notice from the table above, that your final accumulation at the end of year-2 can be written as FV = $1,000 * 1.06^2 while at the end of year-3 it can be written as FV = $1,000 * 1.06^3

Therefore, we can generalize this equation to reflect the future value at any given period N as

$$FV = PV * (1 + i)^N$$

The process of calculating a FV from a given PV is called compounding. There are four ways to solve a TVM problem like this one. You can use the equation we just developed, perhaps with the assistance of a calculator that has a base-exponent function. You can also look at compound interest tables, which is what we had to do before calculators became widely available. You can use a spreadsheet like Exel, or you can use a financial calculator, like the HP10BII or HP10BII+ (the simplest of the two calculators allowed for the CFP certification examination). By far the fastest and easiest way to solve most TVM problems is with a financial calculator, which comes with all the TVM functions (equations) already preprogrammed. You only need to learn how to enter the information properly, and the financial calculator does the rest.

For this example, you will need to set the calculator at one (1) compounding period per year, meaning you only earn interest once every year. So enter 1, Orange button □ (shift operator), and P/YR.

HP10BII FV Calculation

1	□ P/YR	
3	N	
6	I/YR	
$1,000	+/-	PV
	FV	**$1,191.0160**

Notice, that you need to enter the $1,000 as a negative number (+/- changes the sign) to let the HP10BII know this is a cash outflow, as funds leave you and go to a bank account. Therefore, the calculator understands this to be an investment calculation, and calculates a positive FV for your final accumulation. Any time funds come to you this is a cash inflow (positive), and any time funds leave from you this is a cash outflow (negative). If you enter for example, a positive $1,000 for PV, the calculator understands you receive a cash inflow now, indicating a loan, and calculates a negative FV as you will have to repay the loan with interest. (Try it on your HP10BII.) Financial calculators need to know whether the transaction is a loan or an investment to keep you from making calculation errors.

Example: If Linda invests $3,000 into an account which is expected to grow at 6.5% per year, what can she expect to be the account balance after 7 years?

Since Linda invests her money now this is a cash outflow for Linda, and it happens at the present time, so it reflects the present value (PV) of this transaction. She is looking to grow her investment to something larger in the future, so she is looking to calculate a future value (FV).

Using the equation:

$$FV = PV * (1 + i)^N$$
$$FV = \$3{,}000 * (1 + 0.065)^7$$
$$FV = \$3{,}000 * 10.065^7$$
$$FV = \$3{,}000 * 10.554$$
$$FV = \$4{,}661.9596$$

Using the HP10BII

1	□ P/YR
7	N
6.5	I/YR
$3,000	+/- PV
	FV $4,661.9596

So Linda's future account balance after 7 years should be $4,661.9596, assuming no withdrawals of principal or earned interest during this period.

Even at this early point of our TVM discussion, it should be coming clear to you how much easier it is to perform these calculations on HP10BII. It is important to familiarize yourself with the financial calculator as soon as possible, as the situations we examine in the following sections of this chapter and the next will become more complicated, thus the equations will become more complicated.

2.1.2 Practical Application: Does It Pay to Go to College?

Michael Milford, age 15, is rebellious about the idea of going to college and the prospect of spending four more years in school. His father Ric has done all he can do to convince his son that being an educated man should be something he should aspire to. Michael however believes he has learned enough, and more schooling is not necessary. Ric knows Michael likes money and wants to maintain a good lifestyle when he grows up, so he asks a Certified Financial Planner™ to give him some hard numbers about the economic benefit of college education that will convince his son to go to college.

The Certified Financial Planner™ examines two scenarios. The first shows the wage prospects of Michael the high school graduate, over a 40-year career. The second shows the wage prospects of Michael the college graduate, over a similar length career.

As a high school graduate, Michael may earn $10 per hour working 40-hour weeks for 50 weeks per year, totaling $20,000 ($10*40*50) per year. The training he will acquire at his job will probably be very specific to that particular job, and not easily transferable to another job at another industry. Without upward job mobility, he will only average 2% annual pay raises to compensate for the higher cost of living. After 40 years his income is projected to be $44,160.7933.

As a college graduate, depending on the market demand for his major, Michael can earn an average starting salary of $40,000 per year. Because his college education will provide him with universal skills for his career, Michael will be able to move from one job to another, and perhaps from shrinking older industries to growing new industries with greater ease. Therefore, he will manage to gain an average of 4% annual pay raises over his career. After 40 years his income is projected to be $192,040.8251 or $147,880.0318 more than the first scenario. And that's just for one year, the fortieth year of his career.

Certainly there are upfront costs in terms of money, time and effort associated with earning a college degree, but the lifetime reward of higher incomes during your career outweighs the upfront

HP10BII FV of Income Calculation

High School Graduate			College Graduate		
1	☐ P/YR		1	☐ P/YR	
40	N		40	N	
2	I/YR		4	I/YR	
20,000	+/–	PV	40,000	+/–	PV
	FV	**$44,160.7933**		**FV**	**$192,040.8251**

costs. There are more elements (like the choice of major and the cost of private vs. public college) complicating the issue, which we will address in Chapter 6, Education Funding. But the point of this illustration is to show Michael that his higher projected future value of annual salaries as a college graduate is due to both a higher starting salary and a higher annual growth rate that can be achieved only because of the portability of his education. Stay in school Michael!

2.1.3 Present Value of a Sum

Suppose you were offered the choice of receiving $1,191.016 in 3 years or $X today. Assuming there is no doubt the $1,191.016 will be paid after the 3-year waiting period, and you don't need the money immediately, therefore the money would be deposited in your bank savings account earning 6% per year, what dollar amount should you be offered today to make this offer fair?

In this situation you know the promised future value (FV) after 3 years (N), and you are interested in finding how much it is worth today, when the interest rate is 6%. In other words, you are interested in finding the present value (PV) of a future cash flow. Recall from Section 2.1.1, that $1,000 deposited at your savings account, earning 6% per year, for 3 years produces a FV of exactly $1,191.016. Therefore, working backwards you can conclude that the "fair" value today of a promised FV of $1,191.016 in 3 years (when the available interest rate is 6%) is $1,000. Finding a PV is called <u>discounting</u> and it is the reverse of the compounding process.

Solving our future value of a sum equation $FV = PV*(1+i)^N$

for the PV yields: $PV = \frac{FV}{(1+i)^N} = \frac{\$1,191.016}{(1.06)^3} = \frac{\$1,191.016}{1.191} = \$1,000$

or using the financial calculator:

HP10BII PV Calculation

1	☐ P/YR
3	N
6	I/YR
$1,191.016	FV
	PV–$1,000

Notice, that the calculator output shows a negative present value. The reason is we entered a positive future value (cash inflow). The only correct transaction where you receive a cash inflow in the future is an investment, which requires an upfront cash outflow, thus a negative PV.

Example: If Linda wants to have $8,000 to use as a down payment to buy a car 5 years from today, how much must she invest now in an account earning 4% per year?

You know how much Linda needs in the future (FV), and you are interested in finding out how much she needs to invest today (PV) to achieve her goal. Solving our equation for the present value:

$$PV = \frac{FV}{(1+i)^N} = \frac{\$8,000}{(1.04)^5} = \frac{\$8,000}{1.2167} = \$6,575.4169$$

Or using the financial calculator:

HP10BII PV Calculation

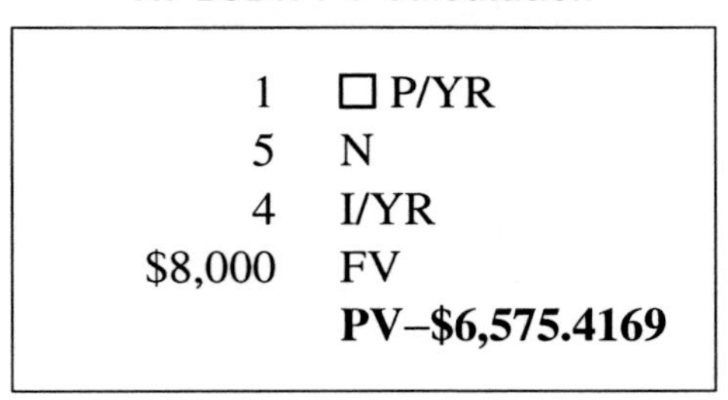

1	☐ P/YR
5	N
4	I/YR
$8,000	FV
	PV–$6,575.4169

Linda will need to deposit today $6,575.4169 in her bank account, earning 4%, so she can have $8,000 for the down payment of her car after 5 years. Notice again the calculator output is negative, indicating Linda will have to suffer a cash outflow (PV) today, to receive a cash inflow (FV) in the future.

2.1.4 Interest Rate

Suppose you needed to determine the interest rate (or investment return) at which your $1,000 investment grew to $1,191.016 in exactly 3 years. Notice that up to this point in the chapter, we have been working with one equation which has only four variables: FV, PV, i, and N. As long as you have information about three of these variables, you can always solve for the fourth one. In this case the beginning balance amount will be the present value (PV), the ending balance amount will be the future value (FV), the time period the investment lasted will be your number of periods (N), and the only unknown variable is the interest rate (i).

Solving our future value of a sum equation $FV = PV*(1+i)^N$ for the interest rate i yields:

$$(1+i)^N = \frac{FV}{PV} \Rightarrow (1+i) = \left(\frac{FV}{PV}\right)^{\frac{1}{N}} \Rightarrow i = \left(\frac{FV}{PV}\right)^{\frac{i}{N}} - 1 \Rightarrow i = \left(\frac{\$1{,}191.016}{\$1{,}000}\right)^{\frac{1}{3}} - 1 \Rightarrow i = 0.06$$

or using the financial calculator:

HP10BII i Calculation

1	☐ P/YR	
3	N	
$1,000	+/-	PV
$1,191.016	FV	
	I/YR	**6**

So the interest rate (or rate of return) for this investment was 6%. The equation will produce the result in a decimal format (0.06) which you can convert to a percentage format by multiplying it by 100 (0.06*100 = 6%). The financial calculator will produce the result in a percentage format, thus no modification is required. Notice however, that you have to enter two cash flows (PV and FV) into your financial calculator to find the interest rate. One cash flow has to be negative and the other has to be positive for the calculator to give you a solution. If you enter both PV and FV positive (or negative) your calculator will give you a "No Solution" for an answer, as there is no valid transaction with only positive (or only negative) cash flows. So if you ever see a "No Solution" answer in your financial calculator, just adjust the signs of the cash flows. Remember, the calculator is trying to help you avoid errors.

Example: Linda wants her $10,000 to grow to $25,000 over 10 years. What annual interest rate must the account earn to achieve her goal?

Using the equation:

$$i = \left(\frac{FV}{PV}\right)^{\frac{i}{N}} - 1 \Rightarrow i = \left(\frac{\$25{,}000}{\$10{,}000}\right)^{\frac{1}{10}} - 1 \Rightarrow i = (2.5)^{0.1} - 1 \Rightarrow i = 1.096 - 1 \Rightarrow i = 0.096$$

Or using the financial calculator:

HP10BII i Calculation

1	☐ P/YR	
10	N	
$10,000	+/-	PV
$25,000	FV	
	I/YR	**9.5958**

Linda will have to find the appropriate investment if she is to achieve her goal of growing $10,000 into $25,000 over a 10-year period. In her case, the appropriate investment will be one that is expected to generate an average annual return of 9.5958% for 10 years. This example indicates that sometimes it is your desired required rate of return that dictates the investment vehicle you need to choose to achieve your desired goal.

2.1.5 Practical Application: Rate of Return

Vanessa Milford and her younger sister Julia inherited $25,000 each from their grandmother Louise, when she passed away 9 years ago. Vanessa was starting a family at the time, so she decided to be conservative with her windfall. Therefore, she invested in a corporate bond fund yielding a 6% average annual return. Julia on the other hand, was single at the time and decided she could afford to take more risk with her inheritance. She chose to invest in a stock fund that was expected to generate, on average, a 12% annual return over long time periods. Julia has been making fun of her conservative sister ever since, so Vanessa decided to visit a Certified Financial Planner™ to seek expert advice on the issue. Is it possible her kid sister was right to be more aggressive with her investment choice?

The Certified Financial Planner™ showed Vanessa the following table, comparing the estimated investment results for both sisters over a 40-year period. Vanessa was shocked to see the results.

While Vanessa's investment was estimated to grow the inherited amount 9 times over during the 40-year horizon, Julia's investment was estimated to grow the same inherited amount 93 times over during the same time period. The two siblings made the same sacrifice (postponed consumption), for the same time period, and yet they will end up with amazingly different results. Clearly, the rate of return on your savings and investments is critical to your success in accumulating wealth.

HP10BII Calculation

Vanessa's Bond Fund Investment			**Julia's Stock Market Fund Investment**		
1	☐ P/YR		1	☐ P/YR	
40	N		40	N	
6	I/YR		12	I/YR	
$25,000	+/–	PV	$25,000	+/–	PV
	FV	**$257,142.9484**		**FV**	**$2,326,274.2610**

2.1.6 Number of Periods

Suppose you are asked to determine the length of time it would take $1,000 to grow to $1,191.016, when the interest rate is 6%. Once again, we are working with the same equation that has four variables (FV, PV, i, N). If you have information about three of these variables, you can always calculate the value of the fourth one.

Solving $FV = PV * (1 + i)^N$ for N yields:

$$(1+i)^N = \frac{FV}{PV} \Rightarrow \log\left\{(1+i)^N\right\} = \log\left\{\frac{FV}{PV}\right\} \Rightarrow N * \log\{1+i\} = \log\left\{\frac{FV}{PV}\right\} \Rightarrow N = \frac{\log\left\{\frac{FV}{PV}\right\}}{\log\{1+i\}}$$

$$\Rightarrow N = \frac{\log\left\{\frac{\$1{,}191.016}{\$1{,}000}\right\}}{\log\{1.06\}} \Rightarrow N = \frac{\log\{1.191016\}}{\log\{1.06\}} \Rightarrow N = \frac{0.1748}{0.0583} \Rightarrow N = 3$$

or using the financial calculator:

HP10BII N Calculation

1	□ P/YR	
6	N	
$1000	+/-	PV
$1,191.016	FV	
	N	**3**

It will take 3 years to grow $1,000 to $1,191.016 when the interest rate is 6%. Once again the HP10BII performs this tedious calculation in a matter of seconds. By this point, most students are convinced the financial calculator is the way to go. If you are not one of them, keep reading and you will have more chances to change your mind in the following sections.

2.1.7 Practical Application: Rule of 72

The Rule of 72 is a rule-of-thumb, or a crude approximation to the number of periods it will take you to double your beginning balance, given the rate of interest you can earn. The rule states that if you divide the number 72 by the interest rate (or rate of return) on a particular investment, you will find the approximate number of periods until you double your original investment. Suppose you have $10,000 and want to know how long it will take you to double your money. Well, it depends on the rate of return on your investments: 7%, 8%, 9%, 12%..........

RULE OF 72: 72/i	HP10BII N Calculation
	1 □ P/YR
	$10,000 +/– PV
	$20,000 FV
72/7 = 10.2857	7 I/YR N **10.2448**
72/8 = 9	8 I/YR N **9.0065**
72/9 = 8	9 I/YR N **8.0432**
72/12 = 6	12 I/YR N **6.1163**

This approximation works well for interest rates within a normal range between 5% and 20%. Still, it is a very useful rule to remember, particularly if you happen to be without your financial calculator, while trying to evaluate some investment opportunities. Clearly, the faster an investment promises to double your principal, the more attractive it becomes. Of course, the emphasis should be on the word "promises." As with all investments, risk should be factored into your financial analysis. Chapter 7 discusses in greater length the risk and return relationship.

Let's assume that you are willing to undertake some risk with your investment capital in order to generate a 12% average annual rate of return. The Rule of 72 will tell you quickly that you can double your capital in 6 years (72/12). If you are 22 years old, over the next 48 years you may be able to double your capital 8 times (48/6). This is a powerful realization. By the time you turn 70 years old (22 + 48 = 70) your original capital will have been multiplied by the factor $2^8 = 256$, assuming of course you could sustain such a high average rate of return over the next 48 years. A $10,000 original investment could grow to almost $2.5 million, while a $50,000 investment could grow to almost $12.8 million, and so on. (The actual accumulation depends on the compounding frequency, which is discussed in Chapter 3.) So plan to double your capital as many times as you can in your lifetime, and you will be a wealthy individual.

2.2 Annuities

An annuity is a series of recurring equal payments, at fixed time intervals, for a specified number of periods. If the payments (PMT) occur at the end of each period, then it is called an ordinary or deferred annuity. Examples of ordinary annuities are car loans and mortgage loans. If however, the payments occur at the beginning of each period, then it is called an annuity due. Rents and leases are examples of annuities due. Since ordinary annuities tend to be more common than annuities due, when we refer to an annuity we assume it is an ordinary type, unless otherwise indicated.

2.2.1 Future Value of an Annuity

Ordinary Annuity

Suppose you are to receive an annuity that will pay you $10,000 at the end of each year, for the next 3 years. You can deposit these payments in an account paying 6% annually. How much will your account balance be at the end of the 3-year period?

In the case of an annuity you have multiple cash flows to deal with, instead of a single amount.

All of these cash flows will have to be compounded to find the future value (FV) of the annuity. It helps to draw a time line to picture the timing of the cash flows. The time line starts with period-0 for the beginning of the first period, and ends with the number of the last period for which there is a cash flow. In our example, the time line starts with 0 and ends at period-3. At the end of every period (ordinary annuity) you will receive a $10,000 cash flow. Vertical lines at every time period indicate the occurrence of a cash flow. Once a cash flow occurs, it can be deposited to your account to earn interest, for the number of periods remaining until the end of the time line. For instance, the first $10,000 cash flow occurring at the end of year-1 can earn interest for 2 years. The second $10,000 cash flow occurring at the end of year-2 can earn interest for 1 year, as there is only one year left to the end of the time line. The third and last $10,000 cash flow has no time left to earn any interest. When you compound these cash flows individually, each for the appropriate number of periods, and you add their future values together, you get the future value of the annuity (FVA), $31,836.

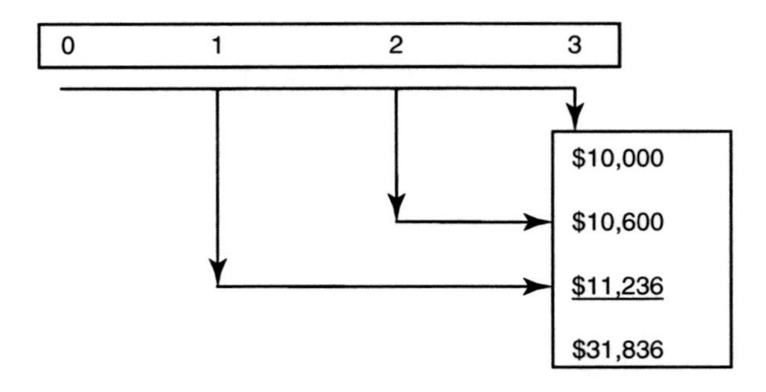

Mathematically, the FVA is just the sum of all the future values of the individual cash flows:

$$FVA = PMT * (1+i)^{N-1} + PMT * (1+i)^{N-2} + \cdots + PMT(1+i)^{N-N} = PMT * \sum_{t=1}^{N} (1+i)^{N-t}$$

As you may recall, in Section 2.1 we warned you that as the transactions get more complicated, the equations will get more complicated too. Fortunately, annuities have equal payments, so the calculations can be simplified by using PMT as a common factor to multiply the sum of all the future value interest factors. The FVA equation can be reduced to:

$$FVA = PMT * \frac{(1+i)^N - 1}{i}$$

And for our example,

$$FVA = PMT * \frac{(1+i)^N - 1}{i} = \$10{,}000 * \frac{(1.06)^3 - 1}{0.06} = \$10{,}000 * 3.1836 = \$31{,}836$$

Or using the financial calculator,

HP10BII FVA Calculation

1	□ P/YR	
3	N	
6	I/YR	
0	PV	
$10,000	+/–	PMT
	FV	**$31,836**

Notice that since you have a series of equal payments you need to use the PMT function of your calculator to enter all these identical cash flows. You also need to enter them as cash outflows (negative sign) since you deposit the payments to a bank account as they occur.

Annuity Due

Suppose now you are to receive an annuity that will pay you $10,000 at the beginning of each year, for the next 3 years, and you can deposit these payments in an account paying 6% annually. How much will your account balance be at the end of the 3-year period?

With an annuity due the payments occur at the beginning of the periods, so on your time line the first cash flow appears at period-0, which is the beginning of the first period. The second cash flow appears at period-1, which is the beginning of the second period. The third cash flow appears at period-2, which is the beginning of the third period. Compared to the ordinary annuity, the annuity due cash flows occur one period earlier, therefore all three cash flows have more time to earn interest.

Notice that the future value of the annuity due (FVA_D = $33,746.16) is greater than the future value of the ordinary annuity (FVA = $31,836). Intuitively this makes sense, as each cash flow

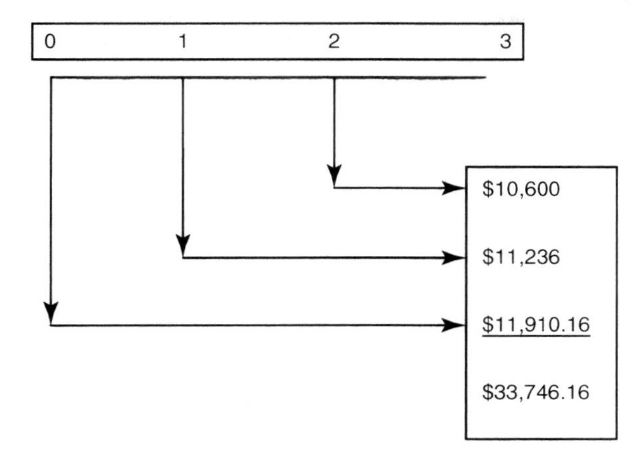

occurs one period earlier, therefore each one is compounded for an extra period generating a higher FV. Mathematically, the relationship between the future values of the two types of annuities is:

$$FVA_D = FVA * (1+i)^1 \Rightarrow FVA_D = \$31,836 * (1.06)^1 \Rightarrow FVA_D = \$33,746.16$$

As long as the interest rate is positive ($i>0\%$), then the annuity due is more valuable than the ordinary annuity ($FVA_D > FVA$).

Using the financial calculator, you need to tell the calculator you are dealing with an annuity due by pressing the orange button (shift operator) and then the Begin/End button (□ BEG/END). The BEGIN indicator will appear on your HP10BII display. Then you enter the information the same way as with the ordinary annuity.

HP10BII FVA_D Calculation

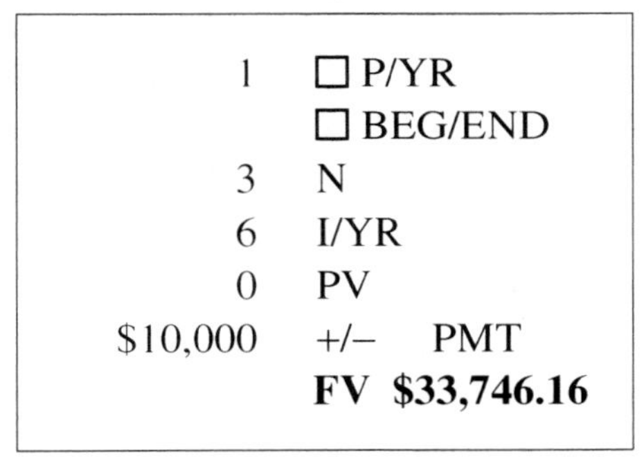

2.2.2 Practical Application: Save the Change

Back in the days when people use to carry money for their transactions instead of cards, a common practice to increase their savings was to leave all the loose change at home, perhaps in a jar. Every day they would come home, they would empty their pockets from the loose change into the jar. Occasionally, the jar and its contents made the trip to the bank, and voila a new deposit to the savings account.

Old and trivial as this practice may seem, we can all learn a lesson or two from the previous generations. After all, they created everything we all have come to know and use in our modern days. So assume you want to imitate this practice, even though you don't use too many paper bills and coins. You can decide to invest every year, for the next 50 years, just $365 the equivalent of $1 per day. Since you are young and modern, a savings account may not excite you, so you invest at an index stock fund with an average expected annual return of 12%. You may get in the practice of investing either at the end or the beginning of the year. It's your choice.

HP10BII FVA_D Calculation

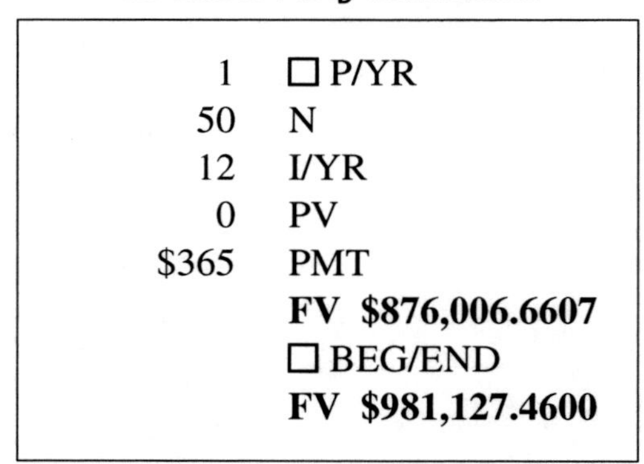

1	☐ P/YR
50	N
12	I/YR
0	PV
$365	PMT
	FV $876,006.6607
	☐ BEG/END
	FV $981,127.4600

Making the investments at the beginning, instead of the end, of each year yields a larger future value. If you start this practice when you are 20 years old, by the time of your retirement you have the opportunity to build a substantial accumulation. Not bad for an old timer ritual!

2.2.3 Practical Application: IRA Account

An individual retirement account (IRA) is a tax favored account to help you save for your retirement. Current tax law allows you to contribute up to $5,500 per year ($6,500 if you are 50+ years old) tax deductible as long as your income is below a certain phase-out amount. Investment earnings grow tax deferred until you withdraw the funds out of the account during your retirement. IRAs are discussed in more detail Chapter 9 in Section (9.2.3).

Assume you are 22 years old, and want to take advantage of the opportunity afforded to you by the law to invest in a tax protected account. Once you get a full time job you open an IRA and you invest at the end of every year the current maximum allowed $5,500. You continue with this practice for the next 48 years, when you start taking mandatory withdrawals from the account. Your investments produce an average annual return of 8.5%.

HP10BII FVA Calculation

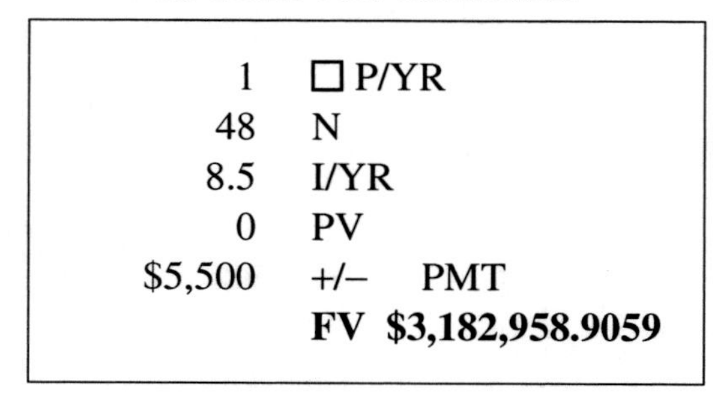

1	☐ P/YR
48	N
8.5	I/YR
0	PV
$5,500	+/– PMT
	FV $3,182,958.9059

It is entirely possible to build a substantial IRA fund over time, which together with your employer sponsored retirement plan will provide you with a very comfortable lifestyle during your retirement years. The law is providing you with the tax protected IRA as an incentive to take control of your financial future. You need to take advantage of the opportunities afforded to you. Becoming wealthy or at least financially secure is an available choice for most people. Choose wisely!

2.2.4 Present Value of an Annuity

Ordinary Annuity

Suppose you were interested in buying an investment instrument that would provide you with a $10,000 payment every year for the next 3 years. The payments will occur at the end of every year, and the investment promises a 6% annual rate of return. How much should you pay for this investment?

The three promised $10,000 payments are future cash inflows, and in order for you to receive them, you will have to incur a cash outflow upfront, the price of this investment instrument. To figure out the "fair" price of this instrument, you need to figure out the "fair" price today of all these future cash inflows. As you may recall from Section 2.1.3, the "fair" price today of a future amount is the present value of the amount, which you can calculate by discounting the amount for the number of periods until the amount is received. So discounting all three cash flows, each for the appropriate number of periods, and adding their present values produces the PVA = $26,730.1195. Therefore you should be willing to pay up to this price for this investment, because it is its "fair" price. If you pay more than $26,730.1195 you will not realize the promised 6% average annual return. You will realize a lower return. Obviously, if you pay less than the "fair" price you will realize a higher return, but it is doubtful that there will be any seller offering the instrument for less than its "fair" value.

Also recall, that when you are dealing with multiple cash flows it is very helpful to draw a time line to visualize the timing of the cash flows.

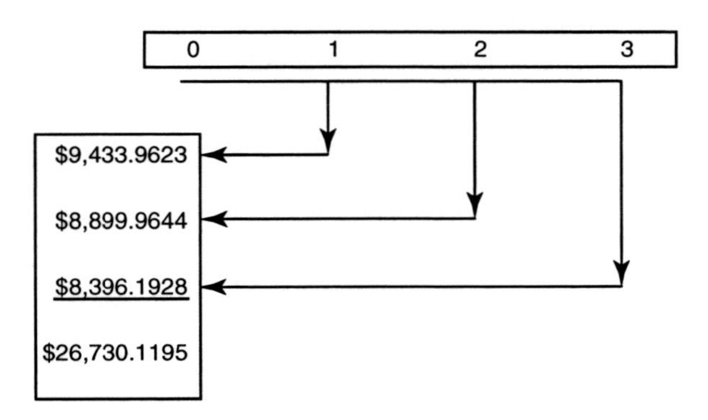

Mathematically, the PVA is just the sum of all the present values of the individual cash flows. Fortunately all annuity payments (PMT) are equal which facilitates the calculation:

$$PVA = \frac{PMT}{(1+i)^1} + \frac{PMT}{(1+i)^2} + \cdots + \frac{PMT}{(1+i)^N} \Rightarrow PVA = PMT * \sum_{t=1}^{N} \frac{1}{(1+i)^t}$$

which can be reduced to:

$$PVA = PMT * \frac{1 - \frac{1}{(1+i)^N}}{i} \Rightarrow PVA = \$10{,}000 * \frac{1 - \frac{1}{(1.06)^3}}{0.06} \Rightarrow PVA = \$26{,}730.1195$$

Despite the apparent complexity of the calculation, the PVA equation really simplifies the process of discounting potentially hundreds of cash flows to calculate the present value of a single financial instrument. Consider for example a 30-year mortgage loan with 360 monthly payments (or cash flows). Solving even an elaborate equation is far more preferable than discounting 360 payments one at a time.

Of course when talking about simplicity you should be thanking your good fortune there is such a device as a financial calculator.

HP10BII PVA Calculation

1	☐ P/YR
3	N
6	I/YR
$10,000	PMT
0	FV
	PV–$26,730.1195

The negative sign for the present value indicates that this is a cash outflow. You have to pay the initial cash outflow (PVA) to receive the series of equal cash inflows (PMT).

Annuity Due

Suppose the investment instrument you are looking to buy would provide you with a $10,000 payment every year for the next 3 years, but the payments will occur at the beginning of every year. The investment still promises a 6% annual rate of return. Does the change in the timing of the cash inflows affect the price you are willing to pay for this investment?

Clearly, the answer is affirmative. The whole idea behind the time value of money concept is that the timing of cash flows is essential for their valuation. With an annuity due all cash flows occur at the beginning as opposed to the end of every period. Therefore, all cash flows shift one period to the left on the time line, and TVM states that money sooner is more valuable than the same amount of money later.

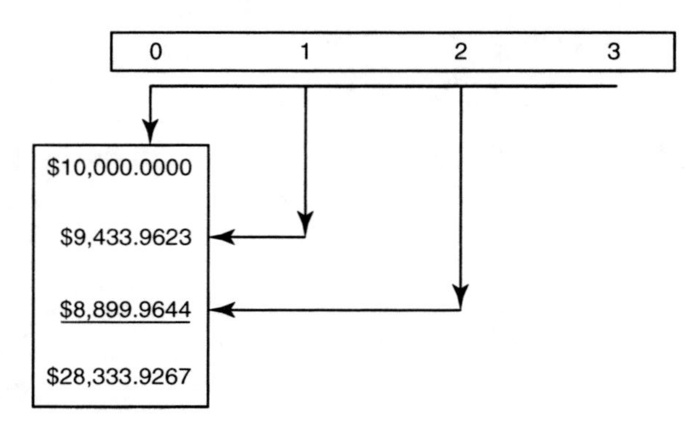

It should be no surprise that the present value of the annuity due exceeds the present value of the ordinary annuity ($PVA_D > PVA$). As a matter of fact, the relationship between the present values of the two annuity types is:

$$PVA_D = PVA * (1+i)^1 \Rightarrow PVA_D = \$26,730.1195 * (1.06)^1 \Rightarrow PVA_D = \$28,333.9267$$

As long as the interest rate is positive ($i>0\%$), then the annuity due is more valuable than the ordinary annuity ($PVA_D>PVA$).

Using the financial calculator, remember to tell the calculator you are dealing with an annuity due by pressing the orange button (shift operator) and then the Begin/End button (☐ BEG/END). The BEGIN indicator will appear on your HP10BII display. Then you enter the information the same way as with the ordinary annuity.

HP10BII PVA_D Calculation

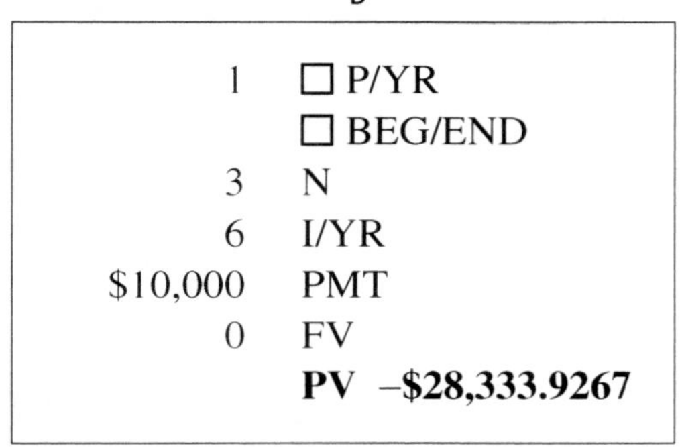

1	☐ P/YR
	☐ BEG/END
3	N
6	I/YR
$10,000	PMT
0	FV
	PV –$28,333.9267

The negative sign for the present value indicates that this is a cash outflow. You have to pay the initial cash outflow (PVA_D) to receive the series of equal cash inflows (PMT).

2.2.5 Practical Application: Lottery Gains

Ric and Vanessa Milford win the $6 million first prize of their state lottery. Deliriously happy they spend the night making plans on how $6 million can change their lives. The party lasts until the next morning, when they visit their state lottery office. There they are informed that their $6 million prize is really an annuity of 30 annual $200,000 payments (30 * $200,000 = $6,000,000) starting today. The Milfords remember reading something about an annuity at the back of their lottery ticket, but with all the excitement such detail seemed unimportant at the time.

The state lottery officials inform the Milfords that if they prefer a lump sum instead of the annuity that can be arranged, as long as the Milfords understand that the lump sum will not be $6 million, but the present value of the series of the annual payments. State officials will discount the future payments at 8% and offer the Milfords the $PVA_D = \$2,431,681.2021$.

HP10BII PVA_D Calculation

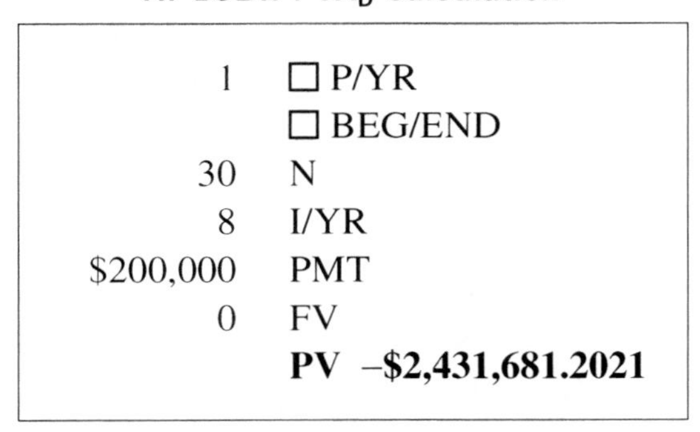

1	☐ P/YR
	☐ BEG/END
30	N
8	I/YR
$200,000	PMT
0	FV
	PV –$2,431,681.2021

Notice that this is an annuity due as the first payment occurs the day the prize is claimed, with all future annual payments occurring at the anniversary of the first payment. You may also notice that the

PV has a negative sign indicating this is a cash outflow. If the Milfords choose the annuity, the state will have to invest the present value at 8% to generate the 30 annual $200,000 payments. The difference between the advertised prize ($6 million) and the lump sum ($2,431,681.2021) paid to the winners immediately, or invested to pay the winners' payments throughout the years is used by the state to cover the operating expenses of the lottery, and to add to the general revenues of the state.

The Milfords have to make a decision. If they choose the lump sum today they walk away with only $2.4 million. If they choose the annuity they will collect all $6 million but it will take 30 years to do so. Suddenly a happy occasion is turned into a dilemma. The Milfords have to consider how drastically they want to change their lives. The less drastic the change, the less likely they are to choose the lump sum. They also have to consider their expected rate of return when they invest their lottery winnings. The less likely to earn more than the state's discount rate (8% in this case), the less likely they are to choose the lump sum.

Finally, the state lottery officials offer the Milfords another valuable piece of information to help them decide the payment option for their prize. If they choose the lump sum, their actual check will only be for $1,400,000 or 58% of the present value of the annuity payments. The state lottery office is obligated to withhold federal and state income taxes from all payouts. With such a big prize the Milfords will certainly be at the top marginal tax bracket for both federal (39.6% currently highest income tax rate) and state (assume 8% highest income tax rate) purposes. Suddenly the prize does not seem so big to the Milfords anymore.

2.2.6 Practical Application: Trusts

Ric and Vanessa Milford are seeking the advice of a Certified Financial Planner™ with respect to arranging the transfer of their assets to their three children, in the event of their demise. Their only concern is the young age of the children. If something were to happen to the Milfords in the next few years, their children could get access to their inheritance when they turned 18 years old. The Milfords fear their young and inexperienced children may squander their inheritance.

The Certified Financial Planner™ suggests the Milfords create trusts for their children, so the funds will be professionally managed for the benefit of the children, who may be receiving annual income from the trusts until the trust assets are distributed to them at an age the Milfords decide. It is possible for the trust assets not to be distributed to the children at all, but for the children to receive annual income payments for life. Trusts are discussed in more detail in Chapter 10.3.

If the Milfords want to provide each of their three children with an annual income supplement of $24,000 for the next 80 years, and the trust could generate an 8% average annual return on the trust assets, then the Milfords need to fund now each trust with $299,364.3460.

HP10BII PVA Calculation

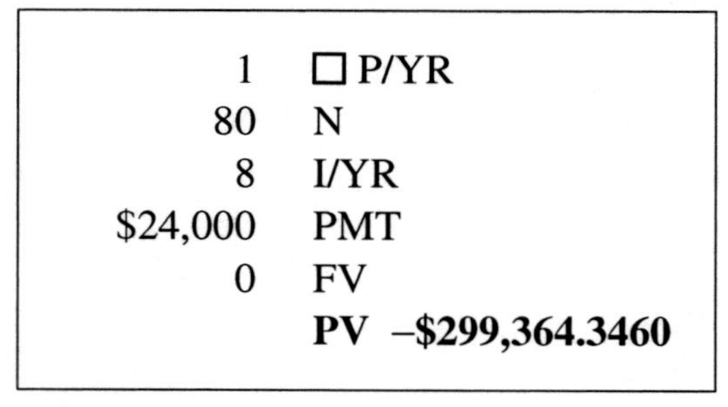

The negative sign indicates a cash outflow. The Milfords will have to fund each trust now (PV), so the trusts can generate the annual cash flows (PMT) for the children.

The Milfords could leave in their will $299,364.3460 for each of their three children, or they could fund a trust for each child with the same amount. While the children may not be happy to find out they will not get an inheritance to spend as they wish, they may be comforted knowing that for the next 80 years they will be receiving $24,000 per year (or $2,000 per month) to subsidize their income. The parents get the peace of mind of knowing they provided a lifetime income for each child. What would you do if you inherited almost $300,000 right now?

2.3 Perpetuities

Perpetuities are annuities with an infinite number of payments. In other words, they are annuities with no maturity ($N = \infty$). They are contracts promising perpetual payments. As long as you have one of these contracts you can be receiving payments forever. There aren't however too many perpetuity contracts around. The British government used to issue them in the nineteenth century to borrow money, and some of these contracts are still around and their owners keep collecting payments.

The reason we are still discussing perpetuities is because they provide valuable insights about asset valuation. The present value of a perpetuity (PV_P) is calculated by dividing the fixed perpetual payment (PMT) by the prevailing long-term interest rate (i). After all, nothing says long term better than infinity. So:

$$PV_P = \frac{PMT}{i}$$

Suppose you track down a perpetuity offering $50 per year forever, and the prevailing long-term interest rate for government issued securities is 5% (for the purpose of this example assume that the credit quality of the UK is similar to the US). You should be willing to pay the "fair" price for this contract or

$$PV_P = \frac{PMT}{i} = \frac{\$50}{0.05} = \$1,000$$

A couple of years later the prevailing long-term interest rate increases significantly, say to 10%. The value of your perpetuity contract would adjust accordingly to:

$$PV_P = \frac{PMT}{i} = \frac{\$50}{0.10} = \$500$$

Your contract loses half of its value when the interest rate doubles. The exact opposite happens when the interest rate decreases. If the rate was to drop from 5% to 2.5%, the value of your perpetuity would double:

$$PV_P = \frac{PMT}{i} = \frac{\$50}{0.025} = \$2,000$$

The observation that interest rates and prices move inversely $\left\{ \begin{matrix} i \uparrow \Leftrightarrow PV \downarrow \\ i \downarrow \Leftrightarrow PV \uparrow \end{matrix} \right\}$ underlies what is known as <u>interest rate risk</u>, an important principal that generally applies to most assets (stocks, bonds, real estate, commodities). When interest rates move, asset prices move to the opposite direction. In a rising interest rate environment most asset classes will get hurt. This is an important relationship to remember whether you manage your clients' assets or just your own personal investments.

Summary

In this chapter we introduced the concept of time value of money and its mathematics. We discussed transactions involving a single amount or series of payments, with finite or perpetual payments. Consequently we covered the three basic building blocks of interest rate calculations: the single amount equation, the annuity equation, and the perpetuity equation. The lump sum equation is used for finding the value of an amount of money at another point in time. The annuity equation is used for finding the total value today or in the future of a series of equal payments. The perpetuity equation is used for finding the total value today of an infinite series of regular payments made in the future. Equipped with these three equations, and some adjustments introduced in the next chapter, you can solve any interest rate valuation issue (commonly referred to as "time value of money" calculations).

Review Questions

1. You deposit $5,000 into a bank account paying 7% per year. What will be your account balance in 1 year? 5 years? 10 years?

2. You deposit $5,000 into a bank account paying 14% per year. What will be your account balance in 1 year? 5 years? 10 years?

3. Your employer promises you a $6,000 bonus sometime in the future. If you had the money now you could be earning an 8% annual return. What is the value of this promised bonus if it is paid in 1 year? 5 years? 10 years?

4. Your employer promises you a $6,000 bonus sometime in the future. If you had the money now you could be earning a 16% annual return. What is the value of this promised bonus if it is paid in 1 year? 5 years? 10 years?

5. You are a professional athlete signing up with a new team. The owner of the team offers you a choice between two bonus options. You can get $1,000,000 today or $1,500,000 at the end of your third season with the team. If you could invest today at 11% which one is the better option?

6. Your grandparents deposited $25,000 in a bank account for you the day you were born. After 20 years the account has a balance of $125,000. What average annual interest rate has the bank account earned over this period of time?

7. You have saved $10,000 and want to buy a $40,000 car without borrowing any money. If you can earn a 9% return on your savings, how long will it take you to achieve your goal?

8. You deposit at the end of every year $4,500 in an IRA earning 10% average annual return. You continue this practice for 20 years. What is the balance of your IRA? If you continue this practice for 40 years, what is the balance of your IRA? What is your conclusion from this comparison?

9. You deposit at the beginning of every year $4,500 in an IRA earning 10% average annual return. You continue this practice for 20 years. What is the balance of your IRA? If you continue this practice for 40 years, what is the balance of your IRA?

10. You quit your pack-a-day smoking habit, and invest the $1,500 per year you were spending on cigarettes on a stock fund earning 11.5% average annual return. How much money will you have in the fund after 45 years?

11. An investment promises to pay you $40,000 per year for 10 years. The interest rate is 0%. What is the value today of this ordinary annuity? What is the value of this annuity due?

12. An investment promises to pay you $40,000 per year for 10 years, with 7.5% rate of return. How much should you pay for this investment if the payments are made at the end of each year? How much should you pay for this investment if the payments are made at the beginning of each year?

13. An investment promises to pay you $40,000 per year at the end of the next 10 years. If you pay $300,000 for this investment, what will be your average annual rate of return?

14. You are interested in purchasing an investment paying $60 per year forever. If the interest rate is 8%, what will be a "fair" price for this investment? If after your purchase the interest rate drops to 4%, what will be the value of your investment?

15. In May 2012 the interest rate on 10-year US government securities (called treasuries) was barely 1.78%, while US interest rates in general were at 40-year historic low levels. Should you have advised your clients to buy such securities at the time? Explain.

CHAPTER THREE

Applied Time Value of Money

3.1 Introduction

During the time value of money discussion in the previous chapter, all examples assumed earning or paying interest once a year, which is called annual compounding of interest. This is the simplest case of compounding, and more appropriate for an initial exposition of the material. In real life applications however, most loans require and most investments offer more frequent payments than just once a year. For example:

Bonds may pay coupon interest payments twice a year (semiannual compounding)

Stocks may pay dividend payments four times a year (quarterly compounding)

Consumer loans may require payments twelve times a year (monthly compounding)

Bank accounts may pay interest every day (daily compounding)

The frequency of compounding follows the frequency of payments per year. We will name M the number of payments per year or the number of compounding periods per year. Therefore, M = 2 indicates semiannual compounding, M = 4 quarterly compounding, M = 12 monthly compounding and M = 365 daily compounding.

3.1.1 More Frequent Compounding

Suppose you deposit \$10,000 in a 5-year bank certificate of deposit (CD or time deposit), which pays 6% per year with annual compounding. Typically, time deposits offer a fixed interest rate until the CD matures (expires). From our discussion in Chapter 2 you should be able to calculate the balance of the CD after 5 years.

$$FV = PV*(1+i)^N \Rightarrow \text{FV} = \$10{,}000*(1.06)^5 \Rightarrow$$

$$FV = \$10{,}000 * 1.3382 \Rightarrow FV = \$13{,}382.2558$$

Or using the calculator:

HP10BII FV Calculation M = 1

1	☐ P/YR	
5	N	
6	I/YR	
\$10,000	+/-	PV
	FV	**\$13,382.2558**

Suppose that the bank instead of annual compounding was offering semiannual compounding for its CD. This means that after 6 months, the bank will apply half the annual interest rate on the original balance, and credit the account with the appropriate interest amount. At the end of the next

6 months, the bank will apply the other half of the annual interest rate on the existing balance, and credit the account with the appropriate interest amount. And so on, for 5 years until the CD matures.

Intuitively you may realize that since the account is credited with interest payments more frequently than before, the interest payments—once added to the principal—are earning interest sooner than with the annual compounding case. Therefore your future balance with semiannual compounding should be higher than with annual compounding.

To calculate the future value of your account with semiannual compounding you need to make two adjustments to the single amount FV equation. You need to divide the interest rate i by M (the number of compounding periods per year), and you need to multiply the number of years N by M.

$$FV = PV * \left(1+\frac{i}{M}\right)^{N*M} \Rightarrow FV = \$10,000 * \left(1+\frac{0.06}{2}\right)^{5*2} \Rightarrow$$

$$FV = \$10,000 * 1.3439 \Rightarrow FV = \$13,439.1638$$

To do this with your financial calculator, you need to let the calculator know you are using semiannual compounding, by doing the same two adjustments of the equation. You need to switch your calculator to two (2) compounding periods per year (2 □ P/YR), which takes care of the interest rate adjustment. In other words, by switching to 2 P/YR you don't have to divide the interest rate by M. The second adjustment multiplies the number of years N by the number of periods per year M. You can do it manually and enter the product as N, or you can instruct the calculator to do it instead (□ X P/YR, where X P/YR is the auxiliary function of the N button).

HP10BII FV Calculation M = 2

2	□ P/YR	
5	□ X P/YR	
6	I/YR	
$10,000	+/-	PV
	FV	**$13,439.1638**

As expected, the FV under semiannual compounding exceeds the FV under annual compounding. Notice that if you start with the same principal, and over the same time period, you end up with $56.9080 more under semiannual compounding than annual compounding ($13,439.1638 – $13,382.2558), then you must be earning a higher return than just 6%. There is no other explanation for the higher future value under semiannual compounding. But how is that possible when in both examples the bank is offering 6% for time deposits?

3.1.2 Different Types of Interest Rates

To avoid any confusion in the future and to be able to make good decisions, when it comes to loans and investments, you need to realize that there are different ways to present interest rates:

i) The stated or periodic rate is the interest rate per period of the year. For example, the bank is offering 3% per 6-month period for time deposits.
ii) The annual percentage rate (APR) equals the periodic rate multiplied by M, the number of compounding periods per year. For example,

$$APR = PERIODICRATE*M = 3\%*2 = 6\%$$

Under annual compounding (M = 1), the APR equals the periodic rate. But any time there is more frequent compounding, the APR will be different from the periodic rate, and you may need to calculate the APR.
Keep in mind that the APR is widely used because the truth-in-lending regulations require all lenders to disclose borrowers the APR charged for the loan.
iii) The effective annual rate (EFF or EAR) or annual percentage yield (APY) is the interest rate expressed as if it was compounded once per year.
For example, in the previous section you calculated the FV ($13,439.1638) of the 5-year CD under semiannual compounding. Let's calculate the interest rate (EAR) that would produce this FV under annual compounding:

$$FV = PV*(1+i)^N \Rightarrow i = \left(\frac{FV}{PV}\right)^{\frac{1}{N}} - 1 \Rightarrow i = \left(\frac{\$13,439.1638}{\$10,000}\right)^{\frac{1}{5}} - 1 \Rightarrow i = 0.0609$$

Or i = 6.09%. In our example therefore the "true" interest rate you earn under semiannual compounding is 6.09%, even though the APR is 6%. The EFF is the "true" rate because it reflects the effects of more frequent compounding on the APR.
Under annual compounding (M = 1), the EFF equals the APR and the periodic rate. But any time there is more frequent compounding, the EFF will be different from the APR and the periodic rate, and you may need to calculate the EFF to use the "true" rate in your decision making process.
Following the truth-in-savings regulations, banks disclose the EFF (or EAR or APY) for their deposit accounts. Notice the possible confusion: banks disclose the APR on loans, but the EFF (EAR or APY) on deposits.

You can calculate the EAR by using the following equation:

$$i_{EFF} = \left(1+\frac{i}{M}\right)^M - 1 \Rightarrow i_{EFF} = \left(1+\frac{0.06}{2}\right)^2 - 1 \Rightarrow i_{EFF} = 1.0609 - 1 \Rightarrow i_{EFF} = 0.0609$$

Notice that i is the APR = 6%. Also, the calculated result is in decimal format, but if you multiply it by 100 you can convert it to a percentage format 6.09%.

Financial calculators are really helpful to make conversions from APR to EFF and from EFF to APR, as the equation you just used already programmed in. For our example, the HP10BII needs the APR = 6% (entered as NOM% for nominal rate) and M = 2 to give you the EFF = 6.09%.

The following table shows the "true" rate EFF for a 6% APR with semiannual, quarterly, monthly, and daily compounding:

HP10BII EFF% Calculation

2☐P/YR	4☐P/YR	12☐P/YR	365☐P/YR
6☐NOM%	6☐NOM%	6☐NOM%	6☐NOM%
☐**EFF% 6.09**	☐**EFF% 6.1364**	☐**EFF% 6.1678**	☐**EFF% 6.1831**

As the number of compounding periods (M) increases, so does the EFF. The "true" rate increases because of the effect of more frequent compounding. The sooner interest payments are added to the principal of an account, the sooner they too can earn interest (compounding). Obviously this is significant to realize and to remember. Among instruments with the same APR, the lender (saver) benefits from the most frequent compounding possible, as the FV of savings will increase the most. The borrower however, benefits from the least frequent compounding possible (annual compounding, M = 1), that keeps the loan balance from growing quickly.

3.1.3 Practical Application: Choosing a Savings Account

Ric and Vanessa Milford are looking to open a bank account to deposit the $1,386,058.2852 lump sum of their lottery prize, until they decide what to do with the funds. Confused about the different offers from the banks they visited, they asked for your expert advice as a Certified Financial Planner™ to make sense of all the offers and choose the best one for them.

BANK	**A**	**B**	**C**	**D**	**E**	**F**
APR	7.00%	7.05%	7.10%	7.15%	7.20%	7.30%
M	Daily	Monthly	Quarterly	semiannually	Annually	Annually

You look at the six bank offers and you realize that those from banks E and F have annual compounding (M = 1), therefore their APR equals their effective rate (EFF). Between the two, clearly Bank F is the better offer. The first four bank offers however, use more frequent compounding. You need to calculate the "true" rate (EFF) to decide which one offers the highest yield.

HP10BII EFF% Calculation

A	**B**	**C**	**D**
365☐P/YR	12☐P/YR	4☐P/YR	2☐P/YR
7.0☐NOM%	7.05☐NOM%	7.1☐NOM%	7.15☐NOM%
☐**EFF% 7.2501**	☐**EFF% 7.2823**	☐**EFF% 7.2913**	☐**EFF% 7.2778**

Your ranking of the bank offers according to the effective rate they offer looks like this:

BANK	APR%	COMPOUNDING	EFF%
F	7.30%	ANNUALLY	7.30%
C	7.10%	QUARTERLY	7.2913%
B	7.05%	MONTHLY	7.2823%
D	7.15%	SEMIANNUALLY	7.2778%
A	7.00%	DAILY	7.2501%
E	7.20%	ANNUALLY	7.20%

One could argue that all the offers are so close to each other that it doesn't make a difference which one is the best. However, even small differences in yields can produce significant results given time and a large principal. In this example the Milfords are looking to deposit a significant amount of money. Even if the deposit is for a single year, the difference between choosing the lowest instead of the highest effective rate will result in forgoing $1,386.06 (0.001*$1,386,058.2852) in interest income.

So which offer are you going to recommend to the Milfords? The answer depends on how long they plan to keep the money in the account. If they are planning on leaving the funds in the bank account for at least a full year, Bank F offers the highest yield. However, Bank F offers annual compounding, meaning the interest payment will be credited to the account after exactly one year from the initial deposit. To receive the full promised interest income, the whole principal needs to stay deposited the whole year. So, if the Milfords are likely to withdraw some or all of the money before a full year has passed, Bank F will not be the best choice, and they will be better off choosing Bank C or Bank B, whose yields are also high but offer quarterly and monthly compounding respectively.

3.1.4 Practical Application: Credit Card Offer

Vanessa received a credit card offer in the mail. The card has no annual fee, and carries a 15% annual percentage rate. Vanessa wants your expert advice on whether this is an honest offer.

Well, yes and no. The offer is legal because it discloses the APR, as all lenders are required to do. However, you are now aware that the APR is not the "true" rate when more frequent compounding is involved. Credit cards require card holders to make monthly payments on outstanding balances. Therefore, there is monthly compounding at play here.

HP10BII EFF% Calculation

12	☐ P/YR
15	☐ NOM%
	☐ **EFF% 16.0755**

This results in an effective annual rate of 16.0755%, which is higher than the advertised APR. Is this dishonest behavior from the card issuer? This is equivalent to asking: Does the card issuer have the obligation to provide financial education to Vanessa? It certainly does not have the legal obligation to do so. Is the lender's job to educate people, or is it to provide them with quick and convenient service when they need funds?

Is lending different from other businesses? Is the job of a fast food restaurant to educate people about the terrible nutritional content of its meals, or is it to provide them with quick and tasty meals when they are hungry?

3.1.5 Practical Application: Payday Loans

Ric Milford had some unexpected "expenses" after betting on a basketball game. He needs to cover these "expenses" pretty quickly, before there is a "misunderstanding" with some people who claim to dislike "misunderstandings," yet they seem pretty good at resolving them in their favor. He cannot withdraw the money from the bank, without Vanessa noticing the transaction on the monthly account statement. So he decides to visit a Payday Loan facility to get access to cash.

The Payday Loan facility asks Ric to write them a personal check for $1,100 postdated 7 days (payable in 7 days) in order to give him $1,000 in cash today. If within a week Ric returns with the $1,100 cash, he can have his check back, and no one will ever know of this. Otherwise, the Payday facility will cash the check. Of course, Ric could renew the loan for an additional charge. Feeling desperate Ric takes the deal without many questions. What interest rate is Ric charged on this loan?

The periodic rate is 10%. He pays $100 interest on a $1,000 loan for 1 period.

Since a period here reflects a week, and there are 52 weeks in a year (M = 52).

The annual percentage rate is

$$APR = PERIODICRATE * M = 10\% * 52 = 520\%$$

The effective annual rate is an astonishing 14,104.2932%.

HP10BII EFF% Calculation

52	☐P/YR
520	☐NOM%
	☐EFF% 14,104.2932

So while the 10% rate may seem reasonable, particularly for an unsecured loan, it is really not, because it reflects the cost of borrowing for only one week. When the APR is calculated (520%) it should be obvious how expensive this loan is. Assuming it was possible for Ric to keep renewing this loan for a whole year, under the same terms, then his "true" cost of borrowing would be 14,104.2932% (EFF%). Astonishingly high as this rate seems, think of the following: After the tenth weekly loan renewal, the Payday facility has received $1,000 (10 weeks * $100 interest charge) income for a $1,000 loan. In other words, in terms of cash flows the lender has received its original investment back. Yet Ric will be paying $100 per week to renew a "loan" (which he seems to have repaid) for another 42 weeks and eventually he will have to repay the $1,000 principal back.

Payday loans are incredibly expensive and can get borrowers into trouble very quickly. Borrowers who need emergency cash can "discount" their paycheck to get access to the needed cash.

Unfortunately this means they will have less money than their whole paycheck to make due until their next paycheck arrives. This may prompt them to repeat the transaction week after week, and in a matter of weeks they may not be able to get by without the Payday Loan services. Therefore, some states have attempted to make them illegal and ban them from their jurisdiction. There are however Payday Loan supporters, who argue that states should not deprive people from what could be their only source of financing in an emergency. Payday Loan operators defend the high cost of these loans based on the extremely high risk level of the investment. These are unsecured loans (no collateral used) and have a very high default rate. Would you lend your money to a complete stranger, in exchange for a postdated personal check, which you may not be able to collect from?

3.2 Annuities and More Frequent Compounding

Chapter 2 introduced annuities while this chapter introduces the effects of more frequent compounding. So let's examine how annuities behave under more frequent compounding. Intuitively you may realize that more frequent payments provide the opportunity for more compounding, thus higher FVA, and less discounting, thus higher PVA. Either way, more frequent payments will produce more valuable annuities. You may also expect that you will need to make some adjustments to the annuity equations to accommodate more frequent compounding.

Future Value of an Annuity with More Frequent Compounding

Suppose you decide to eliminate your unlimited calling, texting and data plan on your fancy smart phone, and instead opt for a prepaid plan. The cost difference between the two services is $70 per month ($840 per year), which you direct to your investment account. You invest in a stock index fund yielding 10.9% average annual return. How much will these monthly investments amount to, if you commit to this practice for the next 45 years?

Recall the FVA equation: $FVA = PMT * \frac{(1+i)^N - 1}{i}$

To accommodate for more frequent payments you need to make three adjustments to this equation. First, divide the interest rate (i) by the number of compounding periods per year (M). Remember, the number of compounding periods per year follows the number of payments per year. Second, multiply the number of years (N) by the number of compounding periods per year (M). Third, divide the payment (PMT) by the number of compounding periods per year (M). So your equation will adjust to:

$$FVA = \frac{PMT}{M} * \frac{\left(1+\frac{i}{M}\right)^{N*M} - 1}{\frac{i}{M}} \Rightarrow FVA = \frac{\$840}{12} * \frac{\left(1+\frac{0.109}{12}\right)^{45*12} - 1}{\frac{0.109}{12}} \Rightarrow$$

$$FVA = \$70 * \frac{131.0073}{0.0091} \Rightarrow FVA = \$70 * 14{,}422.822 \Rightarrow FVA = \$1{,}009{,}597.5413$$

Or you can use your financial calculator. Of course you need to do the same three adjustments to let the calculator know you are using more frequent compounding. Remember, by switching your calculator to 12 P/YR you take care of the interest rate adjustment.

HP10BII FVA Calculation

12	□ P/YR	
45	□ X P/YR	
10.9	I/YR	
0	PV	
\$70	+/−	PMT
	FV	**\$1,009,597.4267**

So switching to a cheaper cell phone plan over the next 45 years of your life can provide you with more than a million dollars in savings. As long as you don't pay the cell phone carrier every month, but instead you decide to pay yourself, your monthly savings could grow to a significant amount. The money you spend on your phone service every month has an opportunity cost. The money could be used alternatively to generate wealth for you.

Notice that your total monthly payments are only \$37,800 (\$70 * 12 months * 45 years). You can send these payments to the phone carrier month-by-month, and you will never see them again, or you can send them to your investment account, and they may grow to be more than a million dollars. Throughout the chapters of this book, there are plenty of examples pointing to the realization, that building wealth and financial security is a personal choice. You control your future with your daily decisions.

For comparison purposes, it is very easy to check the difference in outcomes if you decide to make annual (\$840) instead of monthly (\$70) investments. With annual compounding you would commit the same \$37,800 (\$840 * 45 years) amount to the same stock index fund but would generate only \$802,829.6825. You can earn \$206,767.7442 more with monthly investments due to earning interest on interest more often.

HP10BII FVA Calculation

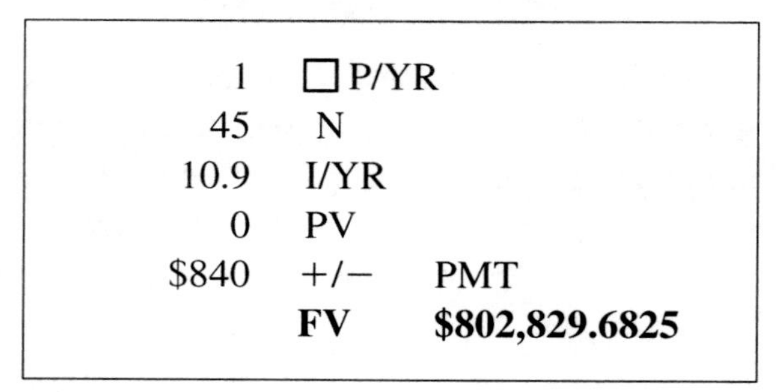

1	□ P/YR	
45	N	
10.9	I/YR	
0	PV	
\$840	+/−	PMT
	FV	**\$802,829.6825**

Present Value of an Annuity and More Frequent Compounding

Suppose you are trying to help your grandparents manage their finances during their retirement years. You suggest to them to buy an annuity which will pay them \$3,000 per month for the next 15 years. The annuity offers a guaranteed 7% annual return, so your grandparents don't have to worry about managing their own investments anymore. How much will such an annuity cost today?

There are several ways to structure this annuity. The annuity may pay at the beginning of the periods (annuity due) or at the end of the periods (ordinary annuity). The annuity can pay \$36,000 once a year or \$3,000 every month. All these possible choices offer different cash flow streams therefore they have a different upfront cost. Suppose your grandparents are interested in monthly payments received at the end of each month. To calculate the cost of this annuity today we need to use the present value of an annuity equation. Recall from Chapter 2:

$$PVA = PMT * \frac{1 - \frac{1}{(1+i)^N}}{i}$$

Like the FVA equation with more frequent compounding, to accommodate for more frequent payments you need to make three adjustments to this equation. First, divide the interest rate (i) by the number of compounding periods per year (M). Remember, the number of compounding periods per year follows the number of payments per year. Second, multiply the number of years (N) by the number of compounding periods per year (M). Third, divide the payment (PMT) by the number of compounding periods per year (M). So your equation will adjust to:

$$PVA = \frac{PMT}{M} * \frac{1 - \frac{1}{\left(1+\frac{i}{M}\right)^{N*M}}}{\frac{i}{M}} \Rightarrow PVA = \frac{\$36,000}{12} * \frac{1 - \frac{1}{\left(1+\frac{0.07}{12}\right)^{15*12}}}{\frac{0.07}{12}} \Rightarrow$$

$$PVA = \$3,000 * \frac{0.6490}{0.0058} \Rightarrow PVA = \$3,000 * 111.2571 \Rightarrow PVA = \$333,771.4286$$

Or you can use your financial calculator. Remember to do the same three adjustments of the equation to the calculator, to let the calculator know you are using more frequent compounding. Remember, by switching your calculator to M P/YR you take care of the interest rate adjustment.

HP10BII PVA Calculation

Monthly Payments	Annual Payments
12 □ P/YR	1 □ P/YR
15 □ X P/YR	15 N
7 I/YR	7 I/YR
$3,000 PMT	$36,000 PMT
0 FV	0 FV
PV −$333,767.8728	**PV −$327,884.9042**

It will cost your grandparents $333,767.8728 upfront to set up a monthly annuity that will provide them with $3,000 at the end of each of the next 180 months. The grandparents will get the peace of mind of guaranteed payments, and guaranteed 7% annual return, without having to worry about chasing investment returns themselves.

Notice the calculator PV result has a negative sign indicating this will be a required cash outflow for your grandparents, in order for them to subsequently receive the 180 monthly cash inflows. Also, notice that the equation PV result and the calculator PV result are $3.5558 apart, due to a rounding error of the equation's manual calculations.

For comparison purposes, it is easy to calculate the cost of an annuity with annual payments of $36,000 at the end of each year. The table above shows the cost of that annuity to be $5,882.9686 cheaper than the monthly annuity, but the grandparents will have to wait until the end of every year to receive their one big cash inflow. Once again, the more frequent the compounding (monthly instead of annual), the more frequent the payments, and the more valuable the annuity.

3.2.1 Practical Application: Vehicle Financing

Michael Milford is about to turn 16 years old, and the only thing on his mind is getting his driving license and a new BMW. His parents have made it clear to him that they are not getting him a BMW. Michael however is a young and spoiled teenager, whose favorite sport is to aggravate his parents on a daily basis. He now threatens to skip college, and get a full-time job right after high school to finance a BMW. His father, Ric has done all he could do to convince Michael about the negative long-term consequences of both skipping college and borrowing too much too early. But the boy is stubborn. Ric figures if Michael will not listen to him, maybe he will be more accepting to the advice of an expert. Ric asks his Certified Financial Planner™ to prepare some figures about vehicle financing for his son, in the hope that Michael will appreciate the size of the mistake he is about to commit and will change his mind.

The financial planner prepares the following realistic car financing scenario for Michael: Price of BMW $40,000, required down payment 10%, 60-month financing, at 12% per year interest rate due to the young age of the borrower.

Michael will need to have a $4,000 down payment ($40,000 * 10%) the day of the purchase. He will finance the remaining $36,000, which will be the present value of the loan. The loan term will be for 5 years, and he will have to make monthly payments to the lender consisting of both principal and interest. Once all monthly payments have been made the loan will be repaid, therefore the future value of the loan is set to $0. Keep in mind that the monthly payments indicate monthly compounding on this loan. Michael's monthly payment will be:

HP10BII PMT Calculation

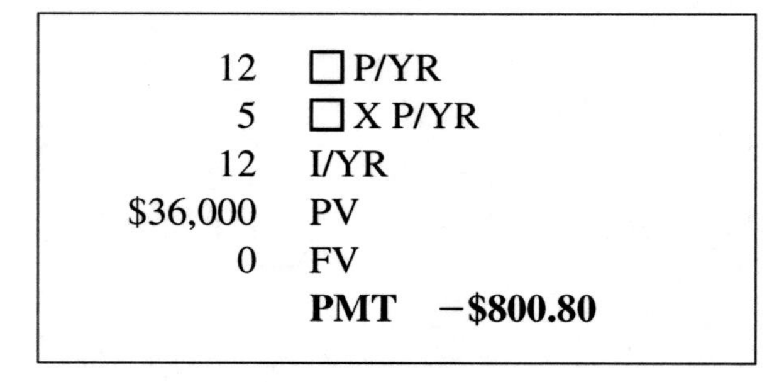

12	□ P/YR	
5	□ X P/YR	
12	I/YR	
$36,000	PV	
0	FV	
	PMT	**−$800.80**

This loan will require a payment of $800.80 per month for 5 years. Over the life of the loan Michael will make 60 such payments for a total of $48,048 ($800.80 * 60). In addition he will pay a

$4,000 down payment, which will bring the total out-of-pocket cost of the car at $52,048 ($48,048 + $4,000). After 5 years on the road however, most vehicles lose more than half their value. Even if the BMW lost only half its original value, it will be worth about $20,000 ($40,000 * 50%) by the time the loan is repaid. This implies that Michael will have paid $52,048 to possess a vehicle with a $20,000 fair market value. This does not look like a wise financial move. Michael will lose with a great degree of certainty $32,048 ($52,048 - $20,000) by financing this vehicle.

To be fair in this analysis, the $32,048 "loss" on this transaction buys a certain degree of "coolness" for young Michael. There is no doubt he will be riding in style for the next 5 years. The question is, should a person lacking $32,048 borrow and spend this amount to buy some "coolness"?

Maybe it would help Michael to see what else he could accomplish with $32,048. In other words, if Michael decided to drive the used vehicle his parents bought for him, he wouldn't buy the new BMW and he wouldn't lose $32,048. He could invest this money for his future. Assume he invested the funds for his retirement in 45 years, earning an average annual return of 10%, Michael could build a $2,335,994.2211 retirement account balance.

HP10BII FV Calculation

1	□ P/YR	
45	N	
10	I/YR	
$32,048	+/−	PV
0	PMT	
	FV $2,335,994.2211	

That's the opportunity cost of the car. By buying the car now, Michael will forgo $2.3 million in retirement funds. The choice comes down to a BMW now, or $2.3 million later. If that doesn't deter Michael from buying the car, then he will suffer the consequences of his action. One thing is for sure. Ric provided his son with the necessary figures to make an informed decision.

3.2.2 Practical Application: 0% Financing vs. Cash Rebate

When looking to purchase big ticket items like vehicles, boats, furniture etc., it is not unusual to be offered special financing terms or other discounts to entice you to make the purchase. The situation can get confusing if there are multiple mutually exclusive promotional offers for purchasing the item. Mutually exclusive means that if you select one promotional offer, you forgo all others.

Suppose you are about to purchase a new car to celebrate your graduation from college. Good news! The manufacturer of the vehicle you desire is currently offering incentives. You can receive EITHER a 0% financing for 4 years OR a $3,500 instant cash rebate, with 5.5% financing for 5 years. If the vehicle price is $35,000 which one is the better offer?

Typically, you cannot tell immediately which one is the "better" offer, as there is no rule that one type of offer is always better than the other. There are however two things you need to consider before deciding which offer to take. First, you need to define what "better" means to you. Does it mean the lowest monthly payment, or does it mean the lowest total cost of the vehicle? Second, you need to run the numbers for both scenarios to figure out which one is the best.

HP10BII PMT Calculation

0% Financing		Cash Rebate	
12	☐P/YR	12	☐P/YR
4	☐X P/YR	5	☐X P/YR
0	I/YR	5.5	I/YR
$35,000	PV	$31,500	PV
0	FV	0	FV
	PMT −$729.1667		**PMT −$601.6866**
$729.1667 * 48 = **$35,000**		$601.6866 * 60 = **$36,101.1965**	

Notice that with monthly payments you have monthly compounding. With the 0% financing, the payment can also be found by simply dividing the principal by the number of periods ($35,000 / 48 = $729.1667). With the cash rebate scenario you only borrow $31,500 as the instant rebate is subtracted from the vehicle price. The payments for both scenarios have a negative sign, indicating they are cash outflows.

The 0% financing scenario results in the lowest total cost for the vehicle, but carries the highest monthly payment. Despite the higher monthly payment, you will save $1,101.20 choosing this scenario. A lot of buyers base their decisions on the affordability of the monthly payment, while overlooking the total cost of the item. As a result they end up overpaying for things.

Once again, there is no rule that one type of offer is always better than the other. Offers can be structured in many ways to be made more or less attractive compared to alternative offers. You need to calculate the total cost of payments under all offers, and choose the offer with the lower total cost for the item.

3.2.3 Practical Application: Mortgage Loan Amortization

Ric and Vanessa Milford purchased a new house for $380,000 on July 1st. To get a conventional mortgage with a low interest rate, they made a 20% down payment and financed the remaining balance for 30 years at 5.25%. They are required to make monthly payments to the lender, starting one month later. The payments will consist of both principal and interest, and after all payments are made, the loan will be paid off or amortized. A time value of money calculation with monthly compounding can tell us the Milford's monthly mortgage payment.

HP10BII PMT Calculation

12	☐P/YR	
30	☐X P/YR	
5.25	I/YR	
$304,000	PV	
0	FV	
	PMT	**−$1,678.6993**

Because of the 20% down payment the loan principal (PV) is $304,000 ($380,000 * 80%). The FV of the loan is set to $0 as it should be completely paid off (amortized) after the 360th monthly payment of $1,678.6993.

Notice that out of the first payment, $1,330 is just interest ($304,000 * 0.0525/12), which means only $348.6993 ($1,678.6993 - $1,330) goes to pay down the loan principal. So after paying $1,678.6993 in their first month, the Milfords will still owe $303,651.3007. They will barely make a dent on the loan! The reason for this is that early on in the life of a loan the balance is too large, and requires most of the monthly payment as interest payment, leaving few dollars for principal repayment. As time goes by however, and the balance shrinks ever so slowly, the interest component of the monthly payment will shrink as well, freeing more dollars for principal repayment.

It is possible to repeat the same calculations for every payment, so the Milfords will know exactly how much of every payment goes for interest, principal, and what is the remaining balance. The outcome is usually presented as an amortization schedule and includes all payments until the last one, when the loan balance equals $0. You can use a spreadsheet to build an amortization schedule, or you can use online tools available for free, like the one on www.bankrate.com.

Your financial calculator has an amortization function, which can help you do these calculations with great ease. Keep in mind that the amortization function follows the PMT calculation you just did, so if you plan to do an amortization calculation you don't want to erase the PMT information from the memory.

The following table lists the HP10BII keystrokes to analyze the loan after the first, fifth, and twelfth monthly payment. The reason to look at the fifth payment is because the Milfords will only make five scheduled payments the year they get the mortgage (August, September, October, November, and December). They may want to know how much mortgage interest they can deduct from their income when they prepare their tax return. (Chapter 5 discusses Income Taxes.) The reason to look at the twelfth payment is just curiosity, as to how much the Milfords will still owe after a year's worth of payments.

HP10BII AMORT Calculation

After First PMT		After Fifth PMT		After Twelfth PMT	
1 INPUT 1		1 INPUT 5		1 INPUT 12	
□ AMORT		□ AMORT		□ AMORT	
= −$348.6993	PRIN	= −$1,758.8190	PRIN	= −$4,286.5615	PRIN
= −$1,330	INT	= −$6,634.6775	INT	= −$15,857.8301	INT
= $303,651.3007	BAL	= $302,241.1810	BAL	= $299,713.4385	BAL

By December, the Milfords will have paid $6,634.6775 in mortgage interest. They can use this information to plan their taxes for the year ahead of time. After 12 payments, totaling $20,144.3916 ($1,678.6993 * 12), the Milfords still owe 98.59% ($299,713.4385 / $304,000) of the loan principal.

If you repeat the amortization calculation once more, to include all 360 monthly payments (1 INPUT 360), you will find out that this loan will cost the Milfords $300,331.7069 in interest expense. So this $304,000 mortgage loan will consume $604,331.7069 of the Milfords money over the next 30 years.

3.2.4 Practical Application: Mortgage Refinancing and Points

Suppose that one year after the Milfords got their original 30-year mortgage loan, interest rates drop significantly. Ric and Vanessa contemplate refinancing their mortgage to lock in a much lower interest rate, possibly repay their loan sooner, and in the process reduce the $300,331.7069 interest expense associated with their current loan.

Their lender now offers 15-year mortgage loans at a 4.00% interest rate. The Milfords are given the option to "buy down" that interest rate by paying "points." A point is typically 1% of the loan principal, and reduces the interest rate by 0.25% for the life of the loan. A borrower can pay more points to permanently reduce the interest rate of the loan.

The Milfords know mortgage interest rates are as low as they can remember, and feel they need to take advantage of this opportunity. But they don't know whether it makes sense to pay points upfront to reduce an already low rate. They seek the advice of their Certified Financial Planner™ to run the mortgage loan figures with and without points, and recommend the best choice for them.

Their financial planner examines two 15-year mortgage loans: one with no points and 4% interest rate, and another requiring 2 points upfront payment, but carrying only 3.5% interest rate. The principal for both loans will be $304,000, the $300,000 of their current mortgage loan balance plus another $4,000 for the closing costs of the new loan. Incurring the refinancing costs will in effect negate the progress the Milfords made paying down the principal during the previous year, but the refinancing could save them a lot in future interest expenses.

HP10BII PMT and AMORT Calculation

15-Year, No Points, i = 4%		15-Year, 2 Points, i = 3.5%	
12	☐P/YR	12	☐P/YR
15	☐X P/YR	15	☐X P/YR
4.00	I/YR	3.50	I/YR
$304,000	PV	$304,000	PV
$0	FV	$0	FV
	PMT −$2,248.6513		**PMT −$2,173.2429**
1 INPUT 180		1 INPUT 180	
☐AMORT		☐AMORT	
= −$304,000.0013	PRIN	= −$303,999.9940	PRIN
= −$100,757.2327	INT	= −$87,183.7280	INT
= −$0.0013	BAL	= $0.0060	BAL

Both 15-year loans have the potential to save the Milfords at least $200,000 in interest expense, compared with their current 30-year mortgage loan. As long as the Milfords can afford the higher monthly payment required under a 15-year loan, they should go ahead and refinance. It will be a sound financial decision which will contribute to their wealth accumulation.

As for the choice between the two 15-year loans, there are two key issues to consider:

First, the loan requiring the 2 points saves $13,573.5047 more in interest expense than the loan without the points. This does not make it necessarily the best choice, as the Milfords will have to pay upfront $6,080 ($304,000 * 2%) to buy down the interest rate. If the Milfords can earn a guaranteed return on their investments of more than 5.5% (see table bellow) they will be better off not paying the points and investing the $6,080. They would earn more over the next 15 years than the $13,573.5047 the lower interest rate could save them in interest expense.

HP10BII I/YR Calculation

1	☐ P/YR	
15	N	
$6,080	+/−	PV
$13,573.5047	FV	
	I/YR	**5.5**

Second, the loan requiring the points comes with a lower interest rate therefore a lower monthly payment. The $75.4084 ($2,248.6513 - $2,173.2429) monthly savings from the lower payment, compared to the non-point loan, are the reward for paying the $6,080 in points upfront. To benefit from the lower monthly payment, the Milfords will need to keep the loan for more than 80.6276 months ($6,080 / $75.4084 per month) or 6 years and 9 months. It will take them that long to recover their initial investment in the points and break even. Keeping the loan for more than 6 years and 9 months will make the investment in the points profitable.

So the decision to refinance into a 15-year mortgage is easy. They will clearly benefit from it. The decision however to pay points on the new loan, or not, depends on the Milfords expected rate of return on their investments, and their expected length of ownership of this house. The longer they expect to stay, the more it pays to pay the points.

Lastly, caution is needed when one is considering paying points on a mortgage loan. Despite the original length of a mortgage (15, 20, or 30 years), the average actual life of a mortgage loan is around 7 years. Homeowners either refinance when they can get better interest rates, or move for employment purposes or due to change in family status (birth, death, divorce). It is not likely anymore to find families that have lived in the same house for several decades. How long has your family lived in its current residence?

3.3 Growing Annuities

By definition an annuity is a series of equal payments in fixed time intervals over a time period. In some cases however, the payments may be increasing to accommodate the cost of living, higher incomes or more generally inflation. In such cases, our annuity formulas will have to be adjusted to accommodate the growing payments. It is also useful to introduce at this point the concept of real interest rate, which can facilitate the calculation of growing annuities.

Nominal Interest Rate vs. Real Interest Rate

Throughout the presentation of the time value of money concepts and calculations you learned to use extensively interest rates or investment returns. In Section 3.1.2, you also learned about different types of interest rates, like the periodic rate, the annual percentage rate, and the effective annual rate. All of these rates are "nominal rates" in the sense that they are the rates quoted by banks, financial publications, news services, etc. nominal rates reflect current prices and do not make an adjustment for inflation.

Inflation is defined in economics as a continuous increase in the aggregate price level. In other words, during a period of inflation prices keep rising and the purchasing power of your money declines, as you need more and more money to purchase the same items you usually purchase. In the presence of inflation (or more accurately expected inflation), lenders require higher nominal interest rates to lend funds, in order to compensate themselves for the expected loss of purchasing power their funds will suffer during the period of the loan.

For example, if a bank was to lend you $1,000 for a year, charging a nominal rate of 5%, you would have to repay the bank $1,050 after one year. The $50 interest would represent the reward of the lender for letting you use the bank's funds. But if during the time of the loan the inflation rate was also 5%, then market prices of goods and services would increase by 5%. Whatever the lender could purchase with $1,000 when the loan was issued, it would cost $1,050 when the loan was repaid. This represents the loss of purchasing power of the lender's money. Despite your $50 interest expense, the lender would not be better off making this loan to you. Adjusted for the increase in prices, the lender would have gained nothing. In "real terms," meaning adjusted for the change in prices, the bank's rate of return on this loan was 0%. It follows then that if in the future the bank expects 5% inflation to prevail, the bank will charge a higher nominal interest rate to compensate itself for inflation, and to make a "real rate of return." Maybe the bank will charge 8% on its new loans, so it can earn a "real interest rate" of 3%. So, the real interest rate is the nominal interest rate adjusted for inflation.

The great monetary economist of the twentieth century, Irvin Fisher, expressed the relationship between the two rates in the following equation:

$$(1 + i_N) = (1 + i_R)*(1 + \pi)$$

Where i_N is the nominal interest rate,
i_R is the real interest rate, and
π is the inflation rate.

Solving the Fisher equation for the real interest rate:

$$(1+i_N)=(1+i_R)*(1+\pi)\Rightarrow i_R=\frac{(1+i_N)}{(1+\pi)}-1$$

And in our example the real interest rate is:

$$i_R=\frac{(1.08)}{(1.05)}-1\Rightarrow i_R=1.0286-1\Rightarrow i_R=0.0286$$

Because it is in decimal format you need to multiply by 100 to get the 2.8571% real interest rate.

3.3.1 Present Value of a Growing Annuity

Suppose you are trying to help your parents plan for their retirement. They expect to live in retirement for 30 years, and they want to receive $50,000 at the beginning of every year. They want these annual payments to increase by 3% to cover inflation, and they believe they can earn 7.5% on their investments. You want to calculate the necessary amount of money they need to accumulate in order to achieve their goal.

This is a growing annuity because your parents want the annual payments to keep increasing, to compensate them for inflation. It is also an annuity due, because the annual payments are desired at the beginning of each year. Recall our annuity PV equation:

$$PVA = PMT * \frac{1 - \frac{1}{(1+i)^N}}{i}$$

For an annuity due we just need to multiply the equation by (1+i) as $PVA_D = PVA*(1+i)$. For a growing annuity we need to introduce to the equation the growth rate of the payments "g". The equation evolves to:

$$PVA_{GD} = PMT * \frac{1 - \frac{(1+g)^N}{(1+i)^N}}{i-g} * (1+i)$$

Substituting the numbers for our example yields:

$$PVA_{GD} = \$50{,}000 * \frac{1 - \frac{(1.03)^{30}}{(1.075)^{30}}}{0.075 - 0.03} * (1.075) \Rightarrow PVA_{GD} = \$50{,}000 * 16.0611 * 1.075 \Rightarrow$$

$$\Rightarrow PVA_{GD} = \$50{,}000 * 17.2657 \Rightarrow PVA_{GD} = \$863{,}284.1250$$

Or you can use your financial calculator. To accommodate for a growing annuity you need to use the real interest rate, as the investments will be growing at one rate (7.5%) and at the same time the payments will be growing by another rate (3%). So the real interest rate in percentage format (multiplied by 100) is:

$$i_R = \left[\frac{(1+i_N)}{(1+\pi)} - 1\right] * 100 \Rightarrow i_R = \left[\frac{(1.075)}{(1.03)} - 1\right] * 100 \Rightarrow i_R = 0.0437 * 100 \Rightarrow i_R = 4.3689$$

HP10BII PVA_{GD} Calculation

1	☐ P/YR	
	☐ BEG/END	
30	N	
4.3689	I/YR	
$50,000	PMT	
0	FV	
	PV	**−$863,291.3875**

Your parents will need to accumulate $863,291.3875 if they are to retire with the living standard they desire. Chapter 9 covers in greater detail retirement planning. Notice the small difference between the equation and the calculator result. Once again it is due to the rounding error of manual calculations required to solve the equation.

3.3.2 Present Value of a Growing Perpetuity

While perpetuities as securities are rare, the perpetuity equation is used by financial planners to make conservative estimates about funding needs. The benefit of using the perpetuity equation is that you can estimate what amount you need to accumulate, in order to secure payments forever. You can see how attractive this concept is in retirement planning. It would be great if retirees could never run out of funds no matter how long they lived.

Let's continue the same example from the previous section, where you were helping your parents prepare for retirement. In your calculations you assumed a 30-year life expectancy at retirement. What if your parents were to live longer? For peace of mind let's calculate how much your parents would need to accumulate to be able to produce inflation adjusted annual payments forever.

The growing perpetuity equation is a slight modification of the simple perpetuity equation:

$$PV_{PG} = \frac{PMT}{i-g} \Rightarrow PV_{PG} = \frac{\$50,000}{0.075-0.03} \Rightarrow PV_{PG} = \$1,111,111.1111$$

So for an extra \$247,819.7236 (\$1,111,111.1111 - \$863,291.3875) your parents can receive their inflation adjusted retirement payments for as long as they live.

3.3.3 Future Value of a Growing Annuity

Planning for achieving a financial goal typically requires commitment to a savings program with periodic contributions for a time period. In such instances a future value of an annuity calculation can be very helpful. Suppose you decide to start saving \$4,000 per year, for the next 40 years, and your average annual return is 10%. You know already how to use the future value of an annuity equation, or how to use your financial calculator, to find your final accumulation after 40 years.

$$FVA = PMT * \frac{(1+i)^N - 1}{i} \Rightarrow FVA = \$4,000 * \frac{(1.10)^{40} - 1}{0.10} \Rightarrow$$

$$FVA = \$4,000 * 442.5926 \Rightarrow FVA = \$1,770,370.2227$$

HP10BII FV Calculation

1	□ P/YR
40	N
10	I/YR
0	PV
\$4,000	+/− PMT
	FV \$1,770,370.2227

As expected, the final accumulation of a steady stream of savings contributions, over four decades will be a significant amount. The power of compound interest in action!

What could be a more realistic scenario however, is to expect that as your income increases in the future, your ability to save will increase as well. If your income increases by an average 3% per year, and your savings are linked to your paycheck, then your savings will increase by the same percentage every year. In other words, the annual savings will keep increasing year after year, resulting in a "growing annuity." You can calculate the future value of the growing annuity by introducing the payment growth rate "g" to the original FVA equation. The modified equation looks like this:

$$FVA_G = PMT * \frac{(1+i)^N - (1+g)^N}{i-g}$$

So your final accumulation under a growing annuity will be:

$$FVA_G = PMT * \frac{(1+i)^N - (1+g)^N}{i-g} \Rightarrow FVA_G = \$4,000 * \frac{(1.10)^{40} - (1.03)^{40}}{0.10-0.03} \Rightarrow$$

$$FVA_G = \$4,000 * 599.9609 \Rightarrow FVA_G = \$2,399,843.60$$

This is a more realistic scenario for you. Your income in the later years of your career will probably be much higher than at the beginning years. Your income will reflect the fact that you will be more productive, experienced, matured, possessing specific industry knowledge and a network of professional relations. This higher income will afford you to save more, and increase your final accumulation by an additional $629,473.3773 ($2,339,843.60 - $1,770,370.2227). Your future looks brighter already!

3.3.4 Serial Payments

"Serial payments" is another name for the increasing payments of a growing annuity. There are situations that you may want to save for a specific goal, and you would like to know how much you need to save each period to reach your goal, taking into account that inflation will keep making this goal more expensive while you are saving for it. It is possible to address this problem with a regular annuity, but the required payment may be too high to be affordable. A growing annuity however uses increasing payments (serial payments), which start low and progressively increase, making the payments more affordable in the early periods.

Suppose you are planning to buy a house in 5 years and you need $60,000 for the down payment in today's prices. Prices are expected to keep rising at an average annual rate of 3%, while your investments can generate a 9% average annual return. You also prefer to start saving less now and more each year thereafter, as your income is expected to keep increasing, to keep pace with inflation.

The down payment for the house is quoted at today's prices. Five years later with 3% inflation the house will be more expensive, and the required down payment will be:

$$FV = PV *(1 + i)^N \Rightarrow FV = \$60,000 * (1.03)^5 \Rightarrow FV = \$69,556.4445$$

Using the future value of a growing annuity equation and solving for the payment:

$$FVA_G = PMT * \frac{(1+i)^N - (1+g)^N}{i-g} \Rightarrow PMT = \frac{FVA_G}{\frac{(1+i)^N - (1+g)^N}{i-g}} \Rightarrow$$

$$PMT = \frac{\$69{,}556.4445}{\frac{(1.09)^5 - (1.03)^5}{0.09 - 0.03}} \Rightarrow PMT = \frac{\$69{,}556.4445}{6.322498} \Rightarrow PMT = \$11{,}001.4182$$

This is the first year's payment. The payment for the second year needs to be 3% higher to compensate for the effect of inflation (π) during that year. The third year will need to be 3% higher than the second year payment, and so on. The following table shows the required payments over the next 5 years and their future values by the end of year-5:

Serial Payments

Serial PMT	**PMT_t * (1+π) = PMT_{t+1}**	**N**	**FV**
First	$11,001.4182	4	$15,529.3996
Second	$11,001.4182 * (1.03) = $11,331.4607	3	$14,674.5703
Third	$11,331.4607 * (1.03) = $11,671.4045	2	$13,866.7957
Fourth	$11,671.4045 * (1.03) = $12,021.5466	1	$13,103.4858
Fifth	$12,021.5466 * (1.03) = $12,382.1930	0	$12,382.1930

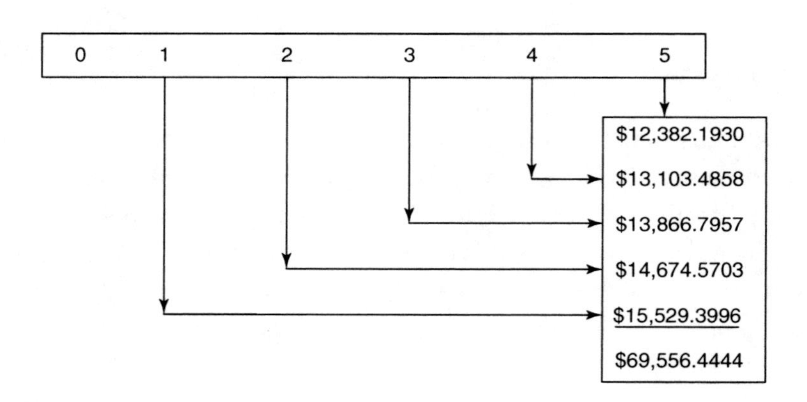

As indicated by the time line above, the serial payments compounded at 9% for the appropriate number of years produce the inflation adjusted down payment.

You may also use your financial calculator to calculate serial payments. You will need to use the real interest rate to accommodate for inflation, but you can use the down payment in current prices. Once you find the PMT you need to multiply it by (1+π) to accommodate for inflation the first year. Multiply again to get the second PMT and so on.

$$i_R = \left[\frac{(1+i_N)}{(1+\pi)} - 1\right] * 100 \Rightarrow i_R = \left[\frac{(1.09)}{(1.03)} - 1\right] * 100 \Rightarrow i_R = 0.0583 * 100 \Rightarrow i_R = 5.8252$$

HP10BII SERIAL PMT Calculation

1	□ P/YR		
5	N		
5.8252	I/YR		
0	PV		
$60,000	FV		
	PMT	**−$10,680.9885**	* 1.03 = $11,001.4182
			* 1.03 = $11,331.4607
			* 1.03 = $11,671.4045
			* 1.03 = $12,021.5466
			* 1.03 = $12,382.1930

Notice that these annual payments are identical to the ones calculated with the FVA equation. Therefore, when they are invested at 9% for the appropriate number of periods, they will add up to the inflation adjusted down payment of $69,556.4444.

Summary

This chapter introduced more involved time value of money scenarios and calculations. The chapter covered more frequent compounding, the different types of interest rates, and a variety of real life practical applications like how to make decisions based on the "true" interest rate, payday loans, car loans, choosing between rebates and low promotional finance terms, mortgage loans, amortization, and paying points on loans. The chapter also covered growing annuities, perpetuities, and serial payments. There is a lot of material in this chapter, and if you want to master it, you will need to go over the examples and applications a few times, until you get comfortable with them.

Review Questions

1. Maria is looking to open a time deposit account. She contacted three banks and got the following offers. Which offer should Maria choose if she plans to keep the deposit for more than a year?

Bank	APR	Compounding
A	10.0%	Monthly
B	10.1%	Quarterly
C	10.2%	semiannually

2. Your credit card issuer is charging you 1.75% interest per month. What interest rate is the credit card issuer required to report to you to be compliant with the truth-in-lending regulations? What is the "true" rate you are charged on this credit card?

3. Mark pawns his car, which has a $10,000 fair market value, for a $5,000 loan. The pawn shop charges 25% interest per month. If Mark returns to the pawn shop in 3 months, how much does he have to repay in principal and interest to pick up his car? What if he was to wait one more month?

4. Juan deposited $10,000 in a savings account paying 8% per year. The bank uses daily compounding on its savings accounts. What will be Juan's account balance after 5 years?

5. Natasha made an investment 6 years ago. Today its value is $45,666.57 which represents a 14% annual return. If the investment offered quarterly compounding, what was Natasha's original investment amount?

6. Bill is in the market for a new automobile. His chosen vehicle comes with a price tag of \$30,000 and two promotional offers. The first option offers 1.9% financing for 4 years. The second option offers a \$4,000 rebate and a 5.9% financing for 5 years. What is the monthly payment under each option? Which is the better offer?

7. Steve and Cathy bought a \$400,000 house with a 20% down payment and a 6.5% 30-year mortgage loan. What is their monthly payment? How much do the still owe on the loan after 3 years? What is the total interest expense for the life of this loan?

8. Steve and Cathy refinance \$310,000 of their 30-year mortgage loan (from the previous problem) into a 15-year mortgage loan with 4.5% interest rate. What will be their new monthly payment? What is the total interest expense for the life of this loan? Did it make sense for Steve and Cathy to refinance their original loan?

9. Bob and Carol have saved \$500,000 and would like to use this money to buy an annuity that will pay them a fixed \$4,000 at the beginning of each month, to supplement their Social Security income at retirement. If the annuity yields 6% annual return, how long will the payments last?

10. In the previous problem, if Bob and Carol wanted their monthly payments to increase by 3% each year to accommodate inflation, how long would the annuity payments last?

CHAPTER FOUR

Personal Financial Scorecards

4.1 Introduction

The financial planning process requires the collection of personal financial information, its organization into useable formats and its detailed analysis to establish one's financial situation. Based on this and the client goals, the financial planner can formulate strategies to help the client achieve his or her financial goals. Important components of the analysis are the determination of the client's current level of wealth (or net worth), and the client's annual income and expenses. Financial ratios and benchmarks can identify strengths and weaknesses in the client's financial life, which will need to be explored and addressed by the recommended strategies. The analysis and the quantitative aspects of the planner's recommendations should be reflected in a proposed budget that should guide the client to financial success.

4.1.1 Financial Statements

Personal financial statements are a key source of financial information. They record, organize and communicate vital information about the financial condition, asset performance and significant activities or events in the life of a household. For example, a big family vacation will certainly appear as an increase in recreational expenses, and either as a decrease in monetary assets or as an increase in debt, depending on how the vacation was paid for.

There are several types of financial statements that can be constructed. For financial planning purposes however, the two necessary ones are the balance sheet and the income statement. With the balance sheet you can determine one's current wealth level. With the income statement you can determine the flow of funds over a period of time. In other words, how much income is earned and how much is spent per period.

Personal financial statements are pretty straightforward to construct. The art is not so much in building them, as it is in analyzing them, interpreting them and getting insights about one's financial life, from the information listed on these statements. A slight confusion may occur because statements may appear in some publications with different names. For example, the income statement is also referred to as the income and expense statement. Another source of possible confusion may arise from the fact that personal financial statements are similar in nature to business financial statements, but not all accounts are the same or reported the same way. The purpose and mechanics however are the same, and with some training you will be able to adjust your analysis for the appropriate unit, whether it is a household or a business.

4.1.2 Balance Sheet

A balance sheet is a convenient way to organize and summarize what you own (called "assets"), what you owe to third parties (called "liabilities") and the difference between the two (called "net worth") at a given point in time. In other words, the information reported on the balance sheet is valid as of the particular date listed on the statement. For example, your 2012 balance sheet is accurately reflecting the values of all listed accounts as of December 31, 2012. Past that date the information may not be accurate anymore, as you may engage in transactions that alter the account balances. For example, January 3rd you pay your credit card bill from your checking account. Both your debts and your cash balances will now be lower than what is reported on your most recent balance sheet.

The following table shows a model, which you can follow to create your own personal balance sheet.

Balance Sheet

Personal Balance Sheet	
Your Name	
As of December 31, 20XX	
Monetary Assets	**Current Liabilities**
Cash Equivalents	Unpaid Bills
Savings Accounts	Credit Card Balances
Money Market Accounts	Auto Loan
Time Deposits (CDs)	Student Loans
	Mortgage Loan
Investment Assets	**Long-Term Liabilities**
Brokerage Account	Auto Loan
Retirement Account	Student Loan
Businesses	Mortgage Loan
Personal Use Assets	**Total Liabilities**
House	
Furnishing/Appliances	**Net Worth**
Clothing/Jewelry	
Automobile/Boat	
Total Assets	**Total Liabilities and Net Worth**

This statement is called a balance sheet because the left column and the right column totals need to be exactly the same amount, so the statement will "balance." Let's look at the components of this financial statement.

Assets

Typically a balance sheet will first list the stuff you own. You may own them by yourself or jointly with others, or they may not be fully paid off. For jointly held assets you only record the value of your share of ownership. If there is a debt associated with the asset, you record the value of the asset in the Asset column, and the debt in the Liabilities column.

Assets can be classified in the following categories:

- Monetary assets are those that are very liquid, and are either in cash or expected to be converted in cash within the next 12 months. They are held primarily for making scheduled payments and covering emergencies or unexpected expenses. Monetary assets include cash and cash equivalents like checking accounts, savings accounts, money market funds and time deposits (CDs) with less than 12 month maturity. Typically all these assets offer low return and low risk. Their primary attribute to your portfolio of holdings is their liquidity. So despite their low return you still need to allocate a percentage of your assets to this category.

- Investment assets are those held primarily for producing earnings and generating wealth. They include time deposits with more than 1 year maturity, bonds, stocks, mutual funds, retirement accounts, pension plans, education savings accounts, cash values of life insurance policies, real estate held for income purposes and businesses. Typically these are your "top producing" assets. They are risky but also have the potential to generate high returns. The reason you have them in your portfolio is to create wealth. The more assets you allocate to this category, the wealthier you will become.
- Personal use assets are those tangible assets that you own primarily for your own personal usage, like vehicles, real estate, furniture, appliances, electronics, clothing and jewelry. Typically these assets offer no return. Their purpose is to provide you with utility in your daily life. Aside perhaps from your residence, the value of all these assets is expected to decline drastically as they are used up. The more assets you allocate in this category, the higher your current lifestyle will be, and the lower your wealth will become. "Living it up" in the present leaves less to be invested for your future.

Keep in mind that all assets need to be reported at their current fair market value. The price you paid to acquire them is not relevant. Recall, the balance sheet reports the accounts as of a particular date. So your assets need to be reported at their fair market value as of the reporting date.

Usually, monetary and investment assets are easy to value any given day. Bank accounts, brokerage accounts and retirement accounts all offer online access to balances based on daily valuations. Business interests are harder to value and you may need to wait for the annual appraisal of the business.

Some personal use assets can also be difficult to value. If you own a vehicle, you can estimate its fair market value based on its condition and mileage by visiting the website of Kelly Blue Book at www.kbb.com. If you own real estate, you can get an estimate of its current value by visiting the website of a company specializing in real estate valuations, like Zillow at www.zillow.com. If you either lease a vehicle or rent a home or apartment, you don't need to value them, because you don't own them, therefore you should not be listing them as your assets.

However, when it comes to furnishings, appliances, electronics and clothing, there is no easy or standard method for their valuation. You need to come up with their fair market value, meaning what a willing buyer would pay a willing seller, taking into account the age and condition of the item. Your possessions are certainly not worth as much as what you paid for them when they were new, but they are not completely worthless either. Somewhere in between the two extremes lies the fair market value of these items. The accuracy of your net worth depends on the accuracy of your asset valuations.

Liabilities

Liabilities reflect your debts. They can be classified in the following categories:

- Current liabilities are those that you need to pay off within the next 12 months. They include current unpaid bills (utilities, rent, medical services, taxes, etc), overdue bills, credit card balances, and the portion of long-term loans due this year.
- Long-term liabilities are those that are not due during the next 12 months, or have remaining balances too large to be repaid within 12 months. Mortgage loans, car loans and student loans are all included in this category.

When it comes to liabilities, only the unpaid principal of a loan is recorded as a liability. Interest is not a liability, unless it has already accrued. For example, if you have a car loan with 3 more years of scheduled payments, the principal to be repaid this year is a current liability, the principal to be repaid the next 2 years is a long-term liability and the interest for all 3 years has not accrued yet. If you decide today to pay off the loan early, none of this interest will be charged to you. The loan amortization calculations in Chapter 3.2.3 are very helpful in determining the correct amount of the loan principal to be repaid each year.

Net Worth

The net worth reflects the amount of assets on your balance sheet that you own, once all liabilities are paid off. In this sense, your net worth represents what is truly yours, and therefore this is the key metric of this statement. To be progressing towards financial success, your net worth should be increasing from one year to the next. The balance sheet is constructed in a way that reflects the fundamental accounting identity:

$$ASSETS(A) \equiv LIABILITIES(L) + NETWORTH(NW)$$

It is an identity because it is always true. What you own (assets) was purchased either with your own means (net worth) or with borrowed means (liabilities). In case something was gifted to you or inherited by you, then it is part of your net worth. Rearranging the fundamental accounting identity to solve for the net worth yields:

$$A - L \equiv NW$$

This is a powerful relationship to use as a guide for your financial decisions. When you are young and focusing on wealth accumulation, try to think of every transaction in terms of this equation. In other words, how do your transactions affect your net worth?

For example, suppose that today you made the following transactions:

i) You paid $40 cash for a pair of sunglasses
ii) You charged $590 on your credit card for a non-refundable flight to Hawaii
iii) You charged $65 on your credit card for a dinner and a movie date, and
iv) Your mutual fund shares increased in value by $200.

Transaction	**A** –	**L** =	**NW**
i)	($40) Monetary Asset $40 Personal Use Asset $0	$0	$0
ii)	$0	$590 Current Liability	($590)
iii)	$0	$65 Current Liability	($65)
iv)	$200 Investment Asset	$0	$200
Total	**$200**	**$655**	**($455)**

The purchase of sunglasses does not affect your net worth immediately, as it is merely a transformation of a monetary asset to a personal use asset. Of course in the long run, the change in your net worth from this transaction depends on whether cash or the sunglasses lose their value faster than the other. Buying a plane ticket reduces your net worth, as you purchase a consumable good/service by incurring debt. The same applies to the purchase of the restaurant meal and entertainment. They are both consumables. Whether you paid with cash or with credit you'll have nothing to show for it, except for the memories. It is only the appreciation of your investment asset that has a positive impact on your net worth. And here lies one of the secrets of creating wealth: Purchasing consumables and personal use assets makes you feel good, but does not make you wealthier. Only acquisition of investment assets has the potential to create wealth for you.

4.1.3 Income Statement

The income statement is an effective way to record and organize your income from all sources and your expenses for all goods and services, over a period of time. Typically the income statement reflects the monthly or annual earning and spending activities of the household. The purpose of constructing this statement is to better track where the money is spent, and to identify your "net income" or "net discretionary cash flow." If the income statement shows a positive net income, then there are funds available to put to work to achieve your financial goals. If the net income is negative, the expenses are greater than the income, and there are no available funds to work with to pursue your financial goals. In this case, the tracking and listing of all expenses will be very helpful in identifying potential future savings, so the net income will turn positive.

The following table shows a model, which you can follow to create your own personal income statement.

Income Statement

Personal Income Statement
Your Name
Period ending December 31, 20XX

Gross Income
Salaries/Wages
Interest/Dividends
Retirement Income
Government Benefits

Taxes
Payroll Taxes (Social Security/Medicare)
Federal Income Taxes
State Income Taxes
Property Taxes

Automatic Savings
Retirement Plans: 401(k), 403(b), 457, IRA, Roth IRA
Education Savings: 529 Plan, Coverdell

Expenses
Housing: Rent, Mortgage, Utilities, Maintenance, Lawn Care
Automobile: Lease/ Loan Payment, Registration, Gasoline, Maintenance, Parking
Food: Groceries, Restaurants
Clothing and Personal Items
Recreation: Entertainment, Vacations, Travel
Insurance: Medical, Life, Disability, Homeowners, Automobile, Liability
Medical: Deductibles/Co-pays for Exams, Tests, Hospitalization, Procedures
Other: Education, Student Loan Payment, Other Debt Payment, Cleaners, Charity
Net Income = Gross Income – Taxes – Automatic Savings – Expenses

Income

Income is typically easy to determine. You need to record the gross income, meaning the full income before any withholdings for taxes or retirement contributions. Taxes and retirement plan contributions are recorded after the gross income, to help you identify your "take home pay." Your gross income will need to include all investment income from securities and business interests. In case you are receiving government benefits like Social Security, disability or unemployment benefits, these will need to be recorded as gross income as well. Finally, retirees will need to also include their pension benefits or their retirement account withdrawals during the period.

Expenses

Expenses can be more difficult to determine for a couple of reasons. First, some of your spending is cash based. Unless you are well organized and keep records and receipts of everything you spend cash on, it will be impossible to accurately track down all these transactions months later.

Second, some of your spending is credit based. This tends to cause some confusion. Do you record an expense when you make the purchase or when you make the payment(s)? Under the cash accounting system, which applies to households and most small businesses, income is recorded when received and expenses are recorded when they are paid. For this reason, the personal income statement tracks very well your actual cash flows. For example, on October 10 of this year, you purchase some furniture on credit. The furniture costs $4,200 and comes with 0% financing for 12 months. To avoid paying any finance charges you plan on making 12 monthly payments of $350 ($4,200/12). For the current year you will record 2 monthly payments (for November and December) or $700 as an Expense. The remaining balance will appear on your end-of-year balance sheet as a current liability. Next year, you will record on your income statement $3,500 in expenses for this purchase.

Third, while it is useful to distinguish between "discretionary" (variable) and "nondiscretionary" (fixed) expenses, it is not always easy to do so with all of them. Discretionary expenses are those over which you have some immediate control, like food, clothing and recreation. These categories would be the prime targets if you were trying to identify ways to reduce expenses. Nondiscretionary expenses on the other hand, are those over which you have no immediate control. Typically, you have to make all contractual payments or bad things will happen. In the short run, you cannot find savings from rent, mortgage payments, car payments, or utilities, unless you are prepared to experience a drastic and possibly traumatic deterioration of your lifestyle. In the long run however, as contracts expire, or you have time to modify them, even your nondiscretionary expenses can be altered. For example, when the rental contract expires, you can move to a less expensive place or find a place with roommates to share the rent.

Yet, there are some expenses like home maintenance or automobile repairs that can be treated as either discretionary or nondiscretionary. Fixing the leaking roof in your house or addressing that painful noise from your car's transmission does not represent a contractual obligation and can be viewed as optional spending. It is doubtful however that postponing for long such "discretionary" expenses will result in real savings.

Net Income

Your net income equals your gross income from all sources once taxes, withholdings, and expenses have been subtracted. In this sense, the net income represents your "available income" or "discretionary cash flow" for financial planning. It affects to a great extent your ability to pursue all your financial goals. If your net income is positive, you can purchase the insurance coverage you lack, or save for a particular goal, etc. If it is not enough to pursue all your goals, then you will need to review all accounts of the income statement to work out a plan (called "budget") that results in higher net income in the future. This is part of financial planning.

If the net income is negative however, then spending exceeds the take home pay. The excess spending is either paid out of your existing assets (savings, investments) or financed with new debt (or both). In either case your net worth will decline, and instead of becoming wealthier you will be getting poorer.

$$A\downarrow - L\uparrow \equiv NW\downarrow$$

In extreme situations, where the net income continues to be negative for a prolonged period of time, assets will be severely depleted. Once your liabilities exceed your assets, your net worth will become negative, and you will become "insolvent." Bankruptcy may not be far off. The need for financial planning is more urgent when faced with negative net income.

Notice that the net income is the link between your income statement and your balance sheet. With a positive net income, you will purchase more assets and increase your net worth. Great, you are becoming wealthier! With a negative net income, you will consume your assets and/or increase your liabilities. Bad news, your wealth is shrinking!

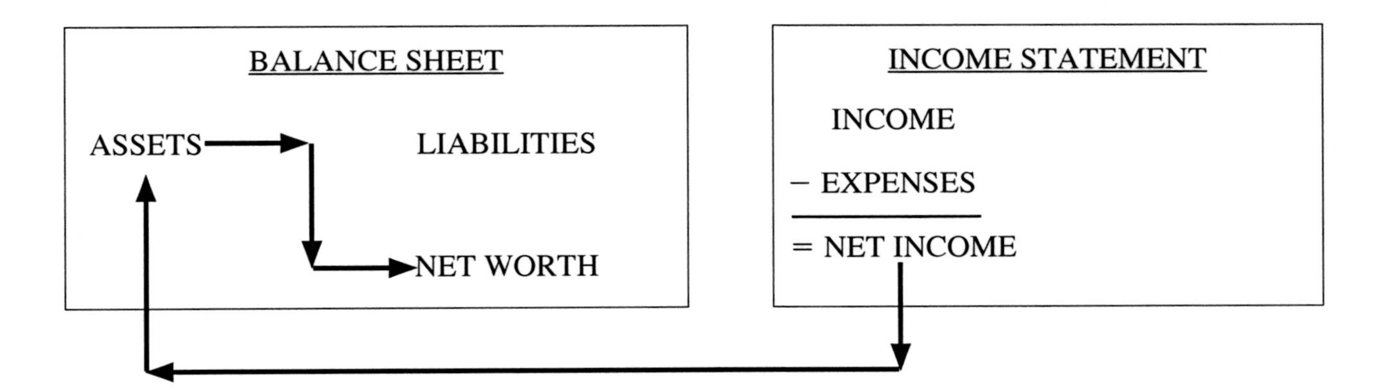

4.1.4 Practical Application: The Milfords' Financial Statements

The Milfords are a working couple in their early 40s (Ric 42, Vanessa 39) raising their two daughters and Ric's son from his first marriage. Both Ric and Vanessa have been contributing from an early age to the retirement plans offered by their employers, and have managed to set aside some money for their children's education. They also have some cash in liquid accounts for emergencies. By far their biggest asset is their house, although there is a mortgage associated with it. Their vehicles are relatively new, but not paid off yet. The Milfords have paid off their student loans and all their credit card debt.

Let's look at this couple's financial statements, in an effort to identify the health of their financial condition from the reported financial information.

Balance Sheet
The Milfords
As of December 31, 20XX

Monetary Assets			**Current Liabilities**		
Checking Accounts	$12,000		Mortgage Loan	$14,800	
Savings Accounts	15,000		Auto Loans (2)	6,000	
Total Monetary Assets		$27,000	Total Current Liabilities		$24,800
Investment Assets			**Long Term Liabilities**		
Ric's 401(k)	108,000		Mortgage Loan	295,200	
Vanessa's 403(b)	31,000		Auto Loans (2)	13,100	
Ric's IRA	23,000		Total Long Term Liabilities		308,300
Ric's Cash Value Life Ins	14,000				
Education Savings (529)	20,000				
Total Investment Assets		196,000	Total Liabilities		333,100
Personal Use Assets			**Net Worth**		347,900
House	400,000				
Vehicles (2)	30,000				
Furniture/Appliances/Elect	25,000				
Clothing	3,000				
Total Personal Use Assets		458,000			
Total Assets		$681,000	**Total Liabilities and Net Worth**		$681,000

Looking at the Milfords' balance sheet you can see that they have $681,000 in assets, but they owe $333,100 to creditors. That leaves them with $347,900 in net worth. Aside from these observations however, you cannot determine whether the assets and the net worth have been increasing or decreasing. In other words, you don't really know if the Milfords are getting richer or poorer.

Furthermore, while looking at the Milfords' balance sheet you can identify the dollar value of their assets, but you cannot identify how these assets came to be theirs. Maybe the education savings were a gift from their parents, who wanted to contribute to their grandchildren's college fund. Maybe some of their cash or the down payment for their house was inherited money from their relatives. Just because the Milfords have assets does not necessarily mean they have been managing successfully their finances.

The only way you could get an idea about the change in assets and net worth, as well as the origin of their assets, would be to have access to balance sheets from previous periods. The comparison between current and past financial conditions would allow you to observe whether the accounts have been increasing or decreasing. It would allow you also to determine whether an asset was purchased with a transfer from another asset category or an increase in debt. Lack of both would suggest a gifted or inherited asset.

Finally, the end result of constructing the balance sheet is the determination of the net worth. While it is clear the Milfords have positive net worth ($347,900), it is not so clear whether this is an appropriate amount for them. Are they ahead or are they falling behind from where they should be? Once again, just looking at a balance sheet will not reveal all the answers to you. Further analysis is required, if you are to get any real insights about one's financial condition.

Let's turn our attention now to the income statement, and try to identify how the Milfords are handling their income, savings and expenses.

Income Statement
The Milfords
Period ending December 31, 20XX

Gross Income		
Salary and Bonus (Ric)	$100,000	
Salary (Vanessa)	50,000	
Investment Income	600	
Total Gross Income		$150,600
Taxes		
Payroll Taxes	11,500	
Federal Taxes	11,200	
State Taxes	7,000	
Property Tax-House	5,000	
Property Tax-Autos	400	
Total Taxes		(35,100)
Automatic Savings		
401(k) Ric	6,000	
403(b) Vanessa	3,500	
IRA Ric	5,000	
529 Plan	6,000	
Total Automatic Savings		(20,500)
Expenses		
Housing	36,400	
Automobiles	11,700	
Food	17,200	
Clothing & Personal	4,000	
Recreation	7,700	
Insurance	13,400	
Medical	2,000	
Other	2,300	
Total Expenses		(94,700)
Net Income		$300

The Milfords are a two-income household. They have steady monthly salary income, and have arranged for automatic retirement and education savings out of their pay checks. The rest of their income is totally consumed by taxes and living expenses. While they earn a comfortable income, they have no meaningful "available income" to pursue any possible financial goals they may have.

Aside from these fairly obvious observations, just looking at the income statement figures provides no insight as to whether the Milfords save enough for retirement and education, or they spend too much on living expenses.

Much like with the balance sheet, there are limitations to the insights you can get just by looking at an income statement. Further analysis of the statements is necessary, if you are to discover any weaknesses in the Milfords' financial life.

4.2 Financial Statement Analysis

Creating or accessing a personal balance sheet and an income statement is a necessary first step in analyzing your finances. Valuable as the information provided by these statements may be however, it is not in a framework that allows for quick discoveries or conclusions, because it is expressed in dollar terms. It is preferable instead, to have financial information expressed in percentages and multiples, to facilitate meaningful comparisons and diagnostics.

Common Size/Common Base Statements

Once the financial statements are prepared, a useful analytical method is to convert them into "common size" and/or "common base" statements.

Common size statements express all accounts on the statement as a percentage of a key account. The common size balance sheet expresses all accounts as a percentage of total assets. The common size income statement expresses all accounts as a percentage of gross income. This allows for immediate discovery of the weight or the importance of every account in the statement. Abnormally small or large weights of accounts create immediate red flags for further analysis.

Common base statements express every account on the statements as a percentage of the same account from a previous year, which is chosen to be the base year. This allows for immediate identification of accounts which have increased or decreased in value compared to the base year account value. Those that have increased (decreased) will be more (less) than 100% of the base year account value. If statements from several years are available, a trend for each account could be identified as well. Again, abnormal or unexpected changes in a trend create a red flag for further analysis.

Ratio Analysis

Financial ratios are relationships between accounts from the financial statements. Since the ratio values are quotients, dollars are cancelled out and the ratios are typically expressed as multiples or percentages. The comparison of ratio values to usual or optimal values for these ratios allows for quick diagnostics of one's financial condition. The different groups of ratios are discussed in Section 4.2.2.

4.2.1 Practical Application: The Milfords' Common Size Statements

Balance Sheet
The Milfords
As of December 31, 20XX

Monetary Assets			**Current Liabilities**		
Checking Accounts	1.76%		Mortgage Loan	2.06%	
Savings Accounts	2.20%		Auto Loans (2)	0.88%	
Total Monetary Assets		3.96%	Total Current Liabilities		3.64%
Investment Assets			**Long-Term Liabilities**		
Ric's 401(k)	15.86%		Mortgage Loan	43.35%	
Vanessa's403(b)	4.55%		Auto Loans (2)	1.92%	
Ric's IRA	3.38%		Total Long-Term Liabilities		45.27%
Ric's Cash Value Life Ins	2.06%				
Education Savings (529)	2.94%				
Total Investment Assets		28.79%	Total Liabilities		48.91%
Personal Use Assets			**Net Worth**		51.09%
House	58.74%				
Vehicles (2)	4.41%				
Furniture/Appliances/Elec	3.67%				
Clothing	0.43%				
Total Personal Use Assets		67.25%			
Total Assets		100.00%	**Total Liabilities and Net Worth**		100.00%

Expressing all balance sheet accounts as a percentage of total assets allows for some quick analytical observations. First, the majority of the Milfords assets are personal use assets (67.25%). They provide for a nice lifestyle, but are counterproductive when it comes to creating wealth. The investment assets on the other hand, which can create wealth, weigh just 28.79% in the asset portfolio. Rebalancing the asset portfolio to become more investment and growth oriented, can be one of the planning recommendations for the Milfords.

Second, you can easily see from the common size balance sheet that the Milfords' net worth is 51.09% of total assets, while their liabilities are only 48.91% of their assets. Obviously, the higher a family's net worth, the better off financially they are. Typically however, it is useful to compare net worth to the total assets of a family, over their life span. Most people go through a "financial life cycle," where it is normal to have a very low, even negative net worth when they are young and just out of college, but as they go through life they build their net worth. There are always exceptions, like the young socialites-heiresses to $400 million fortunes, but for the most part young people start their financial life with few possessions and maybe some student debt. In other words, it is expected to start your adult life insolvent. What is not expected is to end your life insolvent. With care and planning your net worth as a percentage of your assets will keep growing, from a negative number in your early 20s, to 40-50% in mid career, all the way to 90-100% at your retirement time. The Milfords in their early 40s already have a net worth that is more than 50% of their assets. That's an encouraging sign.

Let's see now what the common size income statement reveals about the Milfords.

Income Statement
The Milfords
Period ending December 31, 20XX

Gross Income		
Salary and Bonus (Ric)	66.40%	
Salary (Vanessa)	33.20%	
Investment Income	0.40%	
Total Gross Income		100.00%
Taxes		
Payroll Taxes	7.64%	
Federal Taxes	7.44%	
State Taxes	4.65%	
Property Tax-House	3.32%	
Property Tax-Autos	0.27%	
Total Taxes		(23.32%)
Automatic Savings		
401(k) Ric	3.98%	
403(b) Vanessa	2.32%	
IRA Ric	3.32%	
529 Plan	3.98%	
Total Automatic Savings		(13.60%)
Expenses		
Housing	24.17%	
Automobiles	7.77%	
Food	11.42%	
Clothing & Personal	2.65%	
Recreation	5.11%	
Insurance	8.90%	
Medical	1.33%	
Other	1.53%	
Total Expenses		(62.88%)
Net Income		0.20%

Once the income statement accounts are expressed as a percentage of gross income, it is really easy to make some key observations about the Milfords' saving and spending practices. First, the Milfords pay less than a quarter (23.32%) of their gross income in taxes. This is not bad, given that property taxes are included in this percentage. Further reduction of their taxes is possible, but will require allocating more funds to their tax deferred retirement accounts.

Second, the Milfords savings rate is only 13.60% of their gross income. As you will see in the next section, this is a pretty low portion of income to save, particularly when it includes the education savings (3.98%) for the children's future college costs. Subtracting the education savings, only 9.62% of gross income is saved for the year. Keep in mind, however, that the savings listed on the income statement do not include the employer contributions to Ric and Vanessa's retirement plans. Since there is no information available at this point about the size of these annual employer contributions, this would be a topic to be revisited by their financial planner.

Finally, the Milfords spent almost every dollar that wasn't taken by taxes or committed to automatic savings. There is practically no net income for the year, which is disturbing for a couple of reasons. The obvious one is that no financial goal requiring the commitment of discretionary cash flows can be pursued or accomplished, as there are no discretionary cash flows available. The more subtle cause for worry is that the Milfords' income included Ric's maximum bonus of 25% of his regular salary ($80,000). The question then is: will the Milfords be able to reel in their spending if Ric has a less than stellar year at work and the bonus disappears? Will they have to dip into their savings, consume their assets, and decrease their net worth? This is clearly a red flag for their financial planner, and an area that will certainly draw specific recommendations.

Clearly, the common size financial statements added more and better insights about the Milfords' financial condition, than the regular financial statements. Several red flags were raised requiring further analysis.

4.2.2 Practical Application: The Milfords' Financial Ratio Analysis

Recall from Section 4.2, there are several groups of financial ratios, which a financial planner can use for diagnostic purposes in every area of a client's financial life. Typically three groups of ratios are calculated focusing on the following aspects of the client's financial life: liquidity, debt management and progress ratios.

There are a few things you need to be aware about financial ratio analysis. First, before you even calculate a financial ratio you need to know what constitutes a good, acceptable or poor value for this ratio. In other words, you need to be aware of the benchmark the ratio value will be compared to. Being aware of benchmarks makes you ask the right questions and draw the right conclusions.

Second, there can be many ratios in each group, and each financial planner uses his or her favorites. Furthermore there are variations of these ratios. For example, you can calculate the same ratios using gross income or after tax income. The results will be different, therefore the relevant benchmarks should be different.

Finally, after you calculate the value of a financial ratio you need to pay attention to the units of measurement. Does the ratio value represent dollars, time periods, a percentage, or a multiple? Clearly, the validity of your analysis depends on your understanding of your findings.

So let's look at the different ratios and evaluate the Milfords' financial condition. The account information used for the ratio calculation is found on the Milfords' financial statements, in Section 4.1.4.

Liquidity Ratios

Liquidity ratios measure the ability to meet short term obligations and emergencies.

i) The Current Ratio

$$CurrentRatio = \frac{MonetaryAssets}{CurrentLiabilities} = \frac{\$27,000}{\$24,800} = 1.0887* \geq 1$$

The current ratio measures the client's ability to meet short-term liabilities with available liquid assets. If there was no more income this period, would the client be able to pay all maturing debts? Ideally, the monetary assets will exceed the current liabilities, therefore a value greater than one is desirable for this ratio. However, too high of a current ratio value may indicate that the client is holding too many low yielding liquid assets, forgoing higher potential investment returns. The Milfords can cover their maturing liabilities with their available liquid assets, so they are doing well in liquidity management this far.

ii) The Emergency Living Expenses Coverage Ratio (ELEC)

$$ELEC = \frac{MonetaryAssets}{\frac{LivingExpenses}{12}} = \frac{\$27,000}{\frac{\$94,700}{12}} = \frac{\$27,000}{\$7,891.67} = 3.42 \in \{3-6\}$$

The emergency living expenses coverage ratio measures how long the client can cover living expenses with existing liquid assets. It is useful to know how many months a client can sustain the household expenses in case of loss of income due to job loss, illness, disability etc. The ratio can be calculated using either nondiscretionary expenses or living expenses. Using living expenses is a more conservative method and does not require the arbitrary distinction between discretionary and nondiscretionary expenses. It is also preferable to use annual expenses divided by 12, to estimate average monthly expenses, than to use any random month's expenses, which may not accurately reflect typical monthly expenses.

An acceptable value for this ratio is between 3 and 6 months. In other words, it is a good idea to have enough liquid assets to cover at least 6 months of living expenses, as no one is beyond illness or job loss. Keep in mind that this is just the recommended minimum, as it may take longer to find a new job. For instance, the median duration of unemployment in June 2012 was 9 months. Two-income households or those with available credit lines and disability insurance can afford to be on the lower end of the range, while one-income households and those with difficult to replace jobs may want to have more than a 6-month coverage of living expenses. The Milfords are on the lower end of the range, which is acceptable because they are a two-income household.

Debt Management Ratios

Debt management ratios measure the extent to which the client uses debt and the ability to service this debt.

i) The Debt Ratio

$$DebtRatio = \frac{TotalLiabilities}{TotalAssets} = \frac{CurrentLiabilites{+}LongTermLiabilities}{TotalAssets} =$$

$$= \frac{\$24{,}800{+}\$308{,}300}{\$681{,}000} = \frac{\$333{,}100}{\$681{,}000} = 48.91\%$$

The debt ratio measures the client's debt utilization. It shows the percentage of assets that are acquired with borrowed funds. Typically, young households have very high debt ratios as they carry student loans, car loans, and eventually mortgage loans. As much as 80–90% of their assets are financed by creditors. In time, debt will be paid down, investment assets will appreciate in value, and the debt ratio will decline. By retirement time, the debt ratio should be tiny, as lack of income reduces the ability to service debts. So the benchmark of this ratio is age related. The Milfords have a debt ratio of 48.91%. This means they owe less than half of their assets. Given their young age, this is an encouraging sign for their future financial well-being.

Notice that the portion of assets the Milfords do not owe to creditors, by definition must be their net worth. Dividing both sides of the fundamental accounting identity by assets, and solving for the net worth term yields:

$$A = L + NW \Rightarrow \frac{A}{A} = \frac{L}{A} + \frac{NW}{A} \Rightarrow \frac{NW}{A} = \frac{A}{A} - \frac{L}{A} \Rightarrow \frac{NW}{A} = 1 - 0.4891 \Rightarrow \frac{NW}{A} = 0.5109$$

The percentage of assets not reflected in the debt ratio (L/A), must be reflected in (what can be called) the net worth ratio (NW/A). Currently the Milfords owe 48.91% of their assets and own the remaining 51.09%. In time, the first ratio should decrease and the second ratio should increase, but they will always add up to 1 or 100% of their assets.

ii) The Housing Ratio

$$Housing\ Ratio = \frac{Principal\ \&\ Interest + Tax + Insurance}{GrossIncome} =$$

$$= \frac{\$28{,}452 + \$5{,}000 + \$1{,}000}{\$150{,}600} = \frac{\$34{,}452}{\$150{,}600} = 22.88\% \leq 28\%$$

The housing ratio measures the percentage of gross income committed to housing payments. It includes the rent or the mortgage payment and excludes utilities and maintenance expenses. A mortgage payment typically has four components: principal (P), interest (I), property taxes (T), and homeowners insurance (I). Keep in mind that the housing payment you calculate on your mortgage loan reflects only the lender required principal (P) and interest (I). The relevant property taxes (T) and insurance (I) are added later to form the monthly payment (PITI).

You can calculate the housing ratio on a monthly or annual base. Because banks prefer to approve mortgage loans when the proposed housing payments do not exceed 28% of gross income, the benchmark for this ratio is no more than 28%. Higher housing ratios can lead to financial problems, as there is not enough income left for other debt payments and expenses. The Milfords' annual PITI ($34,452) consists of $28,452 principal and interest, $5,000 property taxes, and $1,000 homeowners insurance. This may seem high, but as a percentage of gross income is only 22.88%, which is well bellow the limit for this ratio. So the Milfords do not overspend on housing.

iii) The Debt Service Ratio

$$DebtServiceRatio = \frac{PITI + AllOtherDebtPayments}{GrossIncome} =$$

$$= \frac{\$34,452 + \$6,000}{\$150,600} = 26.86\% \leq 36\%$$

This ratio expands on the housing ratio. It considers all recurring contractual payments, like housing, car payments, student loan payments, credit card payments etc. The idea here is to measure the percentage of gross income devoted to all debt payments. The ratio can be calculated using either annual or monthly payments. Lenders prefer to extend credit to borrowers whose debt service ratio is no more than 36%. If Debt payments consume more than 36% of gross income, and taxes consume another 30% or more, then there is little left for living expenses and savings. Sooner rather than later, the borrower will be in financial trouble. So the benchmark for this ratio is no more than 36%.

Notice, if a borrower assumes hefty mortgage payments maximizing the housing ratio at 28% of gross income, the borrower in effect limits all other consumer debt payments to 8% of gross income, as the debt service ratio limit is 36%. Conversely, if a borrower assumes too much consumer debt, then the borrower in effect limits the size of his or her available mortgage loan.

Aside from the mortgage loan and the two car loans, the Milfords have no other debt. At 26.86%, their debt servicing ratio is well bellow the established limit. This implies the Milfords have more borrowing capacity available in case they need financing.

Progress Ratios or Savings, Investments and Net Worth Ratios

The progress ratios measure the extent to which the client is preserving income and building assets and net worth to achieve stated financial goals.

i) The Savings Ratio

$$SavingsRatio = \frac{Savings + EmployerContributions}{GrossIncome} = \frac{\$20,500 + \$7,500}{\$150,600} = 18.59\%$$

The savings ratio shows the percentage of gross income that is saved for attaining the client's stated goals. It includes savings in all types of bank, brokerage and retirement accounts. For employer sponsored retirement plans, both the employee and the employer contribution need to be included in the savings. The appropriate value for this ratio depends on the number and cost of the client goals, as well as the available time to save for these goals.

For instance, clients in their 20s, saving only for retirement, can replace their inflation adjusted income at retirement with a 12% savings ratio. But if they want to have a down payment for a house or education funds for their children, then the savings ratio will have to be much higher. Clients in their 40s, just starting saving for retirement, can replace their inflation adjusted income at retirement with a 52% savings ratio (assuming 3% inflation rate, 20 years to retirement, 10% investment yield, and no social security).

So you need to start saving as soon as possible and as much as possible, to have a good chance of achieving your financial goals. Delaying saving can only be justified if you have high interest rate debts. Paying off a credit card loan charging you 21% APR, means you will be saving the 21% interest rate. This is a higher yield than most normal investment returns you can consistently realize.

The department of commerce, bureau of economic analysis, reports the average US personal savings rate to be 3.57% of disposable (or after tax) income during the first four months of 2012. If this personal savings rate was reported as a percentage of gross income, it would be less than 3%. Clearly US households do not save anything remotely close to an adequate savings ratio.

The Milfords' income statement shows \$20,500 in retirement and education savings. In addition Ric and Vanessa received a total of \$7,500 in employer contributions to their 401(k) and 403(b) retirement accounts. Their savings ratio of 18.59% of gross income may seem praiseworthy compared to the average US household, but it may not be adequate given their retirement need and the college education expenses for their three children. Their financial planner will probably have some recommendations for them about their level of savings.

ii) The Investments Ratio

$$InvestmentsRatio = \frac{Investment\,Assets{+}Monetary Assets}{GrossIncome} = \frac{\$196{,}000 + \$27{,}000}{\$150{,}600} = 1.48*$$

The investments ratio measures the extent to which a client has accumulated enough assets to replace his or her gross income for retirement purposes. For a client to be able to replace the preretirement income without taking into account social security, whose benefit is uncertain several decades in to the future, the client needs to build a fund about 20 times the preretirement income. Assuming a 5% real rate of return, the perpetuity formula suggests a fund equal to 20 times the required annual payment from the fund:

$$PV_P = \frac{PMT}{i} = \frac{PMT}{0.05} = \frac{PMT}{\frac{1}{20}} = 20 * PMT$$

Obviously, a lower real rate of return will require a larger investment fund. So, the investments ratio measures the client's progress towards building this fund. The benchmark for this ratio depends on the age of the client. The closer a client is to retirement, the closer this ratio needs to be to 20.

Only the monetary and investment assets are taken into account, as only those can be used for income generation. Personal use assets are intended to support the client's lifestyle now and in the future. They are not intended for income production. To be conservative with your analysis, you can exclude from the numerator all assets committed to goals other than retirement, and use gross income instead of after tax income for the denominator. While there are no payroll taxes for retirement income, there will be income taxes, and maybe at a higher rate, once there are no more dependents and dependent deductions.

The Milfords' investments ratio of 1.48 is clearly not adequate given their age. It is even worse if you exclude from the investment assets the $20,000 in education savings. This brings the investments ratio down to 1.35, which is far away from its target. The Milfords' financial planner will have to address this deficiency.

iii) The Return on Investments Ratio

$$ReturnOnInvestments = \frac{InvestmentAssests_t - InvestmentAssets_{t-1} - Savings_t}{InvestmentAssets_{t-1}} =$$

$$= \frac{\$196{,}000 - \$158{,}000 - (\$20{,}500 + \$7{,}500)}{\$158{,}000} = \frac{\$10{,}000}{\$158{,}000} = 6.33\%$$

The return on investments ratio measures the percentage gain of investment assets over a period of time. Managing to save enough out of your income is half the battle to financial success. The other half is to make your savings work hard to generate returns, that compound over time to create wealth. Obviously, the higher the rate of return on your investment portfolio the sooner you can achieve your financial goals. Remember however, that the rate of return is closely related with the risk level you are undertaking (more on risk and return in Chapter 7).

Historically, a diversified portfolio balanced between bonds and stocks has produced an average annual return of 8–9%. More allocation towards bonds brought the return down towards 5–7%, while more allocation towards stocks raised the returns towards 10–12%. Of course the emphasis is on the term "average" annual returns, which means some periods you experience worse and some periods you experience better returns, but over many holding periods the rate of return converges to some historic average.

To calculate the return on investments ratio you need the ending balance of the investment portfolio (Investment Assets_t), the current period's savings (Savings_t), and the beginning balance of the investment portfolio (Investment Assets_{t-1}). The first two you can find at the current period's financial statements, while the third one you can find at the previous period balance sheet. The Milfords had $158,000 in investment assets at the end of last year. This is their beginning balance for the current year. This year, their balance sheet reveals an ending balance of $196,000 for investment assets, while their income statement reveals $20,500 allocated to savings. In addition, the Milfords received $7,500 in employer retirement contributions this year, which needs to be included in their savings total.

Their 6.33% return on investments is on the low range, and their financial planner will need to address this issue. If such low returns have been the norm over the past years, perhaps they can explain the low multiple of the investments ratio (1.48*). One thing is for sure. It will be difficult for the Milfords to achieve their financial goals with this low rate of return. Perhaps a portfolio reallocation is in order.

iv) The Return on Net Worth Ratio

$$ReturnOnNetWorth = \frac{NetWorth_t - NetWorth_{t-1} - Savings_t}{NetWorth_{t-1}} =$$

$$= \frac{\$347{,}900 - \$286{,}900 - (\$20{,}500 + \$7{,}500)}{\$286{,}900} = \frac{\$33{,}000}{\$286{,}900} = 11.50\%$$

The return on net worth ratio measures the percentage increase in wealth over a period of time. A positive percentage change in net worth signifies real progress towards financial security. The higher the increase in your net worth in any given period, the bigger your progress is. To calculate this ratio you need the ending value of net worth from the current balance sheet, the beginning value of net worth from the previous period balance sheet, as well as the savings allocation from the current income statement.

The Milfords started the year with $286,900 in net worth, and finished with $347,900. during the year they added savings of $20,500, while their employers added $7,500 in retirement contributions. The entire $28,000 in savings needs to be subtracted from the increase in net worth to isolate the return from the influx of the new savings. The Milfords experienced an 11.5% growth rate in their net worth this year, which is really good news for achieving financial security.

Typically, an increase in net worth is the result of asset appreciation, debt paid off or a combination of both. Of course, gifts and inheritances will also increase net worth, but they do not happen very often. So to make progress towards financial security, you can count on investing in assets that tend to appreciate in value, while paying down your debts. Follow the strategy throughout life and you will build your net worth.

Changes in net worth are very important to the economy. When personal wealth increases, households feel more comfortable about their financial condition therefore they tend to spend more. This additional spending expands the economy, creates more jobs and more wealth for all. Economists call this the "wealth effect." It is possible however, to experience a decrease in net worth. If assets decline in value, or households assume new consumer debt to purchase consumables, then wealth will shrink and households will become poorer. A decline in value in the stock market or the real estate market has a negative and profound effect on household balance sheets. Feeling poorer, households may reduce their spending, which can lead to further reductions in the values of stocks and real estate, decimating personal wealth in the process. No wonder people monitor market prices daily, and the number of broadcasting financial networks is proliferating.

Highlights of the Milfords' Financial Statement Analysis

Common Size Balance Sheet

Investment Assets only 28.79% of Total Assets → Greater allocation needed **[PRIORITY]**

Debt level only 48.91% of Total Assets → Good, continue paying debt down

Net Worth at 51.09% of Total Assets → Good for their age

Common Size Income Statement

Savings are 13.60% of Gross Income → Greater allocation needed

Net Income 0.20% of Gross Income → Nonexistent, will have to increase **[PRIORITY]**

Expenses are 62.88% of Gross Income → Have to be trimmed to increase Net Income

Financial Ratios

Current Ratio = 1.0887>1 → Acceptable but at the low end

Emergency Living Expenses Coverage = 3.42 months → Acceptable but at the low end

Housing Ratio = 22.88%<28% → Acceptable to good

Debt Service Ratio = 26.86%<36% → Acceptable to good

Savings Ratio = 18.59% → Inadequate given their goals

Investments Ratio = 1.48* → Too low → Greater allocation needed **[PRIORITY]**

Return on Investments = 6.33% → On the low end → Portfolio review needed

Return on Net Worth = 11.50% → Good

The analysis of the Milfords' financial condition shows that they have good debt management, acceptable but low liquidity, inadequate investment portfolio and nonexistent disposable cash flow to boost savings and pursue their financial goals. Based on this information, their financial planner can offer targeted recommendations to address the deficiencies, starting with those identified as priorities. The recommendations, once accepted by the Milfords, will be introduced to their new budget, so the Milfords can proceed to the implementation step of the financial planning process.

4.3 The Budget

A budget is a detailed plan of your cash flows allowing you to closely monitor both your income and expenses. The starting point for creating a budget is your current income statement. Adjust your gross income for the next year based on your expectations for a new promotion, raise, cost of living adjustment or no change at all. Taxes are adjusted accordingly, based on your expected income changes.

Fixed or nondiscretionary expenses will remain the same (car payment, mortgage payment), but variable or discretionary expenses will have to be adjusted in a couple of ways. First, you will have to adjust them upwards to reflect your inflation expectation for the next year. For example, if you expect prices of goods and services you regularly consume to increase by 3% next year, then your variable expenses will have to be increased by the same percentage. Second, if your financial plan recommends trimming expenses, to increase savings or pay down debts, you will have to identify which expenses you are willing to trim and by how much. This is an area your financial planner can offer only limited assistance, like looking for a cheaper insurance policy or modifying the insurance coverage to save on premiums. But you are the one in control of deciding on the level of your expenses, as it is you that ultimately will have to live within the limits of this budget.

It is easy to be carried away when "trimming" expenses trying to prepare a budget that complies with your financial plan. You have to be realistic however with your expense reductions or the budget will not be followed. The key to a successful budget is to be realistic about both income and expense assumptions, so you can implement it. If you conclude there is no way to trim expenses to the recommended level, you may have to go back and reexamine your stated financial goals. This is preferable to living a lie. One of the benefits of the financial planning process is that it is forcing you to deal with your financial condition in a pragmatic manner, which produces predictable results, thereby reducing the uncertainty in your financial life.

Finally, once you settle on an acceptable and realistic (for you) annual budget, it is useful to convert it to a monthly one by dividing by 12. This will produce an average spending plan which you can monitor more frequently than once a year. If you find yourself for example, spending more on a particular category during a month, then you have the opportunity to adjust your spending the following month, to return to the average monthly budgeted amount. This increases your chances of successfully implementing your budget.

4.4 Practical Application: Good Debt-Bad Debt

Using debt may reduce your freedom and flexibility to allocate your income in the future, but not all usage of debt is bad. It is not debt per se that can cause you problems. It is the way you may be using it which may get you into trouble. If you use debt wisely, you can increase your financial flexibility, and possibly increase your net worth.

While borrowing too much, at high interest rates, to purchase goods and services with a shorter life expectancy than the debt repayment period may be detrimental to your financial future, the opposite behavior is beneficial to you. Borrowing sensible amounts that you can service comfortably, at low interest rates, to purchase items that tend to appreciate in value may be a great opportunity to create wealth.

For example, a 15-year mortgage loan to purchase a house may be beneficial to your net worth. As long as the purchase price is not unreasonably high, the interest rate is low, you can afford the monthly payments and the house is expected to last several decades, then this could be a sound financial decision. You will be using the lender's funds to purchase an asset, which will provide you with a utility yield (you get to live there), and is expected to appreciate over time by the rate of inflation. The value of the house will appear as an asset in your balance sheet, and as the debt will be paid off your liabilities will shrink, creating net worth.

Borrowing to go to college can be a great financial decision, as long as you do not borrow too much, you do not pay too much in interest, and you do not waste your time. In other words, if you need financing to attend college, you will be well advised to attend public institutions, which are cheaper because they are subsidized by the state. This way you will borrow less. Try to get government subsidized student loans which offer lower interest rates, and study a lot on a subject that will increase your marketability in the job market. This way, when you graduate you can easily find a well paying job, which will allow you to repay your student loan quickly to avoid paying interest charges for long. In this case, the lender's funds help you become an educated person (a benefit in itself), and purchase an intangible asset which will increase your earning capacity for life.

Finally, you can use debt to purchase a vehicle. But to make this a good use of debt you may want to borrow for a short time period, like 3 years, to get a lower interest rate and avoid paying interest for long. Once the loan is repaid, you may want to keep the vehicle for a few more years to avoid making new loan payments on the replacement vehicle. Save these payments in interest bearing accounts to earn a return. Before you know it you have created wealth and options for yourself. You can purchase your next vehicle and pay cash to avoid paying finance charges to a lender. Or you can use your accumulated savings to buy an investment asset (like an apartment, a bond etc.) that generates income payments. Use these income receipts to pay your next vehicle's monthly payments. This way, you still get a new vehicle, you still have an investment asset, and the monthly payment does not come out of your pocket!

All these examples indicate that debt is not necessarily a bad thing in your life. It is the way you use it that ultimately will determine whether it is good or bad. If you only use debt when you really need it, and with a focus on creating net worth, then debt can contribute to wealth creation. Instead of demonizing debt, it is better to understand it and learn to use it to your benefit.

Summary

This chapter introduced the scorecards of your financial life. The two major financial statements required in the financial planning process are the personal balance sheet and the income statement. Analysis of financial statements involves the creation and interpretation of common size statements and financial ratios. There are several groups of ratios, with several ratios each, that need to be calculated. The analysis provides insights about the liquidity, debt management, and progress in savings, investments and net worth in your financial life. Specific planning recommendations can target and address all deficiencies to help you achieve your financial goals. The recommendations are reflected on your new budget, which helps you monitor and adjust your income, spending and savings. Finally a practical application presents the beneficial uses of debt.

Review Questions

1. You purchase a new $30,000 vehicle with a 10% cash down payment, and the rest financed over 5 years at 6%. What is the immediate effect on your net worth?

2. Rudy had the following transactions this week. What is their effect on his net worth?

   Purchased a new washer and dryer set for $1,200 with store financing

   Paid off his $800 credit card bill from his checking account

   Charged $140 on his credit card for concert tickets

   Paid $400 for a tuneup to his car with his credit card

Use the following set of information to answer questions 3 to 12.

Brian and Connie have the following financial information:

Current Assets	$18,000	Gross Income	$128,000
Investment Assets	$235,000	Auto Savings	25,000
Personal Use Assets	$400,000	Expenses	$69,000
Current Liabilities	$6,000	Net Income	$5,000
Long-Term Liabilities	$310,000		

3. What is Brian and Connie's current ratio?

4. What is Brian and Connie's emergency living expenses coverage ratio?

5. What is Brian and Connie's debt ratio?

6. What portion of their assets do Brian and Connie truly own?

7. If Brian and Connie received $8,000 in employer retirement contributions, what is their savings ratio?

8. What is Brian and Connie's investments ratio?

9. If last year their investment assets were $180,000 what is Brian and Connie's return on investments?

10. If last year their net worth was $265,000 what is Brian and Connie's return on net worth?

11. If Brian and Connie have a monthly mortgage payment (PITI) of $2,666.67, what is their housing ratio?

12. If Brian and Connie have a monthly mortgage payment (PITI) of $2,666.67, how much in other monthly debt payments are they allowed?

13. You purchase a home with 20 years remaining useable life. Your 30-year mortgage carries a 4.5% interest rate, while inflation is expected to run at 3.5% annually over the same period. Is this good usage of debt?

14. What steps of the financial planning process are involved in this chapter?

CHAPTER FIVE

Income Tax Planning

5.1 Introduction

"Taxes are what we pay for a civilized society" reads the inscription at the front of the internal revenue service building in Washington, DC. Taxes can be seen as our "contribution" to support the public institutions, which provide us with a variety of public services like law enforcement and national defense. The term "contribution" however may imply a voluntary donation, which of course is not the case when it comes to any taxes. Federal, state and local authorities administer and enforce tax collection.

While most states impose their own income taxes, with their own rules and tax rates, the discussion in this chapter will focus on federal income taxes, which apply to all of us living and working in the US. The principles behind the federal income tax system however, are a good representation of the state income tax systems.

5.1.1 Origin of Federal Income Taxes

It is worth noting, that while in our days we perceive federal income taxes to be a natural part of our life as US citizens, this was not always the case. The Founding Fathers of this nation were very worried about the potential for the new federal government to grow in power and interfere with the rights of the states. Therefore, the Constitution allowed for direct taxes, like head taxes and property taxes, but only if they were "apportioned" (distributed) to the states based on their population. So although allowed, federal income taxes were not practical to impose, as the federal government could not use the revenue itself, but had to distribute it to the states based on the census count.

The first serious consideration for a federal income tax was during the War of 1812. Before it was enacted however, the war ended in 1815 and the justification for the tax disappeared. During the Civil War, the Revenue Act of 1862 introduced a personal income tax, but it was viewed as temporary and was repealed 10 years later. The first peace time income tax was passed in 1894, but in 1895 the US supreme court found that according to the Constitution direct taxes on income from personal property (like rental income or interest and dividend income) if imposed have to be "apportioned" to the states based on their population. The federal government found it impractical, if not undesirable, to tax wage income but not property income, so the tax was abandoned.

Eventually, the proponents of a federal income tax managed to pass with a two thirds supermajority by both Houses a proposal to amend the Constitution, and grant the federal government the power to collect income taxes from all sources. By 1913, the required three fourths of the states had ratified the proposal, which became the 16th Amendment to the US Constitution. The Amendment clearly stated that "congress shall have power to lay and collect taxes on income from whatever source derived, without apportionment among the several states, and without regard to any census or enumeration."

The first federal income tax following the 16th Amendment was 1% on net personal incomes above $3,000 with a 6% surtax on incomes above $500,000.

5.1.2 Tax Systems

There are three main personal income tax systems:

Under a progressive tax system, higher incomes are taxed at higher tax rates. under a proportional tax system, all incomes are taxed at the same tax rate. Finally, under a regressive tax system, higher incomes are taxed at lower tax rates, yet the actual dollar tax bill for a higher income is still higher than the tax bill of a lower income. For example, if a person with $40,000 taxable income was paying 20% in taxes ($8,000), while another person with $80,000 taxable income was paying 15% in taxes ($12,000), the tax system would be regressive.

The US has always had a progressive tax system, which means that increasing incomes have always been taxed at increasing tax rates. Table 5-1 shows the 2012 tax rates per filing status. Notice for example, that while a single taxpayer's taxable income in the first tax bracket ($0 to $8,700) is taxed at 10%, additional income beyond $8,700 belongs to the second tax bracket ($8,701 to $35,350) and is taxed at 15%. Taxable income higher than $35,350 belongs to the next tax bracket and it is taxed at a higher rate, and so on. Currently the highest income tax rate is 39.6%.

TABLE 5-1 Year 2013 Income Brackets and Tax Rates

Marginal Tax Rate	Single	Married Filing Jointly or Qualified Widow(er)	Married Filing Separately	Head of Household
10%	$0–$8,925	$0–$17,850	$0–$8,925	$0–$12,750
15%	$8,926–$36,250	$17,851–$72,500	$8,926–$36,250	$12,751–$48,600
25%	$36,251–$87,850	$72,501–$146,400	$36,251–$73,200	$48,601–$125,450
28%	$87,851–$183,250	$146,401–$223,050	$73,201–$111,525	$125,451–$203,150
33%	$183,251–$398,350	$223,051–$398,350	$111,526–$199,175	$203,151–$398,350
35%	$398,351–$400,000	$398,351–$450,000	$199,176–$225,000	$398,351–425,000
39.6%	$400,001+	$450,001+	$225,001+	$425,001+

The taxable income reported on Table 5-1 is the taxpayer's gross income minus numerous deductions and exemptions. In other words, your taxable income is much smaller than your actual income from your work and investments. See Section 5.2 for more details. Also, since 1985 the tax brackets are adjusted upwards every year to reflect the change in incomes due to inflation. Without this adjustment taxpayers would experience "bracket creep" meaning their nominal income would be pushed to the next tax bracket and taxed at higher rates, even though their real incomes have not increased.

It is interesting to look at the results of our progressive tax system almost 100 years from its inception. The internal revenue service (IRS) reports that as of 2009 (last available data) the top 1% of taxpayers paid 35.40% of all income taxes, while having 17.90% of all taxable income. The top 5% of taxpayers paid 57.63% of all income taxes, while having 33.45% of all taxable income. The top 50% of taxpayers paid 97.60% of all income taxes, while having 86.71% of all taxable income. The following IRS table (Table 5-2) shows the shares of income and income taxes, as well as the average tax rate for the different income groups of US taxpayers.

TABLE 5-2 2009 IRS TAXSTATS Table-7 [09in07tr]

Income Group	Income Tax Share	Taxable Income Share	Average Tax Rate
Top 1%	35.40%	17.90%	21.39%
Top 5%	57.63%	33.45%	18.63%
Top 10%	69.64%	44.95%	16.76%
Top 25%	86.66%	66.97%	14.00%
Top 50%	97.60%	86.71%	12.18%

The data from this IRS table imply that the bottom 50% of taxpayers paid only 2.40% of all income taxes in 2009, while declaring only 13.29% of all taxable income! This means that the US is fast approaching (and by now it may have already reached) the point where 50% of the people pay absolutely no income taxes. This is a very dangerous situation for a couple of reasons: First, it is difficult to have a strong nation when only half the people are contributing anything to it. Second, it is exceedingly difficult for a government in a democratic country to reduce spending on any government program, when 50% of the people are net beneficiaries who bear none of the costs of these programs. Consequently, it becomes almost impossible for a government to reduce spending, balance its budget, and stop increasing the nation's indebtedness to foreign nations.

5.1.3 Average vs. Marginal Tax Rate

When referring to tax rates it is important to distinguish between the average tax rate and the marginal tax rate. Table 5-2 uses the average tax rate to show how different income groups are burdened by income taxes. The average tax rate (ATR) can be calculated as:

$$AverageTaxRate = \frac{IncomeTaxesPaid}{TaxableIncome} = \frac{\$7,000}{\$50,000} = 14\%$$

So, if your taxable income is $50,000 and you paid $7,000 in income taxes, your average tax rate is 14%. In other words, 14% of your taxable income is taken by income taxes. The average tax rate is used to determine whether our tax system is progressive, proportionate, or regressive.

The marginal tax rate on the other hand, shows what percentage of an additional dollar of your taxable income will be paid in income taxes, and what percentage you will get to keep. The marginal tax rate (MTR) can be calculated as:

$$MarginalTaxRate = \frac{AdditionalIncomeTaxes}{AdditionalTaxableIncome} = \frac{\$8,561 - \$8,536}{\$50,100 - \$50,000} = \frac{\$25}{\$100} = 25\%$$

For example, according to Table 5-3 which shows an excerpt from the 2012 federal income tax table, if you are filing as single and your taxable income is $50,000, your tax bill is $8,536. However, if you had an additional $100 in taxable income, your tax bill would be $8,561 or $25 more, making your marginal tax rate 25% ($25/$100).

TABLE 5-3 2012 Income Tax Table Excerpt

If Taxable Income is		And You Are			
At least	But less than	Single	Married Filing Jointly	Married Filing Separately	Head of Household
$50,000	$50,050	**$8,536**	$6,634	$8,536	$7,151
$50,050	$50,100	$8,549	$6,641	$8,549	$7,164
$50,100	$50,150	**$8,561**	$6,649	$8,561	$7,176
$50,150	$50,200	$8,574	$6,656	$8,574	$7,189

Notice that your average tax rate at this taxable income level would be 17.07% ($8,536/$50,000). typically the ATR is less than the MTR, unless your taxable income falls in the first tax bracket where the ATR equals the MTR.

The marginal tax rate is very useful when people are making decisions with respect to work or investments. The higher the MTR, the more you need to send to the government, and the less you get to keep out of every additional dollar of your taxable income. Therefore, your incentive to work more or invest more is diminishing.

Keep in mind that the federal income tax is not the only tax applied to your income. for instance, if your federal MTR is 25%, your payroll taxes (Social Security and Medicare) are 7.65%, your state MTR is 5%, and your local (city and/or county) tax rate is 3%, then your effective marginal tax rate is 40.65% (25% + 7.65% + 5% + 3%). So if you were to work a few extra hours or were to get a second job to make a few extra dollars, you would only get to keep 59.35% of this extra money as taxes would consume the other 40.65%.

The marginal tax rate is very important in financial planning, because all decisions about activities like new investments or new jobs have to be evaluated based on your tax bracket, which determines your MTR, and therefore the after tax return on the activity.

5.1.4 Filing Status

As you can see in both Tables 5-1 and 5-3, for any given level of taxable income, your marginal tax rate and the amount of income taxes you will pay are dependent on your filing status, which is determined upon your family situation the last day of the tax year. The most beneficial filing status for tax purposes is the married filing jointly status, while the least beneficial is the Married Filing Separately status. So Congress is promoting marriage and family formation by providing economic incentives through the tax system. Let's look at the five filing status classifications in the order of preferential treatment by our tax system:

Married Filing Jointly (MFJ)

This status can be used only by spouses who decide to combine their gross income, deductions and exemptions and file one (joint) tax return. Typically, most married couples benefit by filing jointly instead of separately. As you can see in Table 5-1, the tax brackets for joint filers are twice as large as those of separate filers, meaning twice as much joint income is taxed at each marginal tax rate before a higher rate is applied.

Qualifying Widow(er) or Surviving Spouse

This filing status can be used by a taxpayer whose spouse has died within the 2 years prior to the tax year, and the taxpayer supports a dependent child, and pays for more than half of the costs to maintain their residence. If all three of these conditions apply, the taxpayer is a qualifying widow(er), and is allowed to file a tax return as married filing jointly. Once the three year period from the death of the spouse has passed, and the taxpayer has not remarried but still has a dependent child, then the taxpayer can file as head of household.

Head of Household

This status can be used by an unmarried taxpayer, who pays for more than half of the costs to maintain a residence for the taxpayer and a dependent child or relative, who lives with the taxpayer more than half of the year. While not as generous as the married filing jointly, this status has broader tax brackets than the single classification, therefore results in lower taxes. Single parents or divorced parents with custody of a child typically use this filing status. Also single taxpayers taking care of a dependent parent can use this status, even if the parent is not living in the same residence as the taxpayer.

Married Filing Separately

Typically married couples file joint returns to benefit from the preferential treatment of that status by the tax code. There can be circumstances however, that the election to file separately makes sense or is necessary. For instance: a) If in a two-income household one of the spouses has several deductible expenses, which may be disallowed under the higher joint income, the couple may find it beneficial to file separate returns for the year. b) Also if a couple is in the process of divorcing, but the divorce is not issued by the end of the year, then the couple is still married. However, the soon-to-be ex-spouses may not want to share information or documents anymore, so they may elect to file separate returns for the year. c) Finally, if a widow(er) remarries the same year the previous spouse died, the new couple will file a joint return for the year, while a separate tax return will have to be filed for the deceased spouse for that year. The deceased spouse's filling status will be married filling separately. Even dead you cannot escape taxes!

Single

This filing status must be used by unmarried, or officially divorced by the end of the year, taxpayers with no dependent children. This is the least generous classification, and typically results in higher taxes for a given income compared to the other classifications.

5.1.5 Types of Income

In the US tax system there are three classifications of personal income: active or ordinary income, investment or portfolio income and passive income. It is important to distinguish each source of income according to its proper classification because different tax treatment applies to each classification.

Active or ordinary income includes all income from work and the active engagement in a business. So wages, salary, bonus, tips, pension and even alimony are all included in this Income classification.

Investment or portfolio income includes earnings derived from investments. So Interest from bank accounts and bonds, dividends from stocks and mutual funds, and finally capital gains from the sale of investment holdings, are all included in this Income classification.

Passive income includes earnings from passive engagement in business activities. Passive means the taxpayer is not actively involved in the management and decision making process of these business activities. Real estate income and limited partnership income is included in this income classification.

Typically, investment income is taxed at lower rates than the other two forms of income. For instance, the maximum tax rate for qualified dividends and long-term capital gains (gains from investment assets held for more that 1 year) is currently 15% for those whose ordinary income is taxed at a marginal tax rate of 25% and higher. For the taxpayers whose ordinary income is taxed at a marginal tax rate of 10% to 15%, qualified dividends and long-term capital gains are tax free (0% tax rate)! Furthermore, investment losses can offset investment income for the year. if the losses exceed the investment income, up to $3,000 of the excess loss can even offset ordinary or passive income! The rest of the excess loss can offset future investment, ordinary or passive income!

Also passive income, representing earnings from real estate and other businesses, enjoys special privileges, like business deductions and write offs. Of course the IRS limits these passive activity write offs to the extent of passive activity income for the tax year, but the point is a lot of the passive activity income can be tax sheltered!

The major realization from this discussion is that our tax system favors investment and passive income over active income. In other words, for tax purposes investment earnings are treated better than working earnings. Congress through the tax code rewards those who invest to grow the economy and create jobs for others, instead of those who just have a job. The tax code message is clear: investing is more useful than working if you want to create wealth.

5.1.6 Tax Accounting Principles

Aside from properly classifying income according to source, taxpayers must also follow one of the approved accounting methods to properly "recognize" income for taxation. income "realization" (when it occurs) can be different from income "recognition" (when it is reported) for tax purposes.

Typically, households and small businesses follow the cash accounting method, which requires income to be recognized (reported for taxation) when it is received, while expenses are to be deducted when they are actually paid.

Larger businesses usually follow the accrual accounting method, which requires income to be reported for taxation at the period it is earned (time of the sale), even if that income is not received by the end of the period. Expenses are also deducted at the period they occur, even if the business did not pay them by the end of the reporting period.

Since this chapter's focus is on personal tax planning, the discussion will follow the cash accounting method, under which income is reported the period it is received. To prevent tax evasion however, there are some exceptions to this method, where households have to report income for taxation even if they did not receive the money during the period.

The first exception is the rule of "constructive receipt," which states that when income is readily available to the taxpayer without any significant restrictions, the income is constructively received during the period, and must be reported for taxation. For example, if you decide not to cash your november and december paychecks this year, but wait until january to do so, you have "constructively received" the income when you received the paychecks. Therefore, the income is taxable this year and not the next. If on the other hand, a bonus was set aside in an account for you, but you had to meet certain performance metrics or a service term to be entitled to the money, then a significant restriction exists that may prevent "constructive receipt" of the income. In this case, the income has not been received yet, and is not taxable this year.

The second exception to the cash accounting method is the "economic benefit" rule, which states that if the taxpayer receives an economic benefit which is deemed to be income according to the IRS rules, then the value of the benefit must be reported for taxation. For example, if your employer was to provide you with a company credit card to use for your personal (not business) expenses, like shopping at grocery stores, department stores, etc, then the value of all these purchases is deemed personal income and must be reported for taxation, even though you did not actually receive "money." Section 5.2.1 includes a list of "fringe" benefits provided by employers that the IRS does not consider income, and their economic value is not reported for taxation.

5.2 Calculating Personal Income Taxes

For financial planning purposes it is important to have a working knowledge of what goes into the calculation of your income taxes. While there are commercially available software programs like Turbo Tax (from Intuit) and TaxCut (from H & R Block Financial) that can calculate your taxes for the year, they cannot do the planning for you. You need to know what types of income are excluded from taxation, what expenses are deductible from your income, and what tax credits you may qualify for, so you can take the appropriate steps throughout the year to minimize your tax bill.

Keep in mind that you are required to file an income tax return for the year by the mid April of the following year. So at the time of filing your tax return it is too late to take any actions to reduce significantly your current tax bill. You can only work on reducing your next year's tax bill. For example, the tax return for 2012 will need to be completed and filed with the IRS by mid-April 2013. While you are preparing your tax return in February or March 2013, you realize you could have paid more of your medical bills during the year to qualify for a deduction, which would lower your tax obligation. Unfortunately, the year is over and the window of opportunity is closed for 2012.

So while there may not be so much value in tax preparation these days, there is great value in income tax planning. Earning income is necessary for creating wealth. protecting that income from overspending in any expense category, including taxes, is critical to your financial success. You will be well advised to acquire as much working knowledge of the income tax code as possible. Table 5-4 shows the process of calculating income taxes.

Sections 5.2.1 to 5.2.4 describe all the elements involved in the income tax calculation in more detail.

5.2.1 Calculating Gross Income (GI)

Your income includes income from all sources regardless of whether it is taxable or not. It includes active income, investment income, and passive income as they are described in Section 5.1.5. Table 5-5 lists common income sources.

Items with an asterisk in Table 5-5 indicate income potentially excluded from taxation. Once exclusions are subtracted from income from all sources, the result is gross income.

TABLE 5-4 Income Tax Calculation Process

	Income from All Sources
-	Exclusions from Income
=	**Gross Income**
-	Adjustments for AGI or Above the Line Deductions
=	**Adjusted Gross Income (AGI)** or (the Line)
-	Deductions from AGI or Bellow the Line Deductions (Standard or Itemized)
-	Personal and Dependent Exemptions
=	**Taxable Income**
*	Tax Rates
=	**Taxes**
-	Tax Withholdings
-	Tax Credits
=	**Tax Due or Tax Refund**

TABLE 5-5 Sources of Income

Salaries/Wages and Some Fringe Benefits *	Social Security Benefits *
Business Income (Self-Employment)	Worker Compensation Benefits *
Income Distributed from Partnerships	Scholarships *
Dividends and Interest *	Life Insurance Proceeds *
Capital Gains from Sale of Assets *	Gifts *
Rental Income	Inheritances *
Pensions and Annuity Distributions	Discharge of Debts *
Retirement Account Distributions *	Foreign Earned Income *
Unemployment Benefits	Alimony Received

Let's examine the exclusions from income in more detail.

The value of certain employee fringe benefits are excluded from taxation. The following employer paid benefits are not taxable income for the employee:

Health Insurance

Group term life insurance up to $50,000 in coverage; premiums for the coverage above $50,000 are taxable income for the employee

Meals at the business facility
Lodging if required for employment
Relocation services
Education assistance up to $5,250 per year
Transportation and parking benefits (within limits)
Gym membership if the gym is located in the employer premises
Employee discounts (up to 20% on services, or up to the gross profit on goods)
Cafeteria plans / dependent care / adoption assistance

Interest income from municipal (state and local government) bonds is excluded from federal income taxation. If you reside in the state which issued the bond, the interest income is excluded from state income taxation as well.

While capital gains from the sale of assets are taxable, the gains from the sale of your personal residence up to $250,000 (if your filing status is single) are excluded from taxation. For married filing jointly the exclusion can be up to $500,000.

While distributions from retirement accounts are generally taxable, qualified distributions from Roth IRAs, Roth 401(k) and Roth 403(b) plans are excluded from taxation. Qualified distributions are those made from an account opened at least 5 years earlier, and for death, disability, or attainment of age $59^1/_2$. Roth IRAs also allow a qualified distribution for a first home purchase. See Chapter 9 for more information about these accounts.

Some of the Social Security benefits are excluded from taxation, but up to 85% of the benefits can be taxable income if income from all other sources exceeds certain limits (hurdles). The limits vary by filing status as indicated in Table 5-6.

TABLE 5-6 Income Limits for Taxation of Social Security Benefits

Limits (Hurdles)	Single, Head of Household	Married Filing Jointly
First	$25,000	$32,000
Second	$34,000	$44,000

So if your income from other sources (modified AGI) plus half of your Social Security benefit exceeds the first hurdle for your filing status, up to 50% of your Social Security benefit is taxable. If your income plus half of your Social Security exceeds the second hurdle for your filing status, up to 85% of your Social Security benefit is taxable.

Workers' Compensation and any other settlements collected for physical injury or sickness are excluded from taxation. However, settlements collected for punitive damages are taxable income.

Scholarships paid to a candidate for a degree, and used for covering tuition (but not room and board) are excluded from taxation. If the candidate receives funds for room and board, that amount is taxable.

The life insurance benefit from the death of the insured is excluded from taxation for the beneficiary. However, if a policy holder surrenders the policy before the death of the insured, any cash received in excess of the premiums paid is taxable income.

Any assets received from gifts and inheritances are excluded from taxation. However, any income subsequently generated from these assets will be taxable income to their new owner(s).

If a debtor receives a discharge of debts, this discharge is a monetary benefit, which may be excluded from taxation only if the fair market value of the debtor's assets is less than the debtor's liabilities immediately after the discharge.

Finally, income earned by US citizens from foreign countries is taxable income in the US, unless the US citizen is a resident of a foreign country, is taxed primarily in the foreign country, and has a physical presence in the foreign country for at least 330 days during the year. If all of these conditions apply, then the foreign earned income is excluded from US taxation.

5.2.2 Calculating Adjusted Gross Income (AGI)

While gross income is the starting point of the income tax calculation, the adjusted gross income (AGI) is a more important income metric for tax purposes. The AGI determines whether some expenses can be deducted from your income, and whether you are phased out of some tax benefits. The lower your AGI, the higher the deductions you qualify for, and the more tax benefits are available to you. Clearly it is in your best interest as a taxpayer to minimize your AGI.

The AGI is derived by subtracting certain expenses from your gross income. Table 5-7 lists the adjustments for adjusted gross income.

TABLE 5-7 Adjustments for Adjusted Gross Income (AGI)

Business Expenses	Moving Expenses
Business Gifts (within limits)	Alimony Paid
Business Entertainment Expenses (within Limits)	Student Loan Interest Paid
Self Employment Tax Paid	Tuition and Fees
Self Employed Retirement Plan Contributions	Contribution to an IRA
Self Employed Health Insurance Deduction	Educator Expenses
Contribution to a Health Savings Account	

The adjustments listed on the first column of Table 5-7 are primarily associated with business ownership, while the adjustments listed on the second column are available to all taxpayers. With half the adjustments for AGI available only to business owners, the message from Congress should be coming apparent: If you want to reduce your AGI, therefore your taxes, you need to own a business!

5.2.3 Calculating Taxable Income

Once you have determined your adjusted gross income, the next step is to calculate your taxable income, which multiplied by the appropriate tax rates will determine your taxes for the year. The tax code allows you to subtract "deductions" and "exemptions" from your AGI in order to determine your taxable income.

Deductions are subtracted from your AGI because congress does not believe you should be taxed on income spent on certain expenses. Table 5-8 lists these deductible expenses.

TABLE 5-8 Deductions from AGI

Medical Expenses in excess of 10% of AGI *
State and Local Income Taxes
Real Estate Taxes (e.g., on the assessed value of your home)
Property Taxes (e.g., on the assessed value of your vehicle, boat)
Home Mortgage Interest Paid
Investment Interest Paid
Charitable Contributions (cannot exceed 50% of AGI) *
Casualty or Theft Losses in excess of 10% of AGI *
Miscellaneous Deductions (job or hobby related) in excess of 2% of AGI *

Notice that there are several deductions in Table 5-8 with an AGI threshold. the lower the AGI, the easier it is to qualify for a deduction. For example, suppose your AGI is $50,000 and because of a minor surgery you incurred $3,600 in unreimbursed (by insurance) medical expenses. The premiums on your health insurance totaled $2,400 for the year. You have $6,000 in medical expenses and a threshold of $5,000 ($50,000 * 0.10). This means you can deduct $1,000 ($6,000 - $5,000) from your AGI for medical expenses. Notice that if your AGI was $60,000 your threshold would be $6,000 ($60,000 * 0.10) therefore, you would not be able to deduct any medical expenses.

The expenses appearing on Table 5-8 are referred to as itemized deductions. The IRS has estimated the average amount a typical household would deduct according to its filing status, and offers that amount as a standard deduction. In other words, you have a choice of "itemizing" your deductions by calculating all your qualifying expenses and maintaining supporting documents as evidence of these expenses, or claiming the standard deduction, no questions asked. Typically, you want to calculate your itemized deductions and compare them to your standard deduction, so you can choose whichever is higher. Table 5-9 lists the standard deduction per filing status.

TABLE 5-9 2013 Standard Deduction

Filing Status	2013 Standard Deduction	2013 Additional Standard Deduction (Blind or 65+)
Married Filing Jointly	$12,200	$1,200
Qualified Widow(er)	$12,200	$1,200
Head of Household	$8,950	$1,500
Married Filing Separately	$6,100	$1,200
Single	$6,100	$1,500

Notice that aside from the basic standard deduction, the IRS is also offering an additional standard deduction for blind, or older than 65 years of age taxpayers. For example, in 2013 a single taxpayer 65 years of age, and blind, can take the basic standard deduction and two additional standard deductions for a total of $9,100 ($6,100 + $1,500 + $1,500). Keep in mind that these amounts are adjusted annually for inflation.

On top of your deductions you also get to subtract personal exemptions from your AGI. The tax code allows for these personal exemptions so everyone will have some untaxed income for basic necessities. For 2013 the personal exemption is set at $3,900 per taxpayer, spouse, and qualifying dependents. Qualifying dependents are those that satisfy all of the following five requirements:

1. Citizenship/Residency: The dependent must be a US citizen, resident, or national. The dependent can also be a resident of Canada or Mexico.
2. No Joint Return: A married dependent is not filing a joint tax return with his or her spouse, unless the return is only for claiming a refund for tax withheld.
3. Relationship: A dependent is a relative (except a cousin). If the dependent is not the taxpayer's relative, then the dependent has to live in the same residence as the taxpayer for the whole year.
4. Gross Income: The dependent's gross income must be less than the personal exemption amount ($3,900 for 2013). This requirement is waived for dependent children under the age of 19 or 24 if they are students.
5. Support: The taxpayer must be providing more than half of the dependent's support (housing, clothing, food, medical, education etc).

For example, in 2013 a married couple with three dependent children could claim five exemptions of $3,900 each, for a total of $19,500 ($3,900 * 5).

So after all deductions and exemptions are subtracted from the adjusted gross income, the taxable income emerges as a much smaller amount than either the gross income or the adjusted gross income.

5.2.4 Calculating the Income Tax Bill

Applying the marginal tax rates from Table 5-1 (Section 5.1.2) to your taxable income you can calculate the appropriate tax amount. For example, if you are single at the end of 2013, with $40,000 taxable income, the appropriate tax amount would be $5,929 (rounded). Table 5-10 reproduces the tax brackets and marginal tax rates for single filers from Table 5-1, and calculates the income tax.

TABLE 5-10 2013 Income Tax Calculation for a Single Taxpayer with $40,000 Taxable Income

Single Filing Status Tax Brackets	Taxable Income in Each Tax Bracket	Marginal Tax Rate	Income Tax
$0–$8,925	$8,925–$0 = $8,925	10%	$892.50
$8,926–$36,250	$36,250–$8,925 = $27,325	15%	$4,098.75
$36,251–$87,850	$40,000–$36,250 = $3,750	25%	$937.50
$87,851–$183,250	**$40,000**	28%	**$5,928.75**
$183,251–$398,350		33%	
$398,351–$400,000		35%	
$400,001+		39.6%	

Notice, that $40,000 of taxable income is spread over the first three tax brackets. The first $8,925 is taxed at 10%. Once the first bracket is exhausted, the next $27,325 (up to the $36,250 upper limit of the second bracket) is taxed at 15%. The final $3,750 of taxable income falls within the third bracket, which is taxed at 25%. The third bracket goes all the way to $87,850. In our example however, the taxpayer's taxable income is only $40,000 so there is no reason to include any income higher than $40,000 in our calculation.

Fearing that taxpayers may be overwhelmed by this calculation, the IRS provides tax tables (like Table 5-3 in Section 5.1.3) and asks filers to identify on them the appropriate tax amount for their taxable income. This really facilitates the tax return preparation.

The tax amount identified on the tax tables may be the appropriate tax for your income level, but it is not what you pay to the IRS. You need to consider a couple more issues before finalizing your tax bill. First, your employer has been withholding income taxes from your paycheck throughout the year. Your employer is obligated by the IRS to do so, to facilitate with the tax collection process. Even if you are self-employed, you are required to pay quarterly estimated income taxes. In other words, the taxpayer in our example may owe $5,929 for his or her $40,000 in taxable income, but the tax withholdings may be $5,200, leaving only a few hundred dollars residual ($729) to be remitted to the IRS.

While the tax withholdings are in effect a pre-payment of taxes, and as such a free loan to the federal government until the tax bill is due, the withholdings do facilitate paying the tax bill. It may be a lot easier for the taxpayer to come up with the $729 residual to send to the IRS in April than to come up with the full $5,929 Tax bill. Of course a better situation would be not to have mandatory withholdings of income taxes, while taxpayers exhibited the necessary self-discipline to save the extra income every month. This way, taxpayers would be prepared to pay their tax bill in April, and they would get to keep the interest generated by these savings.

The second consideration before finalizing your tax bill calculation is to check whether you may qualify for one or more tax credits, which offset dollar for dollar your tax bill. These tax credits can be nonrefundable or refundable. Nonrefundable tax credits can reduce your tax bill all the way to zero, and any excess credit amount can be carried forward to future tax years (or backwards to earlier years). Refundable Tax credits however, not only can reduce or eliminate your tax bill, but they can also produce a tax refund.

The tax code offers tax credits as incentives to influence your decisions towards actions the congress deems beneficial to society. For example, the adoption expenses credit, the alternative fuel vehicle credit, the residential energy efficiency credit, etc. It is in your best interest to be aware of the policies congress is promoting with tax credits because they can reduce your tax bill. Table 5-11 lists some popular tax credits.

TABLE 5-11 Tax Credits

Nonrefundable	Refundable
Foreign Tax Credit	Earned Income Credit
Child and Dependent Care Expenses Credit	Additional Child Tax Credit
Lifetime Learning Education Credit	American Opportunity Education Credit
Child Tax Credit	First-Time Homebuyer Credit
Residential Energy Credit	Excess Social Security Credit
Alternative Fuel Vehicle Credit	

Since tax credit dollars directly offset tax bill dollars, tax credits are more valuable than adjustments or deductions, which only reduce income.

Finally, subtracting tax withholdings and any possible tax credits from your taxable income, yields the tax bill due to the IRS, or the tax refund due to you from the IRS. For example, suppose our single taxpayer with $5,929 calculated tax amount and $5,200 tax withholdings, qualified for $2,500 American Opportunity Education Tax credit, which is up to 40% refundable. The taxpayer would get a $708 tax refund ($5,929 - $5,200 - $2,500=-$1,771*0.40=-$708).

5.2.5 Tax Forms

To help you prepare, and to help itself process your tax return, the IRS requires all taxpayers to file their tax return using Form 1040-US Individual Income Tax Return, or a variation of the form like the 1040EZ or 1040A. These two variations of the Form 1040 are for taxpayers with restricted income sources and very few deductions, requiring a really simple tax return form. Most young taxpayers qualify to file one of these forms because their financial life is not complicated yet. Table 5-12 lists the key requirements for using one of the simpler tax forms.

TABLE 5-12 Requirements to Use a Simpler Tax Form

Form 1040EZ	Form 1040A
Single or Married Filing Jointly Status	Any Filing Status
No Dependents	Dependents allowed
Taxable Income<$100,000 Interest<$1,500	Taxable Income < $100,000
Do not Itemize Deductions	Do not Itemize Deductions
Income: Wages/Salaries, Unemployment	Income: Wages/Salaries, Unemployment, Capital Gains, Interest, Dividends, IRAs, Pensions, Annuities, Social Security
Credits: Earned Income Tax Credit (EIC)	Credits: EIC, Child, Additional Child, Elderly & Disabled, Child & Dependent Care, Education

While the simpler forms may be easier to prepare, they do not allow as many adjustments, deductions and credits as the regular Form 1040. This means that as your financial life develops, you will find it beneficial to switch to Form 1040. Careful tax planning will allow you to take advantage of more adjustments, deductions and credits in order to legally lower your annual tax bill. Typically, it makes sense to switch to Form 1040 when your itemized deductions exceed your standard deduction, or when you start your own business. Your itemized deductions most likely will exceed your standard deduction when you become a property owner, as both the mortgage interest and the real estate taxes are itemized deductions. Itemized deductions are reported on Schedule A of Form 1040.

Looking at the two pages of Form 1040, you can see that the first page is separated in three parts. The top part (until Line 6d) has to do with your personal information, dependents information, and filing status. The middle part (Lines 7 to 22) calculates your gross income, as discussed in Section 5.2.1. the bottom part (Lines 23 to 37) calculates your adjusted gross income, as discussed in Section 5.2.2.

On the second page, Lines 38 to 43 calculate your taxable income, as discussed in Section 5.2.3, while Lines 44 to 77 calculate your tax bill or refund, as described in Section 5.2.4. Finally, all your itemized deductions, as described in Section 5.2.3, appear on Schedule A which accompanies Form 1040.

Other frequently used schedules are: Schedule B (Interest and Dividend Income), Schedule C (Business Profit and Loss), and Schedule D (Capital Gains and Losses). All forms and schedules, as well as instructions for preparing them can be downloaded from the IRS website www.irs.gov

Form **1040** Department of the Treasury—Internal Revenue Service (99)
U.S. Individual Income Tax Return **2012** OMB No. 1545-0074 IRS Use Only—Do not write or staple in this space.

For the year Jan. 1–Dec. 31, 2012, or other tax year beginning , 2012, ending , 20 | See separate instructions.

Your first name and initial	Last name	Your social security number
If a joint return, spouse's first name and initial	Last name	Spouse's social security number
Home address (number and street). If you have a P.O. box, see instructions.	Apt. no.	▲ Make sure the SSN(s) above and on line 6c are correct.
City, town or post office, state, and ZIP code. If you have a foreign address, also complete spaces below (see instructions).		**Presidential Election Campaign** Check here if you, or your spouse if filing jointly, want $3 to go to this fund. Checking a box below will not change your tax or refund. ☐ You ☐ Spouse
Foreign country name	Foreign province/state/county · Foreign postal code	

Filing Status

Check only one box.

1 ☐ Single
2 ☐ Married filing jointly (even if only one had income)
3 ☐ Married filing separately. Enter spouse's SSN above and full name here. ▶
4 ☐ Head of household (with qualifying person). (See instructions.) If the qualifying person is a child but not your dependent, enter this child's name here. ▶
5 ☐ Qualifying widow(er) with dependent child

Exemptions

6a ☐ **Yourself.** If someone can claim you as a dependent, **do not** check box 6a
b ☐ **Spouse**

Boxes checked on 6a and 6b

c **Dependents:**

(1) First name Last name	(2) Dependent's social security number	(3) Dependent's relationship to you	(4) ✓ if child under age 17 qualifying for child tax credit (see instructions)
			☐
			☐
			☐
			☐

If more than four dependents, see instructions and check here ▶ ☐

No. of children on 6c who:
• lived with you
• did not live with you due to divorce or separation (see instructions)
Dependents on 6c not entered above
Add numbers on lines above ▶

d Total number of exemptions claimed

Income

Attach Form(s) W-2 here. Also attach Forms W-2G and 1099-R if tax was withheld.

If you did not get a W-2, see instructions.

Enclose, but do not attach, any payment. Also, please use **Form 1040-V.**

Line	Description	Line box
7	Wages, salaries, tips, etc. Attach Form(s) W-2	7
8a	**Taxable** interest. Attach Schedule B if required	8a
b	**Tax-exempt** interest. **Do not** include on line 8a — 8b	
9a	Ordinary dividends. Attach Schedule B if required	9a
b	Qualified dividends — 9b	
10	Taxable refunds, credits, or offsets of state and local income taxes	10
11	Alimony received	11
12	Business income or (loss). Attach Schedule C or C-EZ	12
13	Capital gain or (loss). Attach Schedule D if required. If not required, check here ▶ ☐	13
14	Other gains or (losses). Attach Form 4797	14
15a	IRA distributions — 15a — b Taxable amount	15b
16a	Pensions and annuities — 16a — b Taxable amount	16b
17	Rental real estate, royalties, partnerships, S corporations, trusts, etc. Attach Schedule E	17
18	Farm income or (loss). Attach Schedule F	18
19	Unemployment compensation	19
20a	Social security benefits — 20a — b Taxable amount	20b
21	Other income. List type and amount	21
22	Combine the amounts in the far right column for lines 7 through 21. This is your **total income** ▶	22

Adjusted Gross Income

Line	Description	Line box
23	Educator expenses	23
24	Certain business expenses of reservists, performing artists, and fee-basis government officials. Attach Form 2106 or 2106-EZ	24
25	Health savings account deduction. Attach Form 8889	25
26	Moving expenses. Attach Form 3903	26
27	Deductible part of self-employment tax. Attach Schedule SE	27
28	Self-employed SEP, SIMPLE, and qualified plans	28
29	Self-employed health insurance deduction	29
30	Penalty on early withdrawal of savings	30
31a	Alimony paid **b** Recipient's SSN ▶	31a
32	IRA deduction	32
33	Student loan interest deduction	33
34	Tuition and fees. Attach Form 8917	34
35	Domestic production activities deduction. Attach Form 8903	35
36	Add lines 23 through 35	36

Form 1040 (2012) Page **2**

Tax and Credits

38	Amount from line 37 (adjusted gross income)			38
39a	Check if: ☐ **You** were born before January 2, 1948, ☐ Blind. ☐ **Spouse** was born before January 2, 1948, ☐ Blind. } **Total boxes checked ▶ 39a**			
b	If your spouse itemizes on a separate return or you were a dual-status alien, check here ▶ **39b** ☐			
40	**Itemized deductions** (from Schedule A) **or** your **standard deduction** (see left margin)			40
41	Subtract line 40 from line 38			41
42	**Exemptions.** Multiply $3,800 by the number on line 6d			42
43	**Taxable income.** Subtract line 42 from line 41. If line 42 is more than line 41, enter -0-			43
44	**Tax** (see instructions). Check if any from: **a** ☐ Form(s) 8814 **b** ☐ Form 4972 **c** ☐ 962 election			44
45	**Alternative minimum tax** (see instructions). Attach Form 6251			45
46	Add lines 44 and 45 ▶			46
47	Foreign tax credit. Attach Form 1116 if required	47		
48	Credit for child and dependent care expenses. Attach Form 2441	48		
49	Education credits from Form 8863, line 19	49		
50	Retirement savings contributions credit. Attach Form 8880	50		
51	Child tax credit. Attach Schedule 8812, if required	51		
52	Residential energy credits. Attach Form 5695	52		
53	Other credits from Form: **a** ☐ 3800 **b** ☐ 8801 **c** ☐ ______	53		
54	Add lines 47 through 53. These are your **total credits**			54
55	Subtract line 54 from line 46. If line 54 is more than line 46, enter -0- ▶			55

Standard Deduction for—
- People who check any box on line 39a or 39b **or** who can be claimed as a dependent, see instructions.
- All others:

Single or Married filing separately, $5,950

Married filing jointly or Qualifying widow(er), $11,900

Head of household, $8,700

Other Taxes

56	Self-employment tax. Attach Schedule SE			56
57	Unreported social security and Medicare tax from Form: **a** ☐ 4137 **b** ☐ 8919			57
58	Additional tax on IRAs, other qualified retirement plans, etc. Attach Form 5329 if required			58
59a	Household employment taxes from Schedule H			59a
b	First-time homebuyer credit repayment. Attach Form 5405 if required			59b
60	Other taxes. Enter code(s) from instructions ______			60
61	Add lines 55 through 60. This is your **total tax** ▶			61

Payments

62	Federal income tax withheld from Forms W-2 and 1099	62		
63	2012 estimated tax payments and amount applied from 2011 return	63		
64a	**Earned income credit (EIC)**	64a		
b	Nontaxable combat pay election **64b**			
65	Additional child tax credit. Attach Schedule 8812	65		
66	American opportunity credit from Form 8863, line 8	66		
67	Reserved	67		
68	Amount paid with request for extension to file	68		
69	Excess social security and tier 1 RRTA tax withheld	69		
70	Credit for federal tax on fuels. Attach Form 4136	70		
71	Credits from Form: **a** ☐ 2439 **b** ☐ Reserved **c** ☐ 8801 **d** ☐ 8885	71		
72	Add lines 62, 63, 64a, and 65 through 71. These are your **total payments** ▶			72

If you have a qualifying child, attach Schedule EIC.

Refund

73	If line 72 is more than line 61, subtract line 61 from line 72. This is the amount you **overpaid**			73
74a	Amount of line 73 you want **refunded to you.** If Form 8888 is attached, check here ▶ ☐			74a
b	Routing number ▶ **c** Type: ☐ Checking ☐ Savings			
d	Account number			
75	Amount of line 73 you want **applied to your 2013 estimated tax** ▶	75		

Direct deposit? See instructions. ▶

Amount You Owe

76	**Amount you owe.** Subtract line 72 from line 61. For details on how to pay, see instructions ▶			76
77	Estimated tax penalty (see instructions)	77		

Third Party Designee

Do you want to allow another person to discuss this return with the IRS (see instructions)? ☐ **Yes.** Complete below. ☐ **No**

Designee's name ▶ Phone no. ▶ Personal identification number (PIN) ▶

Sign Here

Under penalties of perjury, I declare that I have examined this return and accompanying schedules and statements, and to the best of my knowledge and belief, they are true, correct, and complete. Declaration of preparer (other than taxpayer) is based on all information of which preparer has any knowledge.

Joint return? See instructions. Keep a copy for your records.

Your signature	Date	Your occupation	Daytime phone number
Spouse's signature. If a joint return, **both** must sign.	Date	Spouse's occupation	If the IRS sent you an Identity Protection PIN, enter it here (see inst.)

Paid Preparer Use Only

Print/Type preparer's name	Preparer's signature	Date	Check ☐ if self-employed	PTIN
Firm's name ▶		Firm's EIN ▶		
Firm's address ▶		Phone no.		

Form **1040** (2012)

SCHEDULE A (Form 1040)

Department of the Treasury Internal Revenue Service (99)

Itemized Deductions

▶ Information about Schedule A and its separate instructions is at *www.irs.gov/form1040*.
▶ Attach to Form 1040.

OMB No. 1545-0074

2012

Attachment Sequence No. 07

Name(s) shown on Form 1040 | Your social security number

Section	Line	Description	Box		Box	
Medical and Dental Expenses		**Caution.** Do not include expenses reimbursed or paid by others.				
	1	Medical and dental expenses (see instructions)	1			
	2	Enter amount from Form 1040, line 38 [2]				
	3	Multiply line 2 by 7.5% (.075)	3			
	4	Subtract line 3 from line 1. If line 3 is more than line 1, enter -0-			4	
Taxes You Paid	5	State and local **(check only one box):** a ☐ Income taxes, **or** b ☐ General sales taxes	5			
	6	Real estate taxes (see instructions)	6			
	7	Personal property taxes	7			
	8	Other taxes. List type and amount ▶	8			
	9	Add lines 5 through 8			9	
Interest You Paid	10	Home mortgage interest and points reported to you on Form 1098	10			
Note. Your mortgage interest deduction may be limited (see instructions).	11	Home mortgage interest not reported to you on Form 1098. If paid to the person from whom you bought the home, see instructions and show that person's name, identifying no., and address ▶	11			
	12	Points not reported to you on Form 1098. See instructions for special rules	12			
	13	Mortgage insurance premiums (see instructions)	13			
	14	Investment interest. Attach Form 4952 if required. (See instructions.)	14			
	15	Add lines 10 through 14			15	
Gifts to Charity	16	Gifts by cash or check. If you made any gift of $250 or more, see instructions	16			
If you made a gift and got a benefit for it, see instructions.	17	Other than by cash or check. If any gift of $250 or more, see instructions. You **must** attach Form 8283 if over $500	17			
	18	Carryover from prior year	18			
	19	Add lines 16 through 18			19	
Casualty and Theft Losses	20	Casualty or theft loss(es). Attach Form 4684. (See instructions.)			20	
Job Expenses and Certain Miscellaneous Deductions	21	Unreimbursed employee expenses—job travel, union dues, job education, etc. Attach Form 2106 or 2106-EZ if required. (See instructions.) ▶	21			
	22	Tax preparation fees	22			
	23	Other expenses—investment, safe deposit box, etc. List type and amount ▶	23			
	24	Add lines 21 through 23	24			
	25	Enter amount from Form 1040, line 38 [25]				
	26	Multiply line 25 by 2% (.02)	26			
	27	Subtract line 26 from line 24. If line 26 is more than line 24, enter -0-			27	
Other Miscellaneous Deductions	28	Other—from list in instructions. List type and amount ▶			28	
Total Itemized Deductions	29	Add the amounts in the far right column for lines 4 through 28. Also, enter this amount on Form 1040, line 40			29	
	30	If you elect to itemize deductions even though they are less than your standard deduction, check here ▶ ☐				

For Paperwork Reduction Act Notice, see Form 1040 instructions. Cat. No. 17145C **Schedule A (Form 1040) 2012**

5.2.6 Tax Noncompliance and Penalties

Since most taxpayers do not really enjoy paying taxes, income taxation is not voluntary. Voluntary taxation does not seem to work well, mainly because of the "free rider" problem. Suppose you were planning to pay your income taxes, as you always do every April, when from discussions with several friends and coworkers, you discover they have quit this habit long ago. You realize, they actually "free ride" on the public services you help provide. You are taken advantage of, and you will not allow this to continue. Therefore you, and eventually others, quit paying as well. Pretty soon there will not be enough revenues to support the public services society has come to depend upon. Either the public services will have to be curtailed or taxation will have to become mandatory. As mentioned in Section 5.1, in 1913 the people decided to amend the Constitution to allow for federal income taxation, which the IRS not only administers but also enforces.

Enforcement means that you will face penalties if you become cavalier about your tax obligations. The penalties vary in severity according to the severity of the violation. In this chapter we focus on violations exhibiting noncompliance with tax regulations, like failure to file a tax return, failure to pay taxes, fraud, frivolous returns and understatements. Table 5-13 lists these violations and the possible penalties imposed.

TABLE 5-13 Tax Violations and Penalties

Violation	Penalties
Failure to File	5% of the Tax bill per month (or part Month) up to 25% maximum
Failure to Pay	0.5% of the Tax bill per month (or part Month) up to 25% maximum
Fraudulent Return	15% of the Tax bill per month (or part Month) up to 75% maximum
Frivolous Return	20% of the Underpaid Tax amount plus an extra $500 penalty
Understatement	40% of the Underpaid Tax if Understated valuation > $5,000

The penalties for failure to file and failure to pay can be combined, which means the penalty for failure to pay reduces the penalty for failure to file. For example, 3.5 months after the tax filing deadline, James has neither filed a tax return nor requested an extension to file a tax return. Had he filed a tax return his tax bill would be $4,000. Because the failure to file penalty is reduced by the failure to pay penalty, James faces:

$$\textit{FailureToFilePenalty} = (0.05 - 0.005) * \textit{Number Of Months} * \textit{TaxBill} = 0.045 * 4 * \$4{,}000\ \$720$$

$$\textit{FailureToPayPenalty} 0.005 * \textit{Number Of Months} * \textit{TaxBill}\ 0.005 * 4 * \$4{,}000\ \$80$$

So on top of the $4,000 tax bill, James has accumulated $800 ($720 + $80) in penalties this far, and the IRS will charge interest on the $4,000 from the due date of the return.

Failing to file a tax return shows intent to tax evade, which is a serious violation of tax regulations, and it may be impossible to avoid the consequences. While there is a 10-year statute of limitations for the IRS to collect any taxes due, the statute of limitations does not start until a tax return has been filed. Therefore, there is no statute of limitations for the IRS to assess and collect income taxes if you did not file a tax return. Similarly, the statute of limitations does not apply in case of a fraudulent tax return, because it also shows intent to tax evade.

5.3 Practical Application: How Much Do You Have to Earn to File a Tax Return?

Taxpayers are required to file a tax return if their gross income exceeds the sum of standard deductions and personal and dependents exemptions they are allowed for the year. If your gross income is below the sum of your allowed deductions and exemptions for the year, then you have no taxable income, therefore you owe no income taxes, and a tax return is not required. However, you may still want to file a tax return to claim a tax refund for income tax withholdings and any refundable tax credits you may qualify for.

TABLE 5-14 2013 Gross Income Threshold for Required Tax Filing

Standard Deduction Additional Standard Deduction(s) Exemption(s)	Young & Single	65-Year-Old Blind & Single	Young Married Filing Jointly
Standard Deduction	$6,100	$6,100	$12,200
Additional Standard (age 65+)		$1,500	
Additional Standard (blind)		$1,500	
Personal Exemption(s)	$3,900	$3,900	$7,800
Gross Income	**$10,000**	**$13,000**	**$20,000**

Table 5-14 shows the calculation of the gross income threshold for three different taxpayers: a young single individual, a 65-year-old who is blind and single, and a young married couple filing jointly with no dependents.

5.3.1 Practical Application: The Milfords' 2012 Income Taxes

The income statement (Chapter 4) of Ric and Vanessa Milford reveals that the couple had $150,600 income from all sources during the year. They had $11,240 federal income tax withholdings, and $7,000 state income tax withholdings. They contributed $9,500 to their employer sponsored retirement plans, while Ric contributed $5,000 to his IRA. Their property taxes were $5,400 ($5,000 for their home and $400 for their two vehicles). They paid $13,200 in mortgage interest, $2,000 in medical expenses, and contributed $1,200 to charity. The health insurance for the three children was $5,280 and was purchased through Vanessa's employer group plan. Both Ric and Vanessa's health insurance premiums were paid by their employers, and are excluded from taxation.

To calculate the Milfords' 2013 income taxes we need to follow the process outlined in Section 5.2 (Table 5-4), and depicted here in Table 5-15.

TABLE 5-15 The Milfords' 2013 Income Tax Return

Income from All Sources	$150,600	
- Exclusions from Income	− (14,780)	Retirement + Health Insurance
= **Gross Income**	= **$135,820**	
- Adjustments for AGI	− ($5,000)	Ric's IRA
= **Adjusted Gross Income (AGI)**	= **$130,820**	
- Deductions from AGI (Itemized)	− ($26,800)	State + Property + Interest + Charity
- Personal and Dependent Exemptions	− ($19,500)	$3,900 * 5 [2 Parents + 3 children]
= **Taxable Income**	= **$84,520**	
* Tax Rates		
= **Taxes**	= **$12,988**	See Table-16 bellow
- Tax Withholdings	− ($11,240)	Federal Tax Withholdings
- Tax Credits	− ($3,000)	$1,000 Child Tax Credit * 3 Children
= **Tax Due or (Tax Refund)**	= **($1,252)**	**Tax Refund**

TABLE 5-16 The Milfords' 2013 Income Tax Calculation

Married Filing Jointly	Taxable Income in Each Tax Bracket	Marginal Tax Rate	Income Tax
$0–$17,850	$17,850–$0 = $17,850	**10%**	$1,785.00
$17,851–$72,500	$72,500–$17,850 = $54,650	**15%**	$8,197.50
$72,501–$146,400	$84,520–$72,500 = $12,020	**25%**	$3,005.00
$146,401–$223,050	**$84,520**	**28%**	**$12,987.50**
$223,051–$398,350		**33%**	
$398,351–$450,000		**35%**	
$450,001+		**39.6%**	

The Milfords' taxable income is spread over the first three income tax brackets for their filing status. Although the third tax bracket goes up to $146,400, the Milfords' taxable income is $85,020. Therefore we do not include anymore income in our calculation. Since the income in the third tax bracket is taxed at 25%, this is the Milfords' marginal tax rate (MTR). In other words, if they earned one more dollar of taxable income in 2013, they would have to pay $0.25 in federal income taxes.

While the Milfords' tax according to their taxable income is $12,988 (rounded), they qualify for $1,000 child tax credit per dependent child (younger than 18). Since all three of their children qualify for this credit, the Milfords' tax is reduced to $9,988 ($12,988-$3,000). Therefore, their average tax rate is:

$$AverageTaxRate = \frac{IncomeTaxesPaid}{TaxableIncome} = \frac{\$9,988}{\$84,520} = 11.82\%$$

If Congress did not extend the child tax credit, which was set to expire at the end of 2012, then the Milfords' tax would not be reduced by the three $1,000 credits, and their average tax rate would be:

$$AverageTaxRate = \frac{IncomeTaxesPaid}{TaxableIncome} = \frac{\$12,988}{\$84,520} = 15.37\%$$

A congressional action (inaction in this case) not to extend a seemingly insignificant tax credit, would increase the Milfords' average tax rate by 3.55% (15.37% - 11.82%), and would turn a $1,252 tax refund into a $1,748 tax bill ($12,988 tax - $11,240 tax withheld).

5.4 Income Tax Planning Strategies

Tax planning is an essential component of financial planning, because it is so critical to your financial success. Tax planning has nothing to do with tax evasion. instead, it is the careful implementation of strategies, based on existing and expected tax regulations, to avoid paying more in taxes than you legally have to. While in this Chapter we focus only on income tax planning, Chapter 10 deals with estate planning and the tools and strategies employed to minimize wealth transfer taxes.

The following three Sections present income tax planning strategies aiming to exclude income from taxation, defer taxes and minimize taxes.

5.4.1 Exclude Income from Taxation

i) Investing in Municipal Bonds

Municipal bonds are debt securities issued by state and local governments. the big attraction of municipal bonds for investors is that the interest received from these securities is tax-exempt for federal income tax purposes. In other words, municipal bond interest is excluded from gross income. The federal government allows this exclusion from taxation to promote the decentralized ability of the states to borrow and finance their needs. Furthermore, the states provide more incentives for investors who lend them funds. If an investor resides in the state which issued the municipal bond, then the interest is also tax-exempt for state income purposes.

While municipal bonds may have greater credit risk (chance of default) and liquidity risk (few may be traded any given day) than treasury bonds, which are issued by the federal government, the desirability of the tax-exempt feature is so strong that municipal bonds can afford to pay lower yields, than other bonds with similar features and maturity.

Consider for example a corporate bond, issued by a large US corporation, with similar credit and liquidity characteristics as a municipal bond. If the corporate bond offers a 7% yield, and your marginal tax rate is 25%, then your after tax yield is:

$$AfterTaxYieldYield * (1-MTR)7\% * (10.25)7\% * 0.755.25$$

In other words, once you pay income taxes on the interest received from the corporate bond, your return (yield) drops from 7% to 5.25%. Therefore, a tax-exempt municipal bond offering a 5.25% yield would be competitive to the taxable corporate bond offering 7%.

Notice that if your marginal tax rate was higher, your after tax yield would be lower. Suppose your MTR was 35%, then your after tax yield would be:

$$AfterTaxYieldYield * (1–MTR)7\% * (10.35)7\% * 0.654.55$$

So the higher your marginal tax rate is, the less you benefit from taxable bonds and the more you benefit from lower yielding but tax-exempt municipal bonds.

ii) Receiving Tax Free Gains from the Sale of Personal Residence

For most people, their personal residence is one of the biggest assets they will ever have. Mindful of this fact, the tax code allows substantial capital gains from the sale of your personal residence to be excluded from taxable income. The precise amount of the income exclusion depends on your filing status and the fulfillment of three requirements.

For single filers the maximum exclusion is $250,000, while for married couples filing jointly the maximum exclusion is $500,000. The requirements you must satisfy to be eligible for this exclusion are: a) you must have owned the property for at least the last two years, b) you must have used the property as your personal residence for two out of the last five years, and c) you must not have used this exclusion within the last two years.

For married couples filing jointly, while only one spouse could have owned the property during the last two years, both spouses must have used it as their personal residence for two out of the last five years. Also, to make sure the couple is not in the business of "flipping properties" to book tax free capital gains, neither spouse must have used this exclusion in the last two years.

The tax code is also mindful of situations, where you may be forced to sell your primary residence, before the two years of ownership and usage requirements are met. In case of change in employment, change in health, or other unforeseen circumstance (like a divorce), if you are forced to sell the property prematurely, you are allowed a partial exclusion based on the number of months you owned and used the property as your primary residence.

For example, suppose you purchased a home for $300,000 and used it for your personal residence. Twenty-one months later, your employer offers you a promotion, but you have to relocate to another state. You accept the new position, and move immediately. The housing market is strong and within three months your house is sold for $480,000 generating $180,000 in capital gain.

As a single filer, the maximum exclusion from income is $250,000. However, you are only allowed a partial exclusion for the 21 months you used the property as your primary residence.

$$PartialExclusion = \frac{\begin{matrix} NumberOfMonths \\ OwnedandUsed \end{matrix}}{24Months} * MaxExclusion = \frac{21}{24} * \$250,000 = \$218,750$$

Since the $180,000 capital gain from the sale of your primary residence is under the allowed $218,750 partial exclusion, all of your capital gain is tax free!

iii) Transferring Income Generating Assets

If you find yourself taxed at a high marginal tax rate, and you are fortunate to own assets generating substantial income you do not really need, you may want to transfer these assets away from you, and to someone taxed at a lower marginal tax rate. This strategy works well if you happen to have children, who are young adults with low taxable incomes.

Suppose for example, you own a commercial real estate property generating monthly lease income you don't need. While you are taxed at 35% MTR, your two children are in their early 20s and have little taxable income. By transferring ownership of this property to them, all future lease income will be excluded from your income and become your children's taxable income, which will be taxed at a lower MTR.

This strategy may not work well if your children are very young or in college. The IRS does not look favorably upon children declaring "unearned" income (interest, dividends, capital gains, rents, royalties etc) and has passed the "kiddie tax" rule. According to this rule, children under the age of 19 (or 24 if full time students) with unearned income beyond $1,900, are taxed at the marginal tax rate of the parent.

A child with unearned income is entitled to a $950 standard deduction. The next $950 is taxed at the child's MTR (10% for 2012). Unearned income above $1,900 ($950$950) is taxed at the parent's MTR, negating the benefit of this strategy.

5.4.2 Defer Your Taxes

i) Using Tax-Deferred Retirement Plans

Some retirement plans offer "tax favored" accounts like the 401(k), 403(b) and 457, to encourage employees to save more for their retirement. These accounts are "tax favored" because they allow a percentage of your salary to be deposited in such an account with no taxes paid at the time of the deposit. Taxes are due only when the funds are withdrawn from the account, decades later during retirement. In addition, all investment income remains tax sheltered until the funds are withdrawn from the retirement account. This deferral of taxes for decades allows you to use funds, which you would have paid in taxes over the years, to boost your retirement account balance.

Let's compare the retirement savings outcomes between a tax-deferred account, like a 401(k), and a taxable account, like a regular brokerage account. Suppose that for the next 40 years (480 months), you invest at the end of every month $500 out of your paycheck, earning 12% average annual return over this period, while for simplicity your marginal tax rate (MTR) remains constant at 25%.

With the tax-deferred account the whole $500 is invested every month, and you get to keep and reinvest the whole 12% return every year. Since this account balance is sheltered from taxation for the 40-year period, at retirement the whole account balance is taxable at your MTR.

With the taxable account however, you invest after-tax income [$500* (1-0.25) $375], while your annual returns are subject to taxation as well [12%* (1-0.25) 9%]. Therefore, only the after-tax annual returns can be reinvested each year. Since this account is been taxed all along, no taxes are due at retirement. Table 5-17 shows the retirement savings outcomes under the two accounts.

TABLE 5-17 HP10BII-Retirement Savings Calculations

Tax-Deferred Account [401(k)]		Taxable Account [Brokerage Account]	
12 ☐	P/YR	12 ☐	P/YR
40 ☐	X P/YR	40 ☐	X P/YR
12	I/YR	9	I/YR
$0	PV	$0	PV
$500	+/− PMT	$375	+/− PMT
	FV $5,882,386.2551		**FV $1,755,495.1022**
	* (1-0.25)		
	$4,411,789.6914		

Even after the taxation of withdrawals at retirement, the tax-deferred account generates 2.5 times more savings than the taxable account. Deferring taxation is a powerful strategy for wealth creation.

ii) Using Capital Gains for Taxation Time Management

Capital gains are the profits from the sale of investment assets like securities and real estate. gains are "realized" only when assets are sold for "consideration." Until that time, any appreciation in the value of assets reflects only "paper" profits, as no gains have been collected.

Once gains are "realized" however, there are only three choices:

a) The gains are excluded from taxation based on a tax code provision, like the gains from the sale of a primary residence, or
b) The gains are deferred for future taxation, like the IRS Section 1031 "like kind exchanges" for assets used in a trade or business, or
c) The gains are recognized for immediate taxation.

Section 5.4.1 described the common strategies to exclude income and gains from taxation. If you cannot exclude your gains from taxation, and you cannot defer them for future taxation (as business owners may be able to do), then you are left with the worst choice of the three, which is to recognize gains for immediate taxation. In this case, your best strategy may be not to "realize" the gains at all, so you don't have to recognize them and incur a tax obligation. in other words, you can defer "paper" gains for future taxation when you cannot exclude or defer "realized" gains.

Unlike income, capital gains offer you the advantage of selecting the time of taxation. while income is taxable when received, capital gains are not "realized" until you sell investment assets. Holding more assets that tend to appreciate in value (like land, commodities, non-dividend paying stocks), as opposed to assets that generate income (like bonds, dividend paying stocks, and rental properties) allows you more flexibility to choose when you will be taxed.

Clearly, if you have to pay taxes, it will be better for you to delay paying until many years later. This way, you get to keep your assets longer, and they get a chance to appreciate more in value. Furthermore, if you suffer a capital loss along the way, you get the chance to offset some of your gains against your unfortunate loss and pay no taxes at all. Even bad things can be put to good use with proper planning.

5.4.3 Minimize Your Taxes

i) Using Long-Term Capital Gains to Minimize Your Taxes

Recall from Section 5.1.5 that investment income receives preferential treatment in the US tax code. Both qualified dividends and long-term capital gains are currently taxed at a 15% maximum tax rate, for taxpayers facing 25% or higher ordinary income marginal tax rates. They are tax free for taxpayers facing 10% to 15% ordinary income marginal tax rates.

For capital gains to be considered long term, you must have held the investment asset for more than one year. One year and one day is long enough. However, if you sell an asset held for 365 days or less, then the capital gain is considered short term, and taxed at your ordinary income marginal tax rate.

So holding investment assets for the long run, provides you with the opportunity to only "realize" long-term capital gains, which not only allow you to defer your taxes, but also to minimize your taxes with tax rates less than half the maximum ordinary income marginal tax rates.

ii) Shifting Deductible Expenses to Maximize Deductions

Recall from Section 5.2.3, that in the process of calculating your taxable income, you are allowed to subtract from your adjusted gross income (AGI) the greater of the standard deduction for your filing status or your own itemized deductions. Obviously, the greater the itemized deductions, the lower your taxable income will be which minimizes your tax bill.

Some of your possible itemized deductions however, like for medical expenses and miscellaneous expenses, are allowed for amounts exceeding a percentage of your adjusted gross income. Therefore, a useful planning strategy is to maximize such deductions by shifting expenses a few weeks or months, so they all occur within the same tax year.

For example, the strategy works particularly well for the medical expenses of households with multiple dependents. As long as you plan for all household members to have their routine and elective medical, dental, and vision, exams and procedures within a calendar year, you may qualify to deduct some of these expenses.

Another example would be to shift the timing of your gifts and donations to charities so your itemized deductions exceed your standard deduction for a given year, and allow you to reduce your taxable income and minimize your taxes.

All the strategies described in the last three sections can significantly reduce the amount of taxes you will pay over your lifetime, and preserve more wealth for you and your family. The only requirement however, is planning. Tax planning is more of a long-term continuous process rather than a rush to meet the April tax filing deadline.

Summary

This chapter presented the US federal income tax system, which was introduced in 1913 with the 16th Amendment to the Constitution. The system is progressive, meaning higher incomes pay higher average tax rates (ATR). active, passive and investment income are all taxable. There are however, exclusions, adjustments, deductions, exemptions and credits which you need to take into account to calculate your tax bill. Your tax return has to be filed with the Internal Revenue Service (IRS), on Form 1040 or one of its variations. The IRS enforces tax collection, and can impose stiff penalties for noncompliance with tax regulations. While complying with all tax regulations, you can certainly employ tax planning strategies to exclude income from taxation, defer taxes and minimize your tax obligations.

Review Questions

1. James is a single taxpayer whose tax bill for the year is $6,500 on a $42,000 taxable income. What is his average tax rate? If James had $1 more in taxable income how much of this dollar would he have to pay in income taxes?

2. On December 24, 2013 your employer gave you a $3,000 check for your annual bonus. you had no time to deposit the check in your bank account because you had to catch a flight to Hawaii for a 10-day vacation. You deposited the check when you returned from your trip, on January 6, 2014. For which year should the $3,000 bonus count as taxable income? Why?

3. Maria is a young single mother of two children, Jake age 5, and Melissa age 3. Melissa is legally blind. What is Maria's filing status? Maria earned $22,000 this year. Is she required to file a tax return?

4. Bill had a medical emergency during the year that cost him $6,000 in unreimbursed medical expenses. He also paid $2,160 in premiums for his health insurance. If his adjusted gross income (AGI) for the year is $65,000 how much can he deduct from his AGI as medical expenses?

5. Steve had purchased a beach house for $200,000 14 years ago. After his divorce three years ago, the beach house became his primary residence. This year he sold the property for $500,000. How much of this money is taxable? What will be his tax from this sale?

6. Carol did not have the $3,200 to pay her taxes in April, so she did not file a tax return. Six months later, she saved enough money and tried to pay her tax bill. To her surprise, the IRS imposed penalties and interest on top of her original tax amount. How much did the penalties cost her?

Questions 7 to 12 refer to the following set of information:

During 2013, Connie and Brian, a married couple with three young children had $120,000 in active income from salaries, and $1,400 in investment income from interest on corporate bonds. Connie inherited $60,000 from her aunt, who passed away that summer in California. Both Connie and Brian contributed $3,000 each to their IRAs.

7. What is Connie and Brian's gross income? What is their adjusted gross income?

8. If Connie and Brian had during the year $4,200 state income tax withholdings, $3,400 property taxes, $9,000 mortgage interest, and $2,000 in charity donations, should they itemize or take the standard deduction?

9. What is Connie and Brian's taxable income?

10. If Connie and Brian qualify only for the child tax credit, and their federal income tax withholdings were $5,000, what is their tax bill or tax refund? (Use the tax rates in Table 5-1, Section 5.1.2.)

11. What is Connie and Brian's average tax rate?

12. If the child tax credit was eliminated, what would be Connie and Brian's tax bill (or refund) and average tax rates?

Higher Education Planning: Paying for College

6.1 Introduction

It has always been the goal and aspiration of parents to secure a better future for their children. Both as individual families, and collectively as a society, we can measure our progress by the improvement in the standard of living of each successive generation. Education has proven to be a constant and dependable factor determining professional and financial success. In the nineteenth and early twentieth centuries, education allowed people to seek a better quality of life away from the difficult and often hazardous working conditions in the mining, farming and manufacturing sectors of the economy. By the end of the twentieth century, the US was transformed in to a service economy with nearly 90% of its work force employed in the service sector. Competing in a service economy requires higher levels of training and education, intensifying the need of families to plan for their children's higher education.

Historically, higher education was a privilege afforded only to the wealthy, who had the means to pay for tuition and living expenses during the college years. Recognizing the beneficial effect of higher education in labor productivity, and promoting equality of opportunity, Congress passed the Higher Education Act (HEA) of 1965, to assist lower and middle income students pursuing college degrees. This act introduced financial aid for higher education.

6.1.1 Financial Aid

The 1972 Higher Education Amendments renamed the Federal Education programs introduced in 1965 as:

a) Basic educational opportunity grants,
b) Supplemental educational opportunity grants, and
c) National direct student loans.

The US government now provides need-based and merit-based financial aid including grants, work-study programs and loan programs. State governments also provide some $10 billion each year in need-based and non need-based aid, constituting of grants, work-study programs, tuition waivers and scholarships. In 2010, there were 9 federal and 605 state student aid programs in existence.

Individual colleges and universities offer grants, and need-based and merit-based scholarships. Merit-based scholarships are either academic scholarships based on scores and grade point average, or athletic scholarships based on athletic talent.

To receive financial aid a prospective student needs to submit the Free Application for Federal Student Aid (FAFSA) form, directly to the US Department of Education. The FAFSA can be completed by the student and filed online, or by mail, or even prepared and filed by a professional fee-based preparer. The form requires income and net worth data for both the student and the parents, as well as the student dependency status and the household size. Based on the information in the FAFSA, the Department of Education determines the expected family contribution (EFC).

The expected family contribution is an estimate of the amount the parents and the student are expected to pay out of pocket that year, for the student's college cost. Typically, 12% of the parents' net worth, excluding retirement assets and home equity, and 35% of the student's net worth are considered available for the EFC. Therefore, if the family desires to reduce its expected family contribution and potentially qualify for more aid, it is important for the prospective student not to own any assets. It is preferable for the parents to own the assets, since a lower percentage of these assets will then be included in the EFC calculation.

If the parents or the non-dependent student have an adjusted gross income (AGI) of less than $50,000, then their assets are not considered for EFC inclusion, and the student will probably qualify for more aid. If their AGI is less than $23,000, then the EFC is automatically set to zero, and the student will qualify for maximum aid.

The Department of Education sends the FAFSA and EFC information to the institutions the student applies to, and the individual institutions determine the amount of federal, state and institutional aid the student will receive. The calculation typically subtracts the EFC from the cost of attendance of the specific institution, to determine the student's financial need for attending that specific institution. In other words, subtracting the EFC from the different cost of attendance of each school the student applies to produces a different financial need for each school. Therefore, it is possible for a student to have no financial need for attending a public university, while at the same time, to have significant financial need for attending a prestigious private university.

For example, if the Department of Education calculates the EFC to equal $25,000 this year, and the student applies to a private college with $40,000 cost of attendance (COA) and a public university with $16,000 cost of attendance (COA), the student's financial need is:

	COA - EFC = Financial Need
Private College	$40,000 - $25,000 = $15,000
Public University	$16,000 - $25,000 = $0

Since income, net worth, dependency status and household size may change over time, the FAFSA needs to be submitted to the Department of Education every year the student intends to enroll in a college or university in the fall. The EFC and the student financial need are re-determined annually. Filing the FAFSA early on is a good strategy for students to guarantee they receive all the aid they qualify for, as some forms of aid are provided on a first-come first-served basis. However, filing before January is not very practical, because critical family financial documents (like forms W2 and 1099) are not available from employers and financial institutions before the middle to the end of January.

It is worth noting that according to the National Postsecondary Aid Survey (NPSAS), SAT scores have an impact on the size of institutional need-based financial aid. "High SAT and low income" tends to yield more financial aid than "low SAT and low income." So, at least one factor determining aid, academic performance, is at the student's control.

According to the College Board (2011), the great majority of students attending public or private colleges and universities receive one or more of grants, loans, or work study aid, while tax benefits are available to all students, whether they receive any of the other types of aid or not. Table 6-1 shows the percentage of full-time students receiving aid in 2007–2008, per type of institution.

TABLE 6-1 Percentage of Full-Time Students Receiving Financial Aid in 2007–2008

PUBLIC		NON-PROFIT PRIVATE		FOR PROFIT PRIVATE
SELECTIVE	OPEN ADMISSION	SELECTIVE	LESS SELECTIVE OPEN ADMISSION	N/A
60%	75%	75%	80%+	92%

Data from: College Board, Trends in Higher Education, 2011

6.1.2 Financial Aid and Cost of Higher Education

While financial aid has been and continues to be beneficial to generations of college students since its inception, there is a significant negative effect associated with it. Much like with all government subsidies for any activity, the availability of billions of dollars of federal money each year for higher education increases the number of willing recipients, therefore increases the demand for higher education. To accommodate the higher number of students, institutions need to add more classrooms, laboratories, dormitories, athletic facilities, as well as staff and administrators.

According to the College Board (2011), the 30-year average annual inflation-adjusted tuition and fees increase between 1981–1982 and 2011–2012 is 4.44% For public 4-year institutions, 3.46% For public 2-year institutions, and 3.50% For non-profit private 4-year institutions. Inflation-adjusted means these percentage increases are in excess of the average annual inflation level. So if the average annual inflation level over this 30-year period is 3%, the cost of attending a 4-year non-profit private college increased approximately by 6.50% (3% + 3.50%) per year during this period.

Table 6-2 shows the 2011–2012 cost of attending college, and the increase from the previous year, per type of institution.

TABLE 6-2 2011-2012 Cost of Attending College and Annual Cost Increase per Type of Institution

TYPE OF INSTITUTION	TUITION		ROOM and BOARD	
	COST	% INCREASE	COST	% INCREASE
PUBLIC 2-YEAR	$2,727	8.7%	N/A	N/A
PUBLIC 4-YEAR In-State	$7,613	8.3%	$8,549	4.0%
PUBLIC 4-YEAR Out-of-State	$19,648	5.7%	$8,549	4.0%
PRIVATE 4-YEAR Non-Profit	$27,265	4.5%	$9,706	3.9%
PRIVATE 4-YEAR For Profit	$14,040	3.2%	N/A	N/A

Data from: College Board, Trends in Higher Education, 2011

6.1.3 Other Reasons for the Increasing Cost of Higher Education

While both public and private institutions increased tuition and room and board during 2011–2012, the year-over-year increase was higher among public institutions, whether they were 2-year or 4-year institutions. This seems to be in agreement with the recent trend of decreasing state appropriations per college student, and tuition hikes in public institutions. Table 6-3 shows the inflation-adjusted changes in public university tuition and state appropriations per college student, during 2008–2009 and 2010–2011.

TABLE 6-3 Inflation-Adjusted Changes in State Appropriations for Higher Education and Tuition in Public 4-Year Institutions

Academic Year	Change in State Appropriations	Change in Tuition of Public 4-Year Institutions
2008–2009	– 9%	Negligible
2009–2010	– 6%	+ 9%
2010–2011	– 4%	+ 7%

Data from: College Board, Trends in Higher Education, 2011

Public universities are state supported and are more sensitive to changes in state funding. While the data on Table 6-3 cover only the 3-year period following the financial crisis in the US, the data are indicative of the effect of state funding on public university tuition. The deteriorating state finances force state budgets to reduce their appropriations to state universities. Notice on Table 6-3 that tuition changes seem to follow state budget reductions with one year time lag. The 2008–2009 state budget reduction in higher education appropriations, shows up as a state university tuition hike the following year, and so on.

Suppose a public university with $100 million operating budget receives two-thirds support from the state. This implies the student payments provide only one-third of the university revenues or $33.33 million, while the state subsidy amounts to $66.67 million for the year. For simplicity assume no significant donations or endowment income for the year (which tend to dry up during difficult economic times). If the state reduces its support by 9%, the university loses $6 million ($66.67 M * 9%) in revenues. Raising tuition, fees, room and board by 9% to offset the reduction in state support, raises only $3 million ($33.33 M * 9%) in revenues from the students. Therefore, the resulting $3 million revenue shortfall will result in reduction in university offerings and services.

Notice that this example assumes a "unitary" elastic demand for the university services. This simply means the tuition hike does not cause too many students to drop out, as they cannot afford the cost anymore, which would reduce the revenues from students.

So any reduction in public funding of higher education usually turns out to be bad for students, who face higher costs while receiving fewer services and class offerings.

Private colleges and universities are also affected by state reductions in their support of higher education, but to a lesser extent than public institutions. Private institutions are mainly affected by the reduction in state aid to students, who again will have to pay more out of pocket, while possibly receiving fewer services.

Another factor contributing to the increase in the cost of higher education is the number and quality of services provided these days by colleges and universities, as well as, the cost of overseeing all these operations. For example, the College Board (2011) reports that in 2009 only 39% of public institution staff and 37% of private institution staff were primarily instructors. The remaining staff was involved in administration, computer support, financial aid, counseling, library service, etc.

At the same time, the percentage of full-time instructional faculty has steadily declined from 77% in 1971, to 65% in 1991, all the way down to 51% in 2009. Furthermore, the actual cost of teaching has increased very little.

Table 6-4 shows the inflation-adjusted changes in average faculty salaries and tuition, over the 20-year period between 1990 and 2010. While tuition increased 140% in public 4-year institutions during this 20-year period, average faculty salaries increased by only 3%. Private non-profit tuition increased by 74%, while faculty salaries increased by 14.5%. So while students are facing continuously rising costs for higher education, it seems they are paying more for the availability of additional auxiliary services rather than higher education itself.

TABLE 6-4 Inflation-Adjusted Changes in Faculty Salaries and Tuition, 1990–2010

Type of Institution	Change in Faculty Salaries	Change in Tuition
Public 4-Year	3%	140%
Private 4-Year Non-Profit	14.5%	74%

Data from: College Board, Trends in Higher Education, 2011

6.1.4 Does Higher Education Pay?

Despite the rising cost of higher education, the number of students enrolling in college increases every year, and at an increasing rate. Table 6-5 shows the number of all college students enrolled in US colleges and universities, public, private, non-profit and for-profit, between 1990 and 2009, as well as, the percentage change in enrollment, and the growth rate of enrollment. From one decade to the next, not only the enrollment increased significantly, but also the enrollment compound annual growth rate almost tripled in size.

TABLE 6-5 Enrollment in US Colleges and Universities 1990–2009

Year	Enrollment	Change in Enrollment	Enrollment Annual Growth Rate
1990	13,729,000	N/A	N/A
2000	15,540,000	13.19%	1.25%
2009	20,840,000	34.11%	3.32%

Data from: College Board, Trends in Higher Education, 2011

Notice, that the impressive enrollment gains for US institutions between 2000 and 2009 were achieved while it was harder for foreign students to obtain visas, after the terrorist attacks of 2001. This enrollment increase is the result of american households' strong preference for higher education.

It is possible this surge in college enrollment to be the result of affluence and wealth of US households. But this can not be true, as in recent years the US experienced two stock market busts

(2001 and 2008–2009), and a housing market bust (2007). According to the US Census Bureau (6/18/2012), there was a 35% drop in the net worth of US households between 2005 and 2010. Therefore, the most likely explanation for the surge in US college enrollment is the widely publicized effect of higher education on household income. Table 6-6 shows the 2010 median family income based on the education level of the family head. A family headed by a college graduate earns more than twice the income earned by a family headed by a high school graduate.

TABLE 6-6 2010 Median Family Income Based on Education Level of Family Head

Education Level of Family Head	Median Family Income
Bachelor Degree	$99,716
Associate Degree	$67,854
Some College	$58,685
High School Diploma	$48,332
Less than High School	$29,582

Data from: College Board, Trends in Higher Education, 2011

6.2. Types of Federal Financial Aid for Higher Education

With higher education costs already increasing 5% to 9% per year, and states unable to provide more support for their institutions, the trend of rising costs is expected to continue. Families will need to plan very carefully how to save and pay for their children's college education. Those caught unprepared, and unable to pay the full cost of attendance out of pocket, will have to rely on financial aid. Table 6-7 shows the types of federal student aid available for higher education.

TABLE 6-7 Types of Federal Financial Aid for Higher Education

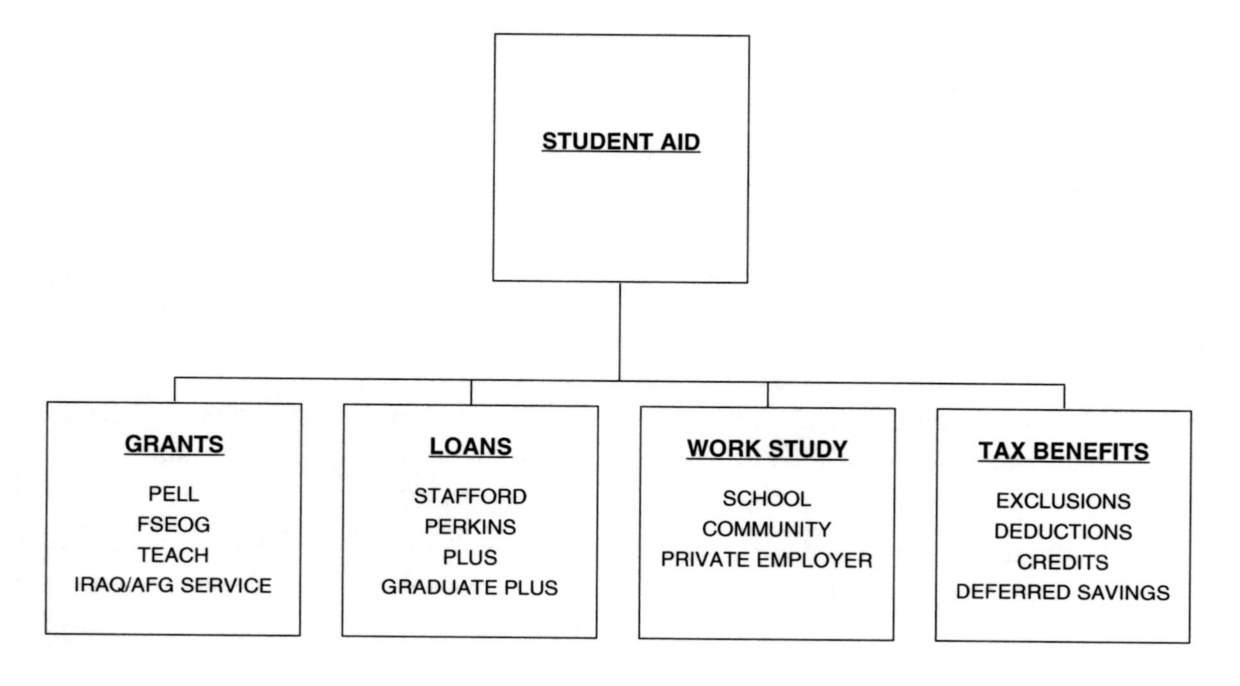

Sections 6.2.1 to 6.2.4 briefly describe each of these types of student aid that can help students and their families hope for a better future. Notice that only grants, loans, and work study are components of financial aid. Tax benefits associated with higher education are available through the US tax code to everyone, whether they receive financial aid or not. Tax benefits are listed here however, because as congress intended, they provide assistance in defraying the cost of higher education, therefore they need to be part of higher education planning.

6.2.1 Federal Grants

Together with scholarships, grants are the best form of aid, because the money does not have to be paid back. Grants are need-based, and awarded mainly for undergraduate studies.

Pell Grant

Recall from section 6.1.1, the 1972 Higher Education Amendments redefined the components of financial aid, which was introduced in 1965 by the Higher Education Act. The primary component of financial aid was the "basic educational opportunity grant," which in 1980 was renamed "federal pell grant," in honor of US Senator Clairborne Pell (1918–2009) from Rhode Island, who had sponsored the Higher Education Act.

The Pell Grant is a need-based aid, and is awarded to students who have not completed a graduate or professional degree. For equality of opportunity, federal Pell Grants are made available to all students (who qualify) to earn a college degree. With limited funds, it would be unfair for some to receive grants for graduate studies, while others would be denied the opportunity to attend college. However, there is an exception to this rule, as federal Pell Grants are made available to those enrolled in a post-baccalaureate teaching certificate program.

The maximum Pell Grant award for 2012–2013 was $5,550. Beginning July 1, 2012, student eligibility for Pell Grants is good only for 12 semesters or its equivalent, in case of partial awards during some semesters. After that, students are no longer eligible for Pell Grants.

Federal Supplemental Educational Opportunity Grant (FSEOG)

The second component of financial aid under the 1972 Higher Education Amendments is the federal Supplemental Educational Opportunity Grant, which is for undergraduate students with exceptional financial need. Only Pell Grant recipients with the lowest expected family contribution (EFC) qualify for FSEOG awards. The amount of the award varies between $100 and $4,000 depending on how early you apply, your financial need and the policies of your institution.

Teacher Education Assistance for College and Higher Education Grant (TEACH)

The College Cost Reduction and Access Act of 2007 created the TEACH Grant, to provide funding for students who intend to teach fulltime, in a high-need subject, in a public or private elementary or secondary school, serving low income families. A high-need subject is one which the Department of Education believes there is a shortage of teachers. Currently, high-need subjects include bilingual education, special education, mathematics, science, foreign language and reading.

The maximum TEACH award is $4,000 per year, and students who receive this grant agree to fulfill their teaching service of 4 years, within the 8 years following the completion of their education program. If they fail to do so, the teach grants they received are converted to unsubsidized Stafford

Loans (described in the next section) and have to be repaid, with interest accrued from the day the funds were awarded.

Iraq and Afghanistan Service Grant

This Grant is for students whose parent or guardian was a member of the US Armed Forces, and died as a result of service performed in Iraq or Afghanistan after September 11, 2001. The student must be under 24 years old, and enrolled in a higher education institution during the parent or guardian's death. The grant amount is equal to the maximum Pell Grant award, and cannot exceed the cost of attendance.

Keep in mind that Congress and the Department of Education make frequent changes to the available grants and the award amounts. For example, the Academic Competitiveness Grant (ACG), and the National Science and Mathematics Access to Retain Talent Grant (SMART) are no longer available. Therefore, it is a good idea to check annually the available grants from the Department of Education by visiting the website www.studentaid.ed.gov.

6.2.2 Federal Student Loans

Federal student loans are the third component of financial aid under the 1972 Higher Education Amendments. These are loans for higher education supported by the federal government, thus they offer students and parents better terms than private sector loans. For instance, they offer low fixed interest rates, income-based repayment plans, deferment options, and even loan cancellation. Unlike grants however, these are borrowed funds and must be repaid with interest.

Stafford Loan

In 1988 Congress renamed the "Federal Student Loan Program" as the "Robert T. Stafford Student Loan Program" in honor of US Senator Robert T. Stafford (1913–2006) from Vermont, for his work on higher education. There are two types of Stafford Loans: Subsidized and Unsubsidized.

"Subsidized Stafford Loans" are need-based higher education loans for undergraduate students, who are enrolled at least half-time in an accredited American institution. The major advantage of the Subsidized Stafford Loan is that while the student is enrolled in college, the federal government pays the interest on the loan. This is the essence of the "subsidy." No interest is accrued and added to the principal of the loan. Effective July 1, 2012 however, Subsidized Stafford Loans are not eligible for the interest subsidy during the 6-month "grace period," from the time the student leaves college and loan repayment begins.

A new development affecting Stafford Loans is introduced by the Budget Control Act of 2011, which eliminates Subsidized Stafford Loans for graduate and professional studies, effective july 1, 2012. Unsubsidized Stafford Loans however, will still be available for graduate students.

"Unsubsidized Stafford Loans" are not need-based higher education loans for undergraduate and graduate students, who are enrolled at least half-time in an accredited American institution. Since the federal government does not pay the interest on the loan while the student is in college, and during the 6-month grace period, interest accrues and is added to the loan principal (capitalized). The interest rates for both subsidized and unsubsidized Stafford Loans are set by Congress. Since the summer of 2013 the rates are linked to the 10-year Treasury Note yield, as determined by the last Treasury auction before June 1 each year. Stafford Loan rates are set at 2.05% above the 10-year Treasury Note yield and are capped at 8.25%. Graduate Stafford Loan rates are set at 3.6% above the 10-year Treasury Note yield and are capped at 9.5%.

The Student Aid and Fiscal Responsibility Act of 2010 eliminated the option of bank-issued Stafford Loans with the guarantee of the federal government (referred to as Federal Family Education Loans-FFEL). Therefore, effective July 1, 2010, all Stafford Loans are issued directly by the Department of Education, and referred to as "Direct Stafford Loans."

According to the Department of Education, 7,400,000 students are expected to get new Direct Stafford Loans in the 2012–2013 academic year, with each student borrowing an average $4,226.

Like federal grants, Stafford Loans do not renew automatically. Students need to re-file annually the FAFSA with the Department of Education to determine their eligibility. Typically, students receive less than the amount borrowed because of the origination fee, which pays for the costs administering the loan, and the funding of a reserve to protect the loan program against borrower default on their loans.

Table 6-8 shows the annual and lifetime borrowing limits for Stafford Loans, based on dependency status, and year of study.

TABLE 6-8 Annual and Lifetime Stafford Loan Borrowing Limits

Year	Dependent Student	Independent Student	Graduate Student
First	$5,500 ($3,500 Subsidized)	$9,500 ($3,500 Subsidized)	$20,500
Second	$6,500 ($4,500 Subsidized)	$10,500 ($4,500 Subsidized)	$20,500
Third & Beyond	$7,500 ($5,500 Subsidized)	$12,500 ($5,500 Subsidized)	$20,500
Maximum	**$31,000 ($23,000 Subsidized)**	**$57,500 ($23,000 Subsidized)**	**$138,500 ($65,000 Subsidized)**

www.studentaid.ed.gov

Perkins Loan

The federal Perkins Loan is a higher education loan for both undergraduate and graduate students, with exceptional financial need. The interest rate is fixed at 5%. unlike the Stafford Loan and the PLUS Loan, the Perkins Loan is made through the college or university financial aid office. In other words, the institution is the lender, and the loan is made with appropriations from the Department of Education.

Since the institution is the lender, the Perkins Loan is available on a first-come first-served basis, according to the funding level of the institutions. So applying early for financial aid is important for students with very high financial need, who could qualify for Perkins Loans.

Unlike the Stafford Loan, the Perkins Loan charges no origination fee. Repayment begins 9 months after graduation, or when the student drops below half-time status, or drops out of school. Perkins loan borrowers have a 10-year period to repay the loan. Table 6-9 shows the annual and lifetime borrowing limits for Perkins Loans.

TABLE 6-9 Annual and Lifetime Borrowing Limits for Federal Perkins Loans

Borrowing Limits	Undergraduate Student	Graduate Student
Annual Limit	$5,500	$8,000
Lifetime Limit	$27,000	$60,000 Including undergraduate Perkins

www.studentaid.ed.gov

PLUS Loans

Federal PLUS Loans allow parents to borrow to cover any undergraduate education costs for their dependent child, not already covered by financial aid. The loan is not need-based. Instead it depends on the parents' credit worthiness. Like the Stafford Loans, effective July 1, 2010 PLUS Loans can only be issued by the Department of Education, through the Direct Loan Program. Therefore, the parents need to apply for PLUS Loans at the institution's financial aid office.

PLUS Loans are useful to families with relatively high expected family contribution (EFC), who have not prepared adequately for their children's higher education costs. The children do not qualify for need-based federal grants, Subsidized Stafford Loans, and Perkins Loans, but can receive Unsubsidized Stafford Loans. The parents can apply for PLUS Loans to cover the remaining costs.

The annual borrowing limit equals the cost of attendance (COA) not covered by financial aid. For example, if the student's COA is $12,000, and the institution determines the financial aid to be $5,000, then the PLUS Loan borrowing limit for the year is $7,000 ($12,000–$5,000). The interest rate for PLUS Loans is set at 4.6% above the 10-year Treasury Note yield and are capped at 10.5%. There is also a 4% loan origination fee.

Payments start 60 days after the PLUS Loan is fully disbursed, but for loans issued on or after July 1, 2008 payments can be deferred while the student is enrolled in college at least half-time, and through the 6-month grace period after leaving college. The repayment period can last 10 to 25 years.

PLUS Loans for Graduate and Professional Students

Graduate students can apply for a PLUS Loan themselves, instead of their parents. The terms of the loan are exactly the same as above, but students have to file a FAFSA to apply for the PLUS Loan. While students' credit scores are not included in the FAFSA, students can not have any defaults, debt discharges, foreclosures, repossessions, delinquencies, or tax liens in the last 5 years to qualify for the loan.

Tips for Loan Repayment

According to the Federal Reserve Bank of New York, student loans grew to a record $904 billion in May 2012, exceeding in size credit card loans. This is troubling. It is important for students borrowing money to attend college, to realize that student loans represent real obligations, which will have to be paid back with interest. In that respect, you need to be as careful when borrowing for higher education expenses, as you would be if you were borrowing to buy a vehicle or a house. All of these loans are long-term obligations, which will require the commitment of your future financial resources for years to come. So, **Tip-1**: Do not borrow too much for your college education. Your education is an investment on yourself, and like all investments, if you overpay it will be hard to make a profit from it.

When it comes to the repayment of the loans, you need to make every effort to stick with the standard repayment method, which amortizes the loans within 10 years. This will minimize the total interest expense you will have to pay for your loans. Although there are alternative repayment methods like the extended, the income based, and the income contingent, which may seem attractive due to lower monthly payments, you will end up paying double or triple the interest expense, as these methods prolong repayment up to 25 years. So, **Tip-2**: Stick with the standard repayment method and pay off your student loans in 10 years or less.

If you ever run into financial trouble, do not stop making your monthly student loan payments. This will cause the student loans to go to default, which will damage your credit record, make it difficult to borrow in the future and invite debt collectors to come after you. You do have some options. You can ask the loan servicer for a "deferment," which allows you to stop making payments for a period, usually if you happen to go back to school or become unemployed. You can also request a "forbearance," which allows you to reduce or stop your payments for up to 3 years, if you are facing really tough times due to an illness, etc. Notice, that both of these options are costly, as the interest accrues and accumulates while you are not making payments. But at least you avoid outright default, which can push you into declaring bankruptcy.

Keep in mind, the federal loans are guaranteed by the government therefore, it is difficult to discharge them by declaring personal bankruptcy. You would have to prove to the bankruptcy court that repaying the student loans would cause you "undue hardship," which apparently is not so easy to prove. The government can garnish up to 15% of your disposable income, or garnish part of your Social Security benefits (if you are receiving any form of benefits), trying to collect on federal student loans. The garnishment could be higher than the monthly student loan payment under the income based repayment method (10% of disposable income). So, **Tip-3**: Do not plan on defaulting on student loans. It is not a good idea.

While it may be difficult to discharge your student loans, it may be possible to have the balances erased without affecting your credit record. The government allows for "cancellation" of federal student loans if you decide to enlist in certain specialties of the Armed Forces (offered as incentive payment), or serve as a nurse for 2–3 years to an "approved eligible" health facility, or you are in public service and you have made 120 monthly student loan payments. Cancellations are also allowed for total and permanent disability or death of the borrower, but you may not want to plan for this course of action. So, **Tip-4**: A few years working in the public sector could erase the balance of your student loans. You may actually discover you enjoy working in the service of your fellow citizens.

6.2.3 Federal Work Study Program

The Federal Work Study Program (FWS) is a federally funded program assisting students paying for higher education, through part-time work. The FWS Program is need-based, and it is available to both undergraduate and graduate students. Students can work on-campus or off-campus. Typical on-campus employment includes tutoring, working in the library etc. Off-campus jobs range from community service with non-profit organizations, to work related to the student's course of study with private employers. Whether working on or off-campus however, students in the Federal Work Study Program receive at least the prevailing federal minimum wage. To participate in the FWS Program, you need to indicate your willingness to be considered for work study when filling in your FAFSA, and to apply early with your institution. This is a first-come first-served program, so when the FWS Program funds are exhausted the aid is gone.

6.2.4 Tax Benefits

While tax benefits for those paying for higher education are not part of financial aid, Congress has introduced many provisions in the US income tax code to alleviate the burden of paying for college, and to provide incentives for families to save for their children's college education. Financial planning would be remiss not to take all the available higher education tax benefits into account. Table 6-10 shows the available tax benefits for higher education per category.

TABLE 6-10 Tax Benefits for Higher Education

EXCLUSIONS (from Income)	TAX DEFERRED SAVINGS
Grants, Scholarships, Fellowships Employer Provided Education Assistance Cancellations of Student Loans Interest from US Bonds EE and I	Prepaid Tuition Plans 529 College Savings Plans Coverdell Education Savings Accounts
DEDUCTIONS (for AGI)	**TAX CREDITS**
Tuition and Fees Student Loan Interest	American Opportunity Lifetime Learning

Caution: Tax credits are incompatible with the other three categories of tax benefits on Table 6-10. In other words, if the student received a scholarship, grant or employer provided education assistance, then the family cannot claim a tax credit for the expenses paid with the grant, scholarship or employer provided education assistance. If education expenses were paid out of a 529 plan or a Coverdell savings account, the family cannot claim a tax credit for the same expenses. Finally, the family cannot claim a tax credit for the same student for whom they decided to deduct tuition and fees for the tax year.

EXCLUSIONS (from Income)

i) Grants, scholarships, and fellowships are tax-free if the recipient is a candidate for a degree at an accredited college or university, and the proceeds are used to pay for "qualified education expenses," such as tuition, fees, and required books and supplies. Any proceeds used for other (non-qualified) expenses, like room and board, living expenses, transportation, etc are taxable income.

ii) Employer provided education assistance reimburses employees for "qualified education expenses," such as tuition, fees, and required books and supplies, up to an annual limit ($5,250 for 2012). Employer assistance above the annual limit, or spent on non-qualified expenses (room and board, living expenses, transportation, etc) are taxable income. The employer provided education assistance must be an existing benefit, listed on the employer's human resources documents, for any reimbursement to be tax-free for the employee.

iii) Cancellations of student loans as described in section 6.2.2, due to 10-year public service, 3-year nursing service at an approved eligible health facility, and serving at certain specialties of the armed forces, are excluded from income and taxation. Cancellations for total permanent disability or death of borrower and for being in repayment past the 25-year limit (reduced to 20 years in 2011) are taxable income. Discharges of student loans are also taxable income.

iv) If US government series EE and I bonds are redeemed to pay for "qualified education expenses," the interest income earned on these bonds is excluded from taxation. The payment of education expenses and the bond redemption must occur in the same year, for the interest income to be tax-free. However, for high income households or for bond proceeds spent on non-qualified expenses (room and board, living expenses, transportation, etc), the interest income is taxable.

DEDUCTIONS (for AGI)

i) Tuition and fees, as well as, other "qualified education expenses" like required books and supplies up to $4,000 per year, can be deducted from gross income, thus reducing the adjusted gross income (AGI). These expenses however, must be either for the taxpayer, spouse, or their dependents, and must be paid directly to the institution. High income households are progressively disallowed this deduction.

ii) Student loan origination fees and student loan interest up to $2,500 per year, for loans used to pay for "qualified" and "non-qualified" education expenses, can be deducted from gross income, thus reducing the adjusted gross income (AGI). Similar to the previous deduction, the student loans must have been used to pay expenses either for the taxpayer, spouse, or their dependents. High income households are progressively disallowed this deduction as well.

TAX CREDITS

i) The American Opportunity Tax Credit (AOTC) is the more generous of the two education tax credits. It provides a tax credit (offsetting dollar for dollar income taxes) up to $2,500 <u>per person</u> per year, for "qualified education expenses" spent by the taxpayer, spouse, or their dependents. So if multiple family members are enrolled (at least half-time) in college during the year, the household can claim the AOTC multiple times. The AOTC however, is only good for the first 4 years of postsecondary education. So it cannot be claimed for graduate studies. The AOTC is calculated as:

(100% * first $2,000 of Qualified Expenses) + (25% * next $2,000 of Qualified Expenses)
Notice that the AOTC is maxed out at $4,000 of Qualified Education Expenses:
(100% * $2,000) + (25% * $2,000) = $2,000 + $500 = $2,500

Up to 40% of the AOTC is <u>refundable</u>, which means it can generate a refund up to $1,000 (40% * $2,500) if the household has a zero income tax bill. High income households are progressively phased-out from claiming this tax credit.

ii) The Lifetime Learning Tax Credit provides a tax credit (offsetting dollar for dollar income taxes) up to $2,000 <u>per family</u> per year, for tuition and fees spent by the taxpayer, spouse, or their dependents. So if multiple family members are enrolled in college during the year, the household can combine the expenses and claim only one Lifetime Learning Tax Credit. This Credit however, is good for all years of postsecondary education. So it can be claimed for graduate studies, or for classes leading to certificates and new job skills. There is no minimum course load requirement. The Lifetime Learning Credit is calculated as:

20% * first $10,000 of Qualified Expenses

The Lifetime Learning Tax Credit is maxed out at $10,000 of family tuition and fees (20% * $10,000 = $2,000). This tax credit is <u>not refundable</u>, and high income households are progressively phased-out from claiming this tax credit.

TAX DEFERRED SAVINGS

Congress has introduced provisions in the tax code that provide tax incentives for households to save for their children's college education. These provisions allow families to save in specific accounts, which offer two advantages: First, the contributions grow tax deferred, thus the accumulations grow larger compared to taxable accounts. Second, the withdrawals are tax-free if used for qualified education expenses. These accounts are very useful to households with children several years away from going to college, as compounding is a function of the number of periods (n) the funds stay invested. An auxiliary advantage of all these accounts is that their assets are considered parental assets for financial aid purposes. Therefore, only 12% of the assets are considered available for the expected family contribution (EFC), which produces more generous financial aid for the children.

i) State prepaid tuition plans allow households to purchase college credits for their children, while the children are growing up. The concept behind these plans is very appealing. Eliminate the uncertainty surrounding the future cost of college education. Families do not accumulate dollars, instead they accumulate college credits. Once they accumulate enough credits, college tuition is paid for. The parents typically pay a premium over the prevailing price per credit at the time of purchase. Given however, the 5% to 9% annual tuition inflation rate, parents feel they save and at the same time hedge against the rising costs of higher education. There are however, a few disadvantages associated with the state prepaid tuition plans.

   First, these are state plans. Households pre-pay for credits in the plan of their domicile state, expecting their children will attend one of the state institutions. If the children want to study out-of-state, or they receive scholarships, or decide college is not for them, then the only recourse for the parents is to get a refund of what they paid over the years, minus administrative charges. The parents in effect forgo the investment returns, which could have been generated if the same payments were invested in a different account.

   Second, while parents may believe they are protected against rising tuition costs, states may be unable to honor the promises they made to these parents. As state appropriations for higher education have been declining (Table 6-3), state institutions are forced to raise tuition higher than was expected by the prepaid plans. As a result, the assets of prepaid plans may not be enough to cover all their liabilities (the promises to parents). It is entirely possible that financially strapped states will renege on their promises, and cover only a percentage of the college credits purchased by parents.

ii) College savings plans (also referred to as 529 plans) are tax-favored investment accounts designed to motivate people to save for the college expenses of their designated beneficiaries. Each 529 plan is managed by the state treasurer or a professional investment management firm appointed by the state treasurer. The contributions to the accounts are typically invested in mutual funds chosen by the plan managers, so there is investment risk involved with these plans. 529 Plans however, offer several advantages:

   First, under the Economic Growth and Tax Relief Reconciliation Act of 2001 (EGTRRA), 529 Plan contributions grow tax deferred and plan distributions for qualified higher education expenses are exempt from income taxation. While there is no deductibility of contributions for federal income taxes, states offer such deductibility for residents who invest in their state's 529 Plan.

   Second, qualified expenses include all post-secondary tuition, fees, books and supplies, computers, and even room and board (or off-campus housing), at ANY accredited institution at ANY state. In other words, parents residing in South Carolina may choose to contribute to the North Carolina State 529 Plan, while their child eventually decides to attend a state university in Virginia. The parents are allowed to use the funds from the North Carolina 529 Plan to pay for the qualified expenses at the university in Virginia.

Third, under the College Cost Reduction and Access Act of 2007, the assets in the account are considered assets of the account owner, and not of the beneficiary. Thus 529 Plans do not reduce significantly the beneficiary's financial aid.

Fourth, in case the beneficiary does not attend college, or there is a left-over balance in the account, the account owner can switch beneficiaries without tax implications, as long as the new beneficiary is a family member of the same generation as the previous beneficiary. Gift taxes or generation skipping transfer taxes are involved if the new beneficiary belongs to a lower generation than the previous beneficiary. See Chapter 10 for more details about these taxes. The account owner can even withdraw the funds from the account and not use them for education expenses. In this case however, the account earnings are taxable income, and subject to a 10% penalty.

Fifth, there is no income phase-out for contributing to a 529 Plan, and contributions are only limited by the total cost of attending college at each specific state. This makes the 529 Plan a useful vehicle for estate planning purposes too. For example, a grandparent could contribute the annual gift tax exclusion amount ($14,000 currently) to the 529 Plan of the grandchild, for its future college education. If the grandparent is married, and the couple elects "gift splitting," the annual gift tax exclusion amount doubles to $28,000. The IRS allows up to five years worth of contributions to be contributed as a lump sum, without incurring any gift taxes. Therefore, the grandparents could reduce their estate by $140,000 (2 * $14,000 * 5) while providing the grandchild with a college education. If they do this for 4 grandchildren, they could reduce their estate by $560,000 ($140,000 * 4), which would reduce or possibly eliminate their estate taxes.

Finally, there is a private 529 Plan which allows parents to buy discounted certificates guaranteed to pay a fixed percentage of tuition (up to 100%) at more than 270 participating private colleges and universities across the country. The participating private institutions guarantee to provide the promised percentage of tuition in exchange for the future value of the certificates. While these institutions hope the investments represented by the certificates will worth at least as much, or more, than the promised cost of tuition, they clearly bear the investment risk of the certificates.

iii) Coverdell Education Savings Accounts (ESAs) are tax-favored accounts providing incentives for families to save for their beneficiaries education expenses. Originally called education IRAs, they were renamed later in honor of US Senator Paul Coverdell from Georgia, who sponsored the bill introducing these accounts. Like 529 Plans, Coverdell education savings accounts allow tax-deferred contributions, and tax-free distributions if used for qualified education expenses. The assets in the accounts are considered parental assets, thus not adversely affecting the beneficiary's financial aid.

The big attraction to Coverdell education savings accounts is that qualified education expenses include the usual tuition, fees, books and supplies, and room and board for elementary, secondary and higher education institutions. In other words, families can use the account funds to pay for private elementary or secondary schools, if they believe their child needs the support at that stage of his or her education. For example, what is the point in saving for attending college in the future, when the child is failing middle school now? Similarly, it may seem counter productive to have savings in accounts that help pay for college, when the child gets diagnosed as having special needs, requiring special education classes early on in its life.

Coverdell education savings accounts however, are more restrictive than 529 Plans in other ways. For instance, annual contributions to a beneficiary's Coverdell ESA cannot exceed $2,000 per year from all donors. Contributions cannot be made after the beneficiary turns 18 years old, while all account assets have to be distributed after the beneficiary turns 30 years old. The account owners can change the account beneficiary without any tax liability, as long as the new beneficiary is another family member younger than 30 years of age. Finally, higher income families are disallowed contributing to Coverdell education savings accounts.

6.2.5 Practical Application: Parents Using Retirement Accounts for College Expenses

A common dilemma among parents, who have not prepared adequately for their children's college education expenses, is whether to cover or to supplement these expenses with funds from their individual retirement accounts (IRAs) and Roth IRAs.

These accounts are covered in more detail in Chapter 9, but for the purposes of this chapter, it is sufficient to know that IRAs and Roth IRAs are tax-deferred accounts, aiming at providing people with incentives to save for their retirement years. Contributions to IRAs are tax deductible (dependent on income limits) and distributions are taxable income. Contributions to Roth IRAs are not tax deductible, but distributions are tax free. Because both accounts aim to boost retirement income, distributions at an early age (less than $59^1/_2$) are generally penalized with an additional 10% tax.

Among the few exceptions to the penalty tax, is the use of the early distributions for higher education expenses. This exception is often misinterpreted by parents to mean that raiding their IRAs and Roth IRAs to pay for college expenses is a legitimate use of these accounts. Parents would be well advised however, to consider the following three issues before raiding their retirement accounts.

First, while there is no 10% tax penalty applied to early distributions used for higher education expenses, there are other negative tax implications. For instance, funds distributed both from IRAs and Roth IRAs lose their tax-deferred status. Furthermore, the early distributions from IRAs are taxable income. For a taxpayer in the 28% federal and 5% state income tax brackets, the college expenses paid with IRA funds cost an extra 33% (28% + 5%) in taxes. This is a steep premium to pay to get (early) access to their own funds!

Second, the early distributed funds from these retirement accounts have an "opportunity cost." Invested for the long run, these accounts could be generating significant annual returns, which will not be realized if the funds are withdrawn early. For instance, according to the Federal Reserve Bank of St. Louis (FRED), the S&P 500 stock index produced 10.6% Average annual return during the 50-year period between 1962 and 2011. Compared to student loan interest rates from section 6.2.2 (currently at 3.86% for Stafford, 5.41% for Graduate Stafford and 6.41% for PLUS loans), it seems that using own retirement funds may be an expensive choice to pay for college expenses.

Third, raiding parental retirement accounts to fulfill the goal of funding the children's higher education, clearly conflicts with another parental goal, that of saving for retirement. Time and again, parents in their 50s with few retirement assets feel the moral and emotional need to help their children go to college, utilizing their scarce retirement funds. While they believe they are addressing a pressing problem, they are in effect creating a bigger one. Since they do not have enough productive years ahead of them, they may not be able to replenish their retirement accounts, thus risking not being able to support themselves during retirement. It is preferable for parents to focus on securing their own financial needs first, while letting the children finance their college education with relatively cheap student loans. While the children have 10 to 25 years to repay the loans, the parents may not have as many working years to rebuild their nest egg.

6.3. Planning for Higher Education Expenses

For parents with a number of years before a child reaches college age, some planning and preparation can help them avoid the tough dilemma of paying for college or saving for retirement. Although parents may like to provide the financial support for their child's college education, they may not know how to prepare for it, or they may become overwhelmed in the process and abandon the whole effort. Financial planning can reduce the uncertainty surrounding paying for future college expenses, and with objective evaluation and analysis of the parents goals versus their financial situation, it can provide parents with a concise plan of required periodic savings to cover the child's future higher education expenses.

Table 6-11 shows the three-step process you can follow to estimate the periodic savings needed to pay for college, and the necessary information needed for every step.

TABLE 6-11 Estimating Required Savings to Pay for a College Education

Steps	Description	Needed Information
Step 1	Estimate the future cost of attendance by inflating the current cost of attendance (finding the FV of the cost of attendance)	Current cost of attendance, years until going to college, college cost inflation rate
Step 2	Estimate the total cost of attendance for all years of college, as of the first day of enrollment in college, by finding the PV of all annual costs	FV of cost of attendance, number of years in college, rate of return on savings, college cost inflation rate
Step 3	Estimate the required periodic savings to raise the total cost of attendance by the year the child enrolls in college	PV of total cost of attendance, years until going to college, rate of return on savings

Once step 3 is completed and the required periodic savings are calculated, the parents with their financial planner should revisit their budget to ensure these periodic savings are feasible. Recall from Chapter 4, the availability of positive discretionary net income (or cash flow) allows pursuing financial goals. If the parents' budget cannot accommodate the necessary periodic savings to produce the needed college fund, there are a few options to be considered.

First, the parents could agree to alter their budget to secure the desired discretionary net income, which will be invested for the child's college education. Clearly, this will require trimming other expenses, which may or may not be desirable or even possible. It depends on how thinly the budget is already stretched, and how high in the priority list of goals is paying for the child's college education.

Second, the parents may consider extending the period of their savings, to include the years the child attends college. For example, adding 4 more years of monthly savings will reduce the size of each payment to a more feasible level. The college fund may not be ready before the child starts college, but better late than never.

Finally, if after trying the first two options, the budget's discretionary net income is still significantly lower than the required periodic savings, it is time to explore cheaper institutions. Repeating the analysis with lower costs of attendance will eventually produce a lower required periodic savings amount, until a realistic college option is identified.

Remember, the benefit of financial planning is to reduce uncertainty in your financial life, by implementing strategies to help you achieve your financial goals. However, it is only when the goals are feasible, and the strategies are realistic that you can achieve financial success.

6.3.1 Practical Application: The Milfords' College Fund

Ric and vanessa milford are ready to get serious about coming up with a plan to pay for their children's college education. The couple has two daughters; Samantha and Cassandra, ages 10 and 7 respectively. No funds have been set aside for their college education. Ric's son from his first marriage, Michael is 15 years old, and Ric has been saving $6,000 per year for the last 3 years for his college expenses. Currently, the account has a balance of $20,000.

Their financial planner, having prepared their financial statements (Chapter 4), knows that the Milfords have no discretionary income available, despite their six-figure income. Therefore, any required monthly contributions to college savings plans will not be easy to come by. On the other hand, it is highly unlikely the children will receive any meaningful financial aid, given their parents' financial situation.

To keep the analysis realistic, the financial planner assumes all three children will attend in-state public universities, unless offered scholarships from out-of-state institutions. The current cost of attendance is $16,162 (Table 6-2) consisting of $7,613 tuition and fees, and $8,549 room and board. The Milfords can earn a nominal rate of return of 9% on their investments, while to err on the side of caution the annual college cost inflation rate is assumed to be 7%. The calculations are prepared separately for each child, and aggregated at the end. This provides a clearer picture, and also allows for scenario analysis in case a child receives a scholarship, or decides not to attend college.

Michael

Table 6-12 presents the calculations for estimating the required monthly savings to fully cover Michael's college expenses. Since Michael is 15 years old, he will start college in exactly 3 years. Given the assumed inflation rate of college expenses, the cost of attendance is expected to be $19,799.145 when Michael enrolls in college.

The present value of the total cost of attendance for 4 years of college, on the day Michael enrolls in college will be $77,043.3986. Notice, that college expenses are paid upfront every period, therefore this is an annuity due, requiring a change to the BEGIN mode on your financial calculator. Also you need to use the real interest rate for this calculation, as the Milfords' investments are expected to grow at 9% per year, while at the same time college costs are expected to increase by 7%. The real rate is:

$$i_R = \left(\frac{1+i_N}{1+\pi} - 1\right) * 100 \Rightarrow i_R = \left(\frac{1+0.09}{1+0.07} - 1\right) * 100 \Rightarrow i_R = 1.8692\%$$

The required monthly savings to fully cover Michael's higher education expenses are $1,236.1393. This is a serious monthly commitment resulting from the fact that there are only 36 months to raise $77,043.3986 And Ric has put aside only $20,000. Recall that with compounding, time is your ally if you start saving early, but it is your enemy if you start late.

TABLE 6-12 HP10BII Calculations for Covering Michael's College Expenses

Step-1 **FV of Cost of Attendance**	**Step-2** **PV of Total Cost for 4 Years**	**Step-3** **Estimate Monthly PMT**
1 □ P/YR	1 □ P/YR	12 □ P/YR
3 N	□ BEG/END	3 □ X P/YR
7 I/YR	4 N	9 I/YR
$16,162 +/– PV	1.8692 I/YR	$20,000 +/– PV
FV $19,799.145	$19,799.145 +/– PMT	$77,043.3986 FV
	0 FV	**PMT -$1,236.1393**
	PV -$77,043.3986	

Samantha

Table 6-13 presents the calculations for estimating the required monthly savings to fully cover Samantha's college expenses. Since Samantha is 10 years old, she will attend college in 8 years. The cost of attendance in 8 years is expected to be $27,769.325. The present value of the total cost of attendance for 4 years of college, on the day Samantha enrolls in college is estimated at $108,057.3517. Given that the Milfords have yet to set any money aside to cover these expenses, the required monthly savings is $772.632 for the next 96 months.

TABLE 6-13 HP10BII Calculations for Covering Samantha's College Expenses

Step-1 **FV of Cost of Attendance**	**Step-2** **PV of Total Cost for 4 Years**	**Step-3** **Estimate Monthly PMT**
1 □ P/YR	1 □ P/YR	12 □ P/YR
8 N	□ BEG/END	8 □ X P/YR
7 I/YR	4 N	9 I/YR
$16,162 +/– PV	1.8692 I/YR	0 PV
FV $27,769.325	$27,769.325 +/– PMT	$108,057.3517 FV
	0 FV	**PMT -$772.632**
	PV -$108,057.3517	

Cassandra

Table 6-14 presents the calculations for estimating the required monthly savings to fully cover Cassandra's college expenses. Cassandra is 7 years old therefore she will attend college in 11 years. The cost of attendance in 11 years is expected to be $34,018.6173. The present value of the total cost of attendance for 4 years of college, on the day Cassandra enrolls in college is estimated to be $132,374.9026. Much like with Samantha's college fund, the Milfords have yet to set any money aside to cover these expenses. Thus, the required monthly savings is $590.4985 For the next 132 months.

TABLE 6-14 HP10BII Calculations for Covering Cassandra's College Expenses

Step-1 FV of Cost of Attendance	Step-2 PV of Total Cost for 4 Years	Step-3 Estimate Monthly PMT
1 ☐ P/YR	1 ☐ P/YR	12 ☐ P/YR
11 N	☐ BEG/END	11 ☐ X P/YR
7 I/YR	4 N	9 I/YR
$16,162 +/– PV	1.8692 I/YR	0 PV
FV $34,018.6173	$34,018.6173 +/– PMT	$132,374.9026 FV
	0 FV	**PMT -$590.4985**
	PV -$132,374.9026	

Notice, that while more funds need to be raised for Cassandra than for Samantha (due to inflation), the monthly required savings for Cassandra are lower than those required for Samantha. The reason is time. The Milfords have 132 months to raise the funds for Cassandra, but only 96 months for Samantha.

Table 6-15 shows the milfords' required monthly savings for all three children and for how long these savings should be budgeted for.

TABLE 6-15 The Milfords' Required Monthly Savings for Higher Education Expenses

First 36 Months (1 to 36)	Next 60 Months (37 to 96)	Last 36 Months (97 to 132)
$1,236.1393 Michael		
$772.632 Samantha	$772.632 Samantha	
$590.4985 Cassandra	$590.4985 Cassandra	$590.4985 Cassandra
$2,599.2698	$1,363.1305	$590.4985

The first 36 months are looking to be very stressful for the Milfords, as they will have to be saving for all three children. With Michael's college expenses covered, the required monthly savings for the two daughters' expenses drop by almost 50%. Once Samantha's expenses are covered too, the monthly burden is reduced to 22.7% Of the initial required monthly savings.

Naturally, it should be expected there will be a struggle producing these monthly savings from a budget with no available discretionary income. It may be down right unrealistic to expect the Milfords will successfully commit to these college savings for the next 132 months (11 years). So some alternatives that could reduce the required monthly savings amount may need to be considered.

For instance, soliciting some contributions from grandparents for 529 Plans or prepaid tuition for their grandchildren could be really helpful at this point. Stretching the monthly savings over a longer time period, perhaps to include the 4 years of college attendance for each child, would also reduce the required monthly savings amount. Finally, if the Milfords cannot come up with the required monthly savings on their budget, junior colleges for the first couple of years of studies may need to be incorporated in their plan.

Once again, an important element of financial planning is setting feasible goals and pursuing them with realistic strategies. Having to save to pay for their children's college education (including junior college), is more painful of a strategy than the children receiving scholarships from Ivy League schools. The first however, is realistic planning while the latter is just dreaming.

Summary

The US Congress in recognizing the importance of higher education for labor productivity is providing multiple programs granting incentives for Americans to attend college. Grants, subsidized loans, guaranteed loans, work-study programs, tax exclusions, tax deductions and tax credits are all federal programs helping people to pay for higher education. In addition, tax-advantaged accounts aim to motivate families to save for their children's future college education. Furthermore, states support and subsidize public university systems, while institutions grant scholarships, fellowships, as well as other forms of grants. All these subsidies may facilitate access to college, but with higher college enrollment come higher college costs. Families with young children should plan to start saving early on to cover the ever increasing costs of higher education.

Review Questions

1. During the year Brian paid out-of-pocket for his daughters' college expenses the following amounts: $6,000 for Julia, who is a senior, and $2,800 for Olivia, a freshman at the local community college. What is the maximum education tax credit Brian can take for the year?

2. During the year Eric paid out-of-pocket $11,000 for his MBA classes, $6,500 for his wife's master in education classes, and $2,600 for his daughter's community college classes. What is the maximum education tax credit Eric can take this year?

3. Mark wants to start saving for his daughter's college education, but he is concerned his little girl is already 4 years old and not talking. Would you recommend a 529 Plan, prepaid tuition, or Coverdell education savings account?

4. Jason and Maria despite their six-figure incomes have not saved anything for their 16-year-old son's college education. They have little available cash and no discretionary income. How should they pay for their son's college expenses?

5. Tyrone's son will start college in 13 years. The cost of attendance this year is $28,000. College costs are expected to keep increasing at an annual rate of 6.5% in the future. Tyrone can earn 10% on his investments. He would like to pay for his son's college education, and to have all the funds available by the time his son enrolls in college. How much will college cost in 13 years?

6. Referring to question 5, how much does Tyrone need to save at the end of every month?

7. Referring to question 6, how much does Tyrone need to save at the end of every month, if he was to stretch the payments for the 4 years his son was in college?

CHAPTER SEVEN

Investment Planning: Creating Wealth

7.1 Introduction

Investment planning is typically associated with the fourth step of the financial planning process, which has to do with developing a plan to achieve financial goals. Once the client's goals are established, the financial planner needs to develop appropriate and realistic strategies to achieve these goals. Accomplishing most financial goals requires investing in productive assets, which help the client accumulate wealth.

Investing is the process of identifying, analyzing, and purchasing assets for the explicit purpose of generating returns. Investing requires deploying capital, which is accumulated through saving. Saving reflects your deliberate effort to defer current consumption for future consumption. While saving is necessary for accumulating capital, it is not sufficient for creating wealth, because it involves no risk and usually offers low returns. For example, a bank savings account or a certificate of deposit provide you with explicit principal protection by the Federal Deposit Insurance Corporation (FDIC), but offer minimal returns which may or may not exceed the inflation rate. Investing on the other hand, implies undertaking calculated risks to generate superior returns.

Investing however, requires thorough analysis in order to identify assets that provide a high degree of safety for both your principal and the returns, over a specific time period. Since all analysis is time-specific, investments are held only as long the analysis is valid. In other words, you need to have a specific investment horizon for every asset in your portfolio of investment holdings. An asset satisfying your safety and return requirements today may not satisfy them two years later, and you may need to purge this asset from your portfolio. Purchasing assets without adhering to this disciplined process of thorough analysis, strict risk and return metrics, and specific investment horizons, provides no safety of principal or returns, therefore it is mainly gambling.

Investment returns have two components. First, is the income stream generated by the asset: rents for real estate, dividends for stocks, interest payments for bonds, etc. Second, is the capital gain resulting from the possible price appreciation of the asset.

When pricing an asset, asset valuation models consider only the first component of return, because the income stream is either promised (rents, interest payments) or reasonably expected (dividends). Even if a corporation currently pays no dividend, to stay in business it will have to be profitable, and it is reasonable to expect that profitable businesses will eventually pay dividends.

The second component of return is not included in valuation models, because while capital gains can be significant, and possibly greater than the income stream, they depend primarily on the demand and supply conditions in the market for the particular asset. For instance, commodities pay no income stream but are subject to wide price fluctuations.

The 2001 average price of gold was $271.04 per ounce, while by 2011 the average price had climbed to $1,571.52 per ounce. An investor who bought an ounce of the precious metal in 2001, and subsequently sold it 10 years later, would have booked an impressive capital gain of $1,300.48.

Of course, the price can move even higher in the future or it can collapse, depending on demand and supply conditions in the market for gold. There is no guarantee a capital gain will be produced within a specific investment horizon. Therefore, buying assets merely hoping to realize capital gains is speculation, rather than investing.

7.1.1 Investment Assets

The typical assets used by investors to grow their wealth are stocks, bonds and mutual funds. Shares of stock are securities representing ownership interest in corporations. Bonds are securities representing debt claims on the bond issuer. Mutual fund shares represent ownership interests in pools of funds investing in stocks, bonds, or both.

Table 7-1 shows the main categories of each of these securities.

TABLE 7-1 Stocks, Bonds and Mutual Funds

STOCKS
Large capitalization (cap) > $10 billion
$2 billion < mid cap < $10 billion
Small cap < $2 billion
Value stocks: Undervalued stocks, paying high dividend yields
Growth stocks: Rapidly growing revenues & earnings, paying low or no dividend yields
BONDS
Treasuries: Debt obligations issued by the federal government, least default risk
Municipal: Debt obligations issued by state and local governments, tax-free income
Corporate: Debt obligations issued by corporations, various degrees of credit quality
Mortgage-backed: Debt obligations collateralized by home mortgage loans
Zero coupon: No periodic income payments, sold at discount from par, repay at par
MUTUAL FUNDS
Load: Charge sales commission either upfront (at purchase) or at the end (at sale back)
No load: Do not charge sales commission
Closed-end: Sell a limited number of shares to public, trade at exchanges thereafter
Open-end: Sell as many shares as the public wants, bought & sold from the fund itself

7.2 Measuring Investment Returns

While investing is necessary for creating wealth, it is very important to be able to measure your investment performance accurately. This allows you to monitor your progress, and adjust your holdings according to their individual performance, as well as their role in your portfolio. However, it is not always easy to measure investment performance, which can lead to embarrassing outcomes.

In the mid 1990s, an investment guide book was published describing the methodology, a group of older ladies had used to "beat" the stock market, 10 years straight. What was remarkable about their story was the consistency of their abnormal positive returns, over a long period of time, given their admitted lack of knowledge and experience when they got started. The story was very appealing to a lot of people, as the group's performance could not be matched by most professional portfolio managers. Naturally, the book received national exposure and news coverage, which attracted scrutiny from investigating reporters.

As it turned out, once the investment returns were calculated accurately, the group not only had not beaten the stock market by a great margin, but had trailed the market's performance by several percentage points each year. The story quickly disappeared from news coverage, and the investment community (presumably the group of ladies too) was reminded that it is highly improbable for anyone to consistently outperform the market, and people need to be careful with their math. In June 2013, the book was still available on Amazon for $0.82 new (hardcover), or $0.01 used. Apparently, there is little demand for investment advice from people who cannot get their numbers right.

Before you dismiss the group's embarrassing story as the silly mistake of amateurs, you need to realize there are different types of returns, each one having its own use and method of calculation.

7.2.1 Holding Period Return (HPR)

Suppose you purchased 100 shares of BP plc at $33.62 each, and sold them when the price per share reached $48.34. During this period BP paid you $5.76 dividend per share. You want to know your return on this particular investment.

When you are interested to know the return on an investment throughout the period you held it, you can use the following equation:

$$HoldingPeriod\,\mathrm{Re}turn = \frac{(EndingValue - BeginningValue) + Income}{BeginningValue} =$$

$$\frac{(\$48.34 - \$33.62) + \$5.76}{\$33.62} = \frac{\$14.72 + \$5.76}{\$33.62} = \frac{\$20.48}{\$33.62} = 0.6092 or 60.92\%$$

Instead of the beginning and ending stock prices, you could use the beginning and ending investment amounts (stock price * number of shares), and the result will be the same. It is simply easier to use just the prices per share.

So your holding period return is 60.92%, comprised of 43.78% ($14.72/$33.62) capital gain and 17.14% ($5.76/$33.62) income (stream) return. Is this a good return?

Well, it is a positive return which means you made a gain on this investment, but as of the quality of the return the HPR metric cannot help you decide if this return is great, good, or simply acceptable. The HPR provides no information about the time period it took for this return to materialize. If you earned 60.92% in a single year, this is a magnificent return. You are either a great stock picker or got extremely lucky. But if you held the stock for 10 years before realizing this gain, the return does not seem as impressive anymore.

7.2.2 Annual Rate of Return

To address the vagueness issue of the holding period return, it is standard practice in finance to report all investment returns on an annualized basis. This way, any asset's investment performance is readily comparable to the performance of all other assets, over the same time frame. Suppose you held the BP shares for 3 years. By multiplying the HPR by the factor 1/N, where N is the number of years you held the asset, you can find the annual return per year the asset was held.

$$AnnualRateof\,\mathrm{Re}turn = HoldingPeriod\mathrm{Re}turn * \frac{1}{N} = 60.92\% * \frac{1}{3} = 0.2031 or 20.31\%$$

So over the 3-year period you held the BP shares, you earned 20.31% per year, which is an enviable investment performance.

Notice, that if you held an asset for less than a full year, you can annualize the return by multiplying the HPR by the factor 365/M, where M is the number of days the asset was held. For example, if you only held the BP shares for 300 days instead of 3 years, the annual rate of return would be an even more impressive 74.12%.

$$AnnualRateof\,\mathrm{Re}turn = HPR * \frac{365}{300} = 60.92\% * 1.2176 = 74.12\%$$

7.2.3 Arithmetic Average Rate of Return

Suppose you held the BP plc shares for 4 years and you realized the following annual returns: 9%, 11%, 20%, −12%. Some of these returns are good, one is very good, and one is bad. You want to know whether BP was a good investment for you. A simple way to find the return on an investment, when several observations (annual returns) are available, is to calculate the simple average or arithmetic average of the available observations.

$$ArithmeticAverage = \frac{\sum_{i=1}^{N} R_i}{N} = \frac{9\% + 11\% + 20\% + (-12\%)}{4} = \frac{28\%}{4} = 7\%$$

The average annual rate of return on the BP investment is only 7%, as the last year's return of −12% drags down the average return. If you had sold the BP shares a year earlier, you would have avoided the loss, and the average return would have been a much healthier 13.33% [(9%+11%+20%)/3]. Holding the shares for the fourth year adversely impacts the average return in two ways: first it increases the denominator by one more year. Second, the loss decreases the numerator's sum of returns.

Obviously, had you known before hand you would suffer a loss that fourth year, you would have sold the BP shares at the end of the third year, and would have booked the 13.33% instead of the 7% average annual return. Of course, that requires perfect foresight of the future, a gift most people do not possess, so that is beyond the point. What is the point however, is that a single loss can ruin a perfect streak of good returns, and transform a great investment to a barely adequate (if not bad) one. No wonder investors despise losses.

Your financial calculator can generate the arithmetic average of a number of observations, as long as you input the observation values. Before entering any data you should always clear the memory (☐ CLΣ or ☐ CLSTAT for HP10BII+) to avoid mixing data from multiple problems.

HP10BII Arithmetic Average Calculation

9	Σ+	
11	Σ+	
20	Σ+	
12	+/−	Σ+
	☐ x̄, ȳ	**7**

7.2.4 Geometric Average Rate of Return

A more precise metric than the arithmetic average is the geometric average, or compound rate of return. It is a more precise metric because it takes into account the effect of all previous periods' re-invested earnings on the average return. In other words, it takes into account the compounding effect of annual returns into the average return. For this reason, the geometric or compound average return is lower than the simple arithmetic average, as it takes a lower compound rate to reach the same dollar return. It can be calculated with the following equation:

$$GeometricAverage\,Return = \sqrt[N]{(1+R_1)*(1+R_2)*.....*(1+R_N)} - 1 =$$

$$= \left[(1+0.09)*(1+0.11)*(1+0.20)*(1-0.12)\right]^{\frac{1}{4}} - 1 =$$

$$= [1.09*1.11*1.20*0.88]^{\frac{1}{4}} - 1 =$$

$$= [1.2777]^{\frac{1}{4}} - 1 = [1.2777]^{0.25} - 1 =$$

$$= 1.0632 - 1 =$$

$$= 0.0632 or 6.3181\%$$

Using the TVM function of your financial calculator, the geometric average or compounded rate of return can be calculated as an interest rate calculation, where the present value is \$1, the future value is the product of all the return terms \$1.2777= (1.09)*(1.11)*(1.20)*(0.88), and the number of periods is 4.

HP10BII Compound Rate of Return Calculation

1	□ P/YR
4	N
1	+/− PV
1.2777	FV
	I/YR 6.3181

As expected the geometric average or compounded rate of return is lower than the arithmetic average rate of return. It is however, more precise. The following example should make this point obvious.

Suppose your investment lost 50% of its value during the first year, but recovered the following year, earning 100%. The arithmetic and geometric average returns are calculated below:

$$ArithmeticAverage = \frac{\sum_{i=1}^{N} R_i}{N} = \frac{-50\% + 100\%}{2} = \frac{50\%}{2} = 25\%$$

$$GeometricAverage\,\mathrm{Re}turn = \sqrt{(1-0.5)*(1+1)} - 1 = \sqrt{0.5*2} - 1 = 1 - 1 = 0 or 0\%$$

The arithmetic average return is 25% while it should be obvious you earned nothing over the 2-year period. If you had invested $1, by the end of the first year you had lost half your money, and you were left with $0.50. By the end of the second year your investment had doubled to exactly $1. Therefore, the correct return over the 2-year period is 0%, as indicated by the geometric average return or compound rate of return.

7.2.5 Weighted Average Portfolio Return

Suppose your investment holdings include more assets than just the BP shares. Let's assume your portfolio is comprised by shares of BP, AT&T, WALMART and AMAZON. You know the annual return of each individual holding (R_A), but would like to find out the more important piece of information, the portfolio return (R_P) of all your holdings together. To do so, you need to "weigh" each asset according to its importance in your portfolio. The weight of an asset (W_A) is simply the percentage of the portfolio value (V_P) allocated to the particular asset (V_A), or

$$w_A = \frac{V_A}{V_P}$$

Then the weighted average portfolio return (R_P) can be calculated as the sum of the products of each asset's weight times its return:

$$R_P = \sum_{A=1}^{N} (w_A * R_A) = (w_1 * R_1) + (w_2 * R_2) + ... + (w_N * R_N)$$

Notice, that the value of an asset is simply the current stock price of the asset (P_A) multiplied by the number of its shares in the portfolio (S_A), or

$$V_A = P_A * S_A$$

Since stock prices change daily, the value of each holding and the value of the portfolio change daily as well. Table 7-2 shows the current market values of your assets, their individual returns, weights, and calculation of your weighted average portfolio return.

TABLE 7-2 Weighted Average Portfolio Return

Stock	Symbol	V_A	w_A	R_A	$w_A * R_A$
AT&T	T	$3,500	$3,500/$25,000 = 0.14	−8%	−1.12%
BP	BP	$4,000	$4,000/$25,000 = 0.16	20%	3.2%
WALMART	WMT	$7,000	$7,000/$25,000 = 0.28	29%	8.12%
AMAZON	AMZN	$10,500	$10,500/$25,000 = 0.42	37.5%	15.75%
Portfolio		**$25,000**			**25.95%**

Or using the equation

$$R_P = \sum_{A=1}^{N} \left(w_A * R_A\right) = \left(w_1 * R_1\right) + \left(w_2 * R_2\right) + \ldots.. + \left(w_N * R_N\right) =$$

$$= \left(0.14 * (-8\%)\right) + \left(0.16 * 20\%\right) + \left(0.28 * 29\%\right) + \left(0.42 * 37.5\%\right) =$$

$$= -1.12\% + 3.2\% + 8.12\% + 15.75\% =$$

$$= 25.95\%$$

Your portfolio had a terrific year, with three out of four assets being big winners, generating a weighted average return of almost 26%. This simple illustration highlights a couple of useful points:

First, expert investment analysis is very important because it can help you identify potential winning asset classes, as well as, specific winning assets within each asset class. It will serve you well to acquire the skills to perform quality investment analysis. You will be able to maximize your portfolio returns, thus building your wealth faster.

Second, no matter how good your investment analysis is, not all of your holdings will be winners during the same year. Since no one has perfect foresight of the future, you are doing well if your winning assets exceed the losing ones at any given period. Therefore, it is important to split your funds into many different assets, or as it is referred to in the investing community to "diversify" your portfolio. The practice of "diversification" reduces the chance of suffering big losses, in case your investment selection skills happen to be a little "off" during a period.

7.2.6 Weighted Average Expected Return

Suppose you are trying to get an idea of the possible return you can earn by investing in a particular asset. A very simple way to form such an expectation would be to look at historical data, and observe how the asset performs during different types of economic environments.

It is reasonable to expect that during vigorous economic expansions ($g > 2.5\%$), as measured by the growth rate (g) of the gross domestic product, there will be growing demand for most assets, and their prices will rise a lot. Modest economic growth ($0\% < g < 2.5\%$) will be accompanied by moderate asset price increases, while economic contractions ($g < 0\%$) will generally be accompanied by declining asset prices.

Suppose that after researching the historic performance of BP stock during the last 50 years, you conclude that during booming economic times the stock's average return is 21%, during years of moderate economic growth the returns average 12%, while during economic contractions the stock loses on average 9% of its value.

With that information at hand, the big question is how do you think the economy will perform during the next 12 months? your knowledge of economics can be very useful while trying to answer this question. For our example, assume you believe there is a 40% probability the economy will expand vigorously, 30% probability it will expand moderately, and 30% probability it will experience a contraction during the next 12 months. You can use your assigned probabilities as weights to calculate a weighted average expected return.

The weighted average expected return is the sum of the products of probabilities that certain economic conditions will prevail, times the returns observed during such economic conditions:

$$E[R_A] = \sum_{i=1}^{N}(p_i * R_i) = (p_1 * R_1) + (p_2 * R_2) + \ldots\ldots + (p_N * R_N) =$$

$$= (0.40 * 21\%) + (0.30 * 12\%) + (0.30 * (-9\%)) =$$

$$= 8.4\% + 3.6\% - 2.7\% =$$

$$= 9.3\%$$

Table 7-3 shows the assigned probabilities for the future state of the economy, the historic average return observed for each state of the economy, and the weighted average expected return calculation.

TABLE 7-3 Weighted Average Expected Return Calculation

State of the Economy	p_i	R_i	$p_i * R_i$
Vigorous Expansion	0.40	21%	8.4%
Moderate Expansion	0.30	12%	3.6%
Contraction	0.30	−9%	−2.7%
$E[R_A]$	**1.00**		**9.3%**

So given your assumptions about the possible state of the economy during the next 12 months, your expected return from an investment in BP shares of stock is 9.3%. There are a few issues with this calculation. First, you need to make sure the probabilities column sums up to 1 (or 100%). Second, it should be obvious that the 9.3% expected return depends heavily on your assigned probabilities about the future of economic growth, as well as the length of the sample you used to calculate the average returns per economic condition. Another investor or analyst could use different probabilities, and/or a sample with different length, thus reaching a different expected return.

Investment analysis is both an art and a science. All analysts may use the same equations, but some of the inputs are at their discretion. As analysts use different assumptions, they reach different conclusions about the desirability of a particular asset. Therefore, there are usually both buyers and sellers for any given asset, any given day.

7.3 Measuring Investment Risk

In the context of investing, risk is the chance the expected return of an investment will not be realized. In the previous section, you calculated the weighted average expected return of holding BP shares of stock to be 9.3%, over the next year. It is highly unlikely the actual return will be exactly 9.3%. You should feel pretty good about your forecasting ability, if the actual return ends up in the "ball park" of the 9.3% expected return. Actual returns tend to randomly "fall around" the average expected return, and are assumed to be distributed "normally" around the mean or average. "normally" means that the frequency distribution of the actual returns resembles the normal or bell-shaped distribution shown in Figure 7-1.

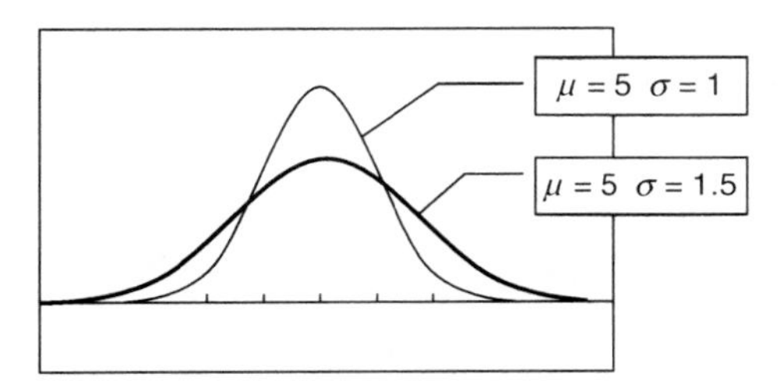

FIGURE 7-1 Normal Distribution

Source: From the Virginia Department of Education

How far from the average expected return the actual returns happen to fall determines the risk level of the asset. If they tend to fall pretty close to the expected return, the bell curve will be tall and thin around the expected return, like the tall one in Figure 7-1 indicating a less risky asset. If on the other hand, the actual returns tend to frequently fall away from the expected return, the bell curve will be short with fat tails, like the shorter one in Figure 7-1, indicating a more risky asset.

7.3.1 Standard Deviation (SD)

The standard deviation is a statistical measure of variability, which can be used to measure investment risk. The standard deviation measures the dispersion or variation of the actual returns around the average expected return. The larger the standard deviation, the more risky the asset, and the more worried you should be about the return on your investment. Not only the expected return (9.3%) will not materialize, but also the actual return can be much higher or much lower than the expected return. While you, along with most investors, will probably not complain about realizing a much higher return than the expected one, the divergence from the forecasted expected return should concern you. Maybe the next actual return will be on the other side of the bell curve, causing you a significant loss.

Recall from Section 7.2.3, your investment had produced the following annual returns: 9%, 11%, 20%, and -12%, with an arithmetic average of 7%. Using these recent historical returns, you can calculate the standard deviation of the returns with the following equation:

$$Standard Deviation = \sqrt{\frac{\sum_{i=1}^{N}\left(R_i - \bar{R}\right)^2}{N-1}}$$

Table 7-4 shows the standard deviation calculation for your BP investment.

TABLE 7-4 Standard Deviation Calculation

R_i	$\bar{R}$	$R_i - \bar{R}$	$(R_i - \bar{R})^2$
0.09	0.07	0.09 − 0.07 = 0.02	0.0004
0.11	0.07	0.11 − 0.07 = 0.04	0.0016
0.20	0.07	0.20 − 0.07 = 0.13	0.0169
-0.12	0.07	−0.12 − 0.07 = -0.19	0.0361
$\Sigma(R_i - \bar{R})^2$			**0.0550**
$\Sigma(R_i - \bar{R})^2/N-1$			**0.0183**
$\sqrt{\Sigma(R_i - \bar{R})^2/N-1}$			**0.1354**

Or using the financial calculator

HP10BII Standard Deviation Calculation

9	Σ+
11	Σ+
20	Σ+
12	+/− Σ+
	□ **S_x, S_y 13.5401**

Given your experience with BP over the last 4 years, the stock returns have a 13.54% standard deviation. Clearly, this value is dependent on the sample size of actual returns included in the calculation. Typically, for investment calculations you may not want to use the whole population of data (annual returns since BP was incorporated), as what happened in 1983 may have no relevance to the 2013 stock risk and return. On the other hand, including very few observations in the sample (as in this example) impairs the accuracy of the estimated variability. The size of the sample is always at the discretion of the analyst. Since investment calculations involve mainly samples out of populations of data, both the equation and the financial calculator solution presented above refer to the sample standard deviation, instead of the population standard deviation. Furthermore, it should also be obvious that when it comes to calculating standard deviations, the financial calculator is the way to go.

7.3.2 Standard Deviation and Confidence Intervals

How does it help you to know that the standard deviation of BP stock returns over the last four years is 13.54%? with some knowledge of elementary statistics, you can use the standard deviation and the average return to determine the probability of any possible return occurring. You can also create zones around the average return, called confidence intervals, showing the probability the actual return will fall within a zone.

Because the sample means (or averages) of returns are distributed "normally," you can use the bell-shaped distribution which has some very desirable properties, to build confidence intervals around the average return. For instance, the probability any annual return will fall within a zone (interval) of one standard deviation around the average return is 68%. The probability an annual return will fall within a zone of two standard deviations around the average return is 95%, while if you extend a zone three standard deviations around the average return, you have a 99% probability the zone will include any annual return.

Figure 7-2 shows the probabilities associated with a normal distribution confidence intervals.

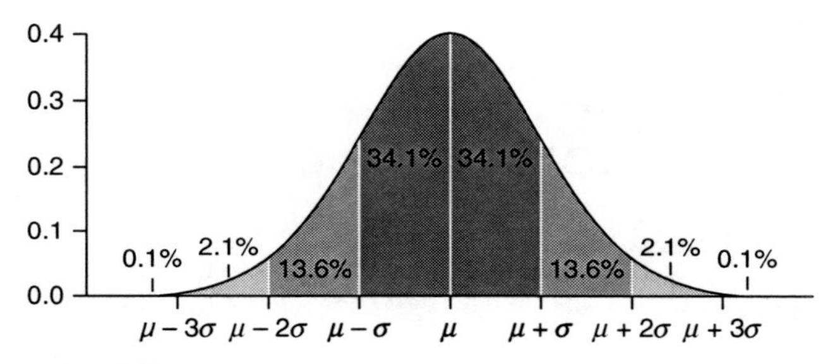

FIGURE 7-2 Confidence Intervals

Source: From the Virginia Department of Education

For the BP sample of returns, the average return (or mean) is 7%, and the standard deviation is 13.54%. Therefore, you can say the next BP annual return has:

68% probability to be within [7%-13.54% & 7%+13.54%] or [-6.54% & 20.54%]

95% probability to be within [7%-(2*13.54%) & 7%+(2*13.54%)] or [-20.08% & 34.08%]

99% probability to be within [7%-(3*13.54%) & 7%+(3*13.54%)] or [-33.62% & 47.62%]

Notice that with 99% of all possible returns falling within the [-33.62% & 47.62%] confidence interval, the next return could be anywhere within this 81.24% (33.62%+47.62%) wide zone. Is this a variability of investment returns you can tolerate?

Furthermore, with 99% of all possible returns falling within the [−33.62% & 47.62%] confidence interval, there is only 1% probability the actual return will fall outside this zone. Because the normal distribution is symmetrical around the mean, half of this probability will be to the upside (the right tail of the distribution) and the other half will be to the downside (the left tail of the distribution). Therefore, there is 0.5% probability (roughly speaking 1 out of every 200 years) that you could lose more than 33.62% of your invested funds in the BP stock. The year of this big loss could be 60 years away, or it can be this year. You never know. That's the essence of risk!

7.3.3 Standard Deviation and the Coefficient of Variation (CV)

The standard deviation, by itself, can help you identify and rank risky assets as long as they have the same average return. For example if two assets, YYY and ZZZ happen to have the same 7% average return as BP, and their standard deviations are 16% and 9% respectively, then you can easily claim that asset YYY is the riskiest of all three, because it has the highest standard deviation. Asset ZZZ is the safest of all three, and bp is moderately risky.

You cannot always claim however, the asset with the highest standard deviation to be the riskiest one. In a more realistic situation, the assets you are analyzing have different average returns and different standard deviations. In this case, you need to use the coefficient of variation (CV), which standardizes variation per unit of return. It is calculated by dividing the standard deviation of the asset with its average return.

$$CoefficientOfVariation = \frac{Standard\ Deviation}{Average\ Return}$$

Assume that the average return of asset YYY is 12%, while that of asset ZZZ is 6%. With all three assets having different standard deviations and average returns, it is not obvious anymore which one is the riskiest. By expressing variation per unit of return, you can identify the riskiest (and safest) assets. Table 7-5 ranks the three assets YYY, ZZZ and BP according to their coefficient of variation.

TABLE 7-5 Coefficient of Variation (CV)

Asset	Average Return	Standard Deviation	Coefficient of Variation
YYY	12%	16%	16% / 12% = 1.3333
ZZZ	6%	9%	9% / 6% = 1.5
BP	7%	13.54%	13.54% / 7% = 1.9343

Looking at the coefficient of variation, the riskiest asset is BP. It has more units of risk per each percentage point of return. The safest asset seems to be YYY despite having the highest standard deviation of the three assets. YYY has the highest chance of realizing a return close to its average return.

7.3.4 Types of Risk

The standard deviation of an asset's returns represents the total investment risk of holding the asset. The total investment risk can be separated into two distinct components: the systematic risk or market risk and the non-systematic risk or business specific risk.

Systematic Risk

The systematic risk reflects all the risk factors associated with the particular economic or market environment the asset exists in, and is influenced by. That's why this type of risk is also called market risk. For example, when the us economy is contracting, the US stock market declines, and most american stocks trade at lower prices. On the other hand, when the US economy is expanding, the US stock market rises, and most american stocks trade at higher prices. As the saying goes "a rising tide lifts all boats." It may not matter much what a particular corporation is or is not doing, a percentage of its return will reflect the overall market movement, upwards or downwards. Nothing short of shutting down operations and going out of business can eliminate the systematic risk, which is why it is also referred to as non-diversifiable risk.

There are several ways the systematic risk can manifest itself, like inflation risk, interest rate risk, exchange rate risk, and political risk.

i) Inflation Risk reflects the chance that rapidly rising prices will prevail and erode the purchasing power of money. In this case, the future income produced by your investments will not be able to purchase the same amount of goods and services it could purchase today. In real terms therefore, your investment return will be negatively affected.
ii) Interest Rate Risk reflects the chance that market interest rates will rise in the future, causing your investment holdings to appear less attractive. If bank deposits and new bonds offer higher interest rates, the returns on stocks and existing bonds will become less competitive and their prices will decline, causing you to suffer capital losses.
iii) Exchange Rate Risk reflects the chance that an appreciating US dollar will reduce the income and capital gains from your foreign investments, when eventually they will have to be converted back to us dollars to be repatriated. A weaker dollar on the other hand, will reduce the real value of the income stream and capital gains from your domestic investments. This is closely related to the inflation risk. Any change in currency value will affect the value of some of your portfolio holdings.
iv) Political Risk reflects the chance there could be political instability, which could adversely affect the economic environment and the value of your investments. For instance, inconclusive elections or partisan politics could render congress and the administration ineffectual in addressing the nation's problems. Domestic unrest or uncertainty about potential conflicts with other nations could lead to significant market downturns.

Non-Systematic Risk

The non-systematic risk reflects the specific risks associated with the particular asset. If the asset is a business or a security issued by a business, then you have to consider all the types of business-specific risk the asset is exposed to. Different businesses operating in different industries are each facing a unique set of challenges and situations, which create additional risks on top of the common market risk. Such risks can be in the form of financial risk, management risk, country risk, and regulation risk.

i) Financial Risk is associated with the amount of debt in the capital structure of the business. The more debt and/or other leveraged contracts held by the business, the higher its exposure to a negative shock, which will affect its ability to meet contractually obligated payments. In case of financial distress, the value of the business and its securities will decline sharply, causing you to suffer capital losses.
ii) Management Risk is associated with the quality of the top management team of the business. In good economic times, even mediocre managers seem to perform adequately for a while. The effects of bad managerial decisions tend to become apparent only in the long run, when it is finally obvious to all that the business has lost its vision, direction, competitive edge, or even the reason to exist. At that point however, the value of your investment may have evaporated.
iii) Country Risk is associated with the specific country exposures of each particular business. Different businesses have operations and subsidiaries in different parts of the world. Furthermore, some multinational businesses earn more than half of their revenues outside of the US. Occasionally, whole regions seem to be in turmoil. Think of the latin america debt crisis of the 1980s, the asian tigers currency crisis of the late 1990s, the arab spring of the early 2010s,

the european debt crisis of the 2010s. If any of your holdings are exposed to a troubled region, your investment returns will suffer.

iv) Regulation Risk is associated with the degree of government oversight to each industry. Some industries are more heavily regulated than others, which may affect the profitability of businesses and your investment returns. Of greater importance however, are unforeseen new regulations or changes in existing regulations, which introduce additional costs and taxes, and can ruin a perfectly good investment.

While non-systematic risk adds another layer of worry to the unavoidable systematic risk, the good news is you do not have to suffer it. It is possible you can reduce it, or even avoid it, through diversification. Holding several different assets from different industries tends to reduce the business-specific risk, as the positive developments from some of your holdings offset the negative ones from other holdings.

For example, while some oil exploration companies with operations in Africa may suffer due to the repeated incidents of local civil unrest, other oil companies with operations in canada will perform extremely well. The supply problems in Africa will raise the price of oil, and increase their profitability. While the high price of oil, and therefore fuel, may hurt the profitability of the airlines, rail companies will enjoy higher profits from handling more shipments of coal, an oil substitute for power generation.

Diversifying your assets among different industries, and different companies in each industry, will reduce or eliminate the non-systematic risk of your portfolio. Therefore, the non-systematic risk is also referred to as diversifiable risk. A well diversified portfolio should be exposed only to systematic risk, thus experiencing reduced variability of returns.

The 1972 research on the issue of diversification, by nobel prize winner william sharpe, shows that while diversification reduces non-systematic risk, the majority of the risk reduction benefit is achieved by the 30th or so different asset holding. Figure 7-3 shows the effects of diversification at reducing non-systematic risk.

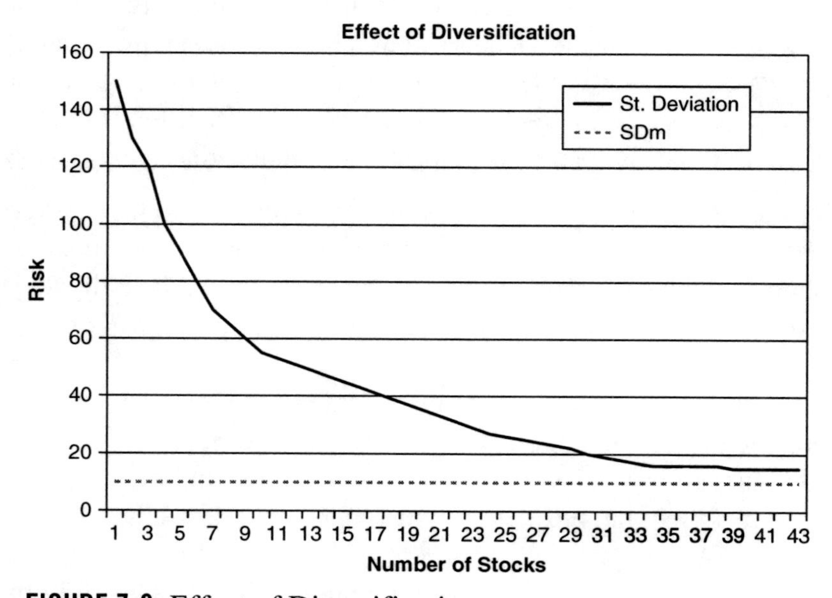

FIGURE 7-3 Effect of Diversification

To completely eliminate the non-systematic risk from the portfolio, you will need to hold all market assets. Practically, this entails investing in domestic and foreign, stock and bond index funds. Table 7-6 summarizes the types of investment risk.

TABLE 7-6 Total Investment Risk = Systematic Risk + Non-Systematic Risk

Systematic or Market or Non-Diversifiable Risk	Non-Systematic or Business-Specific or Diversifiable Risk
Inflation Risk	Financial Risk
Interest Rate Risk	Management Risk
Exchange Rate Risk	Country Risk
Political Risk	Regulation Risk

7.4 Risk Preferences

The first step in the investment planning process is to assess the client's true "risk preference." Risk preference is different from "ability to undertake risk." Your ability to undertake risk typically depends on objective factors like, the nature of the financial goal, the time frame to achieve the financial goal, and the size of your emergency fund or extra funds to cover arising needs.

For example, if the funds to be invested are intended to pay for the down payment of your home or your child's college expenses within three to five years, and you have no other funds available other than a minimum emergency fund, your ability to undertake risk is very limited. You cannot afford to suffer any investment losses, as these financial goals are milestones for your family finances, and are approaching quickly. On the other hand, if the funds represent your speculative portfolio, with no specific time frame attached to it, and you have plenty of other funds and assets to cover arising needs, then your ability to undertake risk is great.

Risk preference however, is completely subjective. It is in your mind, and determined by psychological factors. Financial models assume people are risk-averse although in reality people can be risk-neutral, or even risk-seekers (risk lovers).

A risk-averse individual is one who when presented with a choice between two assets with the same risk level, chooses the one with the highest expected return. In Figure 7-4 for example, between assets A and B the risk-averse individual will choose asset B, because it promises 8% return compared to 6% return for A, while both A and B have the same 10% standard deviation.

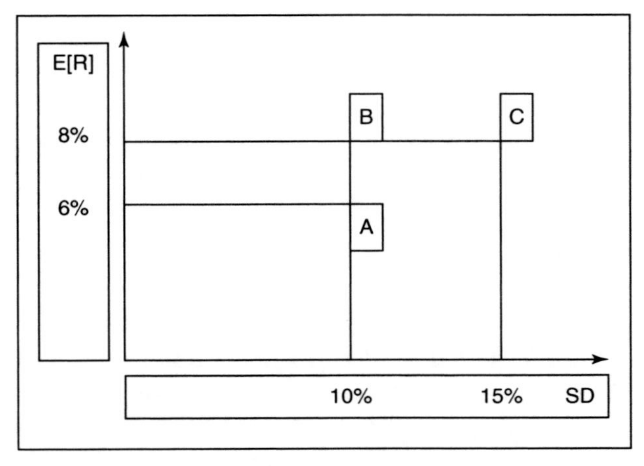

FIGURE 7-4 Risk-Averse Behavior

Also, when presented with a choice between two assets with the same expected return, the risk-averse individual chooses the less risky asset. Between points B and C in Figure 7-4, the risk-averse individual will choose asset B, because it promises the same 8% return as asset C, but its standard deviation is only 10% compared to 15% for C.

Figure 7-5 shows graphically the risk preferences of risk-averse, risk-neutral, and risk-seeker investors.

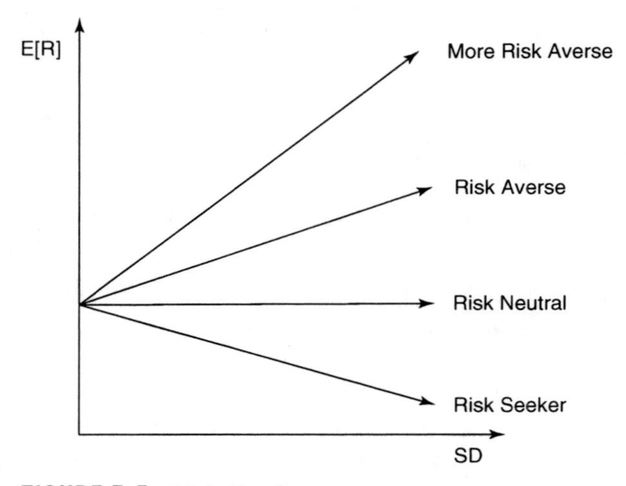

FIGURE 7-5 Risk Preferences

A risk-averse preference is depicted by an upward sloping curve, indicating the investor requires a higher expected return to undertake more risky assets. The more conservative the investor is, the steeper the slope of the curve, indicating the investor requires a very high expected return to consider buying riskier assets. Typically, as people age they become more conservative with their investment choices, because they may not be able to recover potential investment losses with active income from work.

Notice that risk-averse investors may not like risk, but they do invest in risky assets to reach their financial goals. However, they need to be promised an adequate return to buy risky assets.

A risk-neutral preference is depicted with a horizontal line (zero slope line) indicating perfect sensitivity towards the expected return. In other words, a risk-neutral investor is mainly concerned with the promised return of assets, without regard to their risk level.

A risk-seeker preference is depicted with a downward sloping curve, indicating the investor is attracted mainly by the risk level of the assets, rather than their expected return. Although the risk-seeker investor appreciates a good investment return, he or she is after the "thrill of the chase." Returns earned from a gamble are valued more than less risky or risk-free returns.

7.4.1 Assessing risk preferences

While the financial planner has to assess the clients' true risk preference before recommending appropriate investments, this is easier said than done. First, clients may not really be aware of their investment risk preference. Novice investors in particular may not have given any serious thought to this issue before, because they did not have to.

Second, even if people think they know their risk preference, the financial planner cannot assume clients are familiar with the terminology described in the previous section. When a client describes herself as risk-averse, is she trying to communicate she is willing to invest in risky assets for the right expected return, or is she thinking she is stating she does not want anything risky in her portfolio? The financial planner cannot afford to leave this matter unresolved, due to the liability issues involved with investing in assets deemed inappropriate to the client's stated risk preference.

Third, during a meeting with their financial planner, some clients may overstate their investment experience and their willingness to invest in risky assets, out of fear of admitting their anxiety about undertaking investment risks. It is preferable therefore, for the financial planner to have clients fill out a risk tolerance questionnaire that can objectively assess the clients' true risk preference.

Table 7-7 presents some risk tolerance questions that can be found in such questionnaires.

TABLE 7-7 Sample Risk Preference Questions

1. If you received an unexpected large sum of money, how would you choose among the following investment categories and in what percentages?

Stocks	____
Corporate Bonds	____
US Government Securities	____
Stock Mutual Funds	____
Bond Mutual Funds	____
Bank Certificates of Deposit	____
Options	____
Gold	____
TOTAL	100%

2. Listed below are six investment objectives. Rank them in importance, with 1 as most important and 6 as least important.

Current income	____
Growth potential	____
Safety of principal	____
Favorable tax treatment	____
Hedge against inflation	____
Liquidity	____

3. What would a friend who knows you well say about your willingness to take risks?
   (a) Roll the dice
   (b) After careful analysis, you would take a risk
   (c) Cautious
   (d) Not willing to take risks; wears a life preserver in the shower
4. Your close friend is an expert in oil and gas exploration. He approaches you to invest in a new venture, and he says it has a 25% chance of returning 50 times the amount of your investment in five years or it could be a total failure. Assume you have the money available, how much would you invest?
   (a) Zero
   (b) One half of your annual salary
   (c) One month's salary
   (d) Three month's salary
   (e) Your annual salary

(continued)

TABLE 7-7 Sample Risk Preference Questions *(continued)*

5. How many years will it be before you need to make withdrawals for retirement expenses?
   (a) Under five years
   (b) Five to ten years
   (c) Ten to fifteen years
   (d) Over 15 years
6. How much investment experience do you have?
   (a) None
   (b) Limited experience in purchasing and selling stocks and mutual funds
   (c) Many years of experience in purchasing and selling stocks, bonds, and mutual funds
   (d) I have experience in purchasing and selling puts, calls, futures, and commodities
7. What types of property and casualty insurance do you carry?
   (a) Only automobile liability and renter's insurance.
   (b) Complete automobile liability and physical damage plus homeowner's policy.
   (c) Complete automobile liability and physical damage plus homeowner's policy with personal articles floater.
   (d) Complete automobile liability and physical damage plus homeowner's policy with personal articles floater and umbrella coverage.

Such questionnaires are designed to reveal the true risk preference of an individual, and to provide the financial planner with a numerical score, which can be used to objectively classify the client in one of the following risk categories: conservative, moderately conservative, moderately aggressive, aggressive, and very aggressive. Specific portfolio allocations can then be recommended to each risk category.

Once the client's true risk preference is determined, the financial planner will have to reconcile it with the client's ability to undertake risk. It is possible for a client to be in the aggressive or very aggressive risk category, according to the risk tolerance questionnaire score, but not to have the ability to undertake risk, due to the short time horizon of her stated financial goals. On the other hand, a client may have the ability to undertake risk, but to be classified as conservative.

It is only when both the risk preference and the ability to undertake risk point towards investing in risky assets, that those can be included in the portfolio. When the risk preference and the ability to undertake risk point to opposite directions, the financial planner has to err on the side of caution and choose a conservative portfolio allocation, while at the same time educating the client about the risk-return trade-off.

7.4.2 Risk and Return

For conservative clients with the ability to undertake risk, the financial planner will have to inform and educate them about the risk and return relationship, so they can make an educated choice about their portfolio allocation.

Typically, investors are compensated either for "waiting" or for "waiting" and "worrying." "Waiting" indicates deferred consumption with the funds allocated to very safe assets. While there is a compensation or return for investing in assets providing principal and income guarantees, the return is minimal. "Worrying" on the other hand, indicates investment in risky assets with the possibility of a loss of principal, income or both. While worrying about the safety of your funds may not be fun, there is a compensation for worrying, which when added to the compensation for waiting may create an attractive return.

Traditionally, the US Treasury Bills (T-Bills) are considered the safest investment asset, as the principal and interest income are guaranteed by the federal government. The T-Bills mature and repay your principal with interest within a few weeks to a few months, thus allowing for a frequent reevaluation of the safety of your investment. Naturally, investing in such a safe asset will provide you only with a "waiting" return.

If you are willing to commit your funds for a longer time period, Treasury Notes (T-Notes) and Bonds (T-Bonds) maturing anywhere between 2 years and 30 years, guarantee your principal and interest income but only if you hold the securities to maturity. If you need to sell them before their maturity, you may receive more or less than what you paid for them, depending on the prevailing market interest rate for each maturity. This is the interest rate risk described in Section 7.3.4 under systematic or market risk. Naturally, assuming the interest rate risk adds a "worrying" return to the "waiting" return of T-Bills, and T-Bonds offer higher returns than T-Bills.

If you are willing to depart with the guarantees provided by the federal government, you can sample from the myriad of corporate securities, both domestic and foreign. Corporate bonds may pay higher yields than T-Bonds, and corporate stocks may offer dividend income and the potential for capital gains. All these returns are paid if the business performs well. If not, loss of income and principal are to be expected. Naturally, the higher risk level associated with corporate securities is translated to higher "worrying" compensation for your brave soul. The difference between the returns on corporate stocks and Treasury bills is called the "risk premium." It indicates the compensation risky assets pay over and above the compensation paid by risk-free assets.

Table 7-8 shows US historical returns for the S&P 500 stock index, T-Bills, and T-Bonds as well as, the stock risk premiums over T-Bills and T-Bonds for three different time periods.

TABLE 7-8 US Returns and Risk Premiums

Arithmetic Return				Risk Premium	
Time Period	**Stocks**	**T-Bills**	**T-Bonds**	**Stocks vs. T-Bills**	**Stocks vs. T-Bonds**
1928-2011	11.20%	3.66%	5.41%	7.54%	5.79%
1962-2011	10.60%	5.22%	7.24%	5.38%	3.36%
2002-2011	4.93%	1.81%	6.85%	3.12%	−1.92%

Source: www.research.stlouisfed.org/fred2

The data on Table 7-8 are from the Federal Reserve Bank of St. Louis. The T-Bill returns are for the 3-month bill, while the T-Bond returns are for the 10-year bond, reflecting both coupon and price appreciation. The stock returns reflect the total return for the S&P 500 index.

The data on Table 7-8 reveal that over long periods of time stocks have outperformed T-bonds and T-Bills. The difference in performance is reflected on the risk premiums between stock returns and those of the Treasury securities. For financial goals with long investment horizons (several decades), investing in the stock market seems to yield significantly higher returns. Earning 3% to 7% more per year, compounded over 40 years makes tremendous difference in wealth creation.

For example, looking at the 40-year period between 1962 and 2011, investments of $100,000 each in stocks, T-Bonds, and T-Bills would have grown to $5.6 million, $1.6 million, and $0.765 million respectively. With the benefit of hindsight, which one would you prefer to have owned?

HP10BII Future Value Calculation

Stock Investment		T-Bond Investment		T-Bill Investment	
1	☐ P/YR	1	☐ P/YR	1	☐ P/YR
40	N	40	N	40	N
10.60	I/YR	7.24	I/YR	5.22	I/YR
$100,000	+/− PV	$100,000	+/− PV	$100,000	+/− PV
	FV $5,626,069.3181		**FV $1,637,842.7870**		**FV $765,476.5634**

The higher stock returns however, are compensation for assuming risk. Notice on Table 7-8, that during the 2002 to 2011 period the stock returns underperformed the T-Bond returns. The stock market crashed twice during this 10-year period. Recall from Section 7.3.2, confidence intervals can reveal how many really bad years out of every 100 years you can expect from an investment. They don't reveal you however, the time of these bad returns. Once again, this is the nature of risk. In the short run anything can happen, therefore funds for financial goals with short time horizons need to be invested mostly in low risk assets.

If risky assets seem a little scary to you, looking at the returns of the risk-free asset may seem even scarier. Considering that the us inflation rate over the 1950 to 2009 period averaged 3.8%, The real return of T-Bills hovers around 1% annually. It is highly unlikely you can accomplish any of your financial goals, let alone create wealth, with a 1% real annual return.

7.4.3 Portfolio Allocation

Once the financial planner has established a client's risk preference, reconciled it with the client's ability to undertake risk, and determined the investment horizon of the client's financial goals, the planner is ready to make a portfolio allocation recommendation. Table 7-9 lists portfolio allocation suggestions for different risk categories of investors.

TABLE 7-9 Portfolio Allocation Suggestions According to Risk Classification

Risk Classification	Portfolio Allocation
Conservative	80% Bonds, 20% Stocks
Moderately Conservative	60% Bonds, 40% Stocks
Moderately Aggressive	40% Bonds, 60% Stocks
Aggressive	20% Bonds, 80% Stocks
Very Aggressive	Stocks, Derivatives, REITs, MLPs

Notice that the proportion of portfolio assets allocated to stocks increases as the risk classification moves towards the more aggressive categories. However, even the conservative portfolio allocation may include up to 20% of stocks, to provide it with a growth element so it may generate a positive real (inflation adjusted) return.

With the exception of the "very aggressive" risk classification, all other suggested portfolio allocations include varying proportions of bond holdings. Bonds act as the "ballast" in the portfolio, stabilizing the portfolio returns despite the possible violent fluctuations of the stock holdings during the year. This is an application of diversification across asset classes to reduce the overall risk level of the portfolio.

The "very aggressive" portfolio allocation includes no bond holdings. Typically this risk classification is for experienced and affluent investors pursuing superior returns, with possible tax-advantaged treatment. For them, stocks of small and speculative companies are in order, with a possible dose of real estate investment trusts (REITs), and master limited partnerships (MLPs). REITS are funds investing in multiple commercial real estate properties, providing investors with instant diversification in this risky asset class. MLPs are limited partnerships investing in some really speculative projects, like oil and natural gas exploration. Aside from the possible upside of earning big capital gains, MLPs provide favorable tax treatment of distributed profits.

In addition, "very aggressive" investors are prime candidates for including derivatives in their portfolios. Derivatives are highly leveraged contracts, like options and futures, deriving their value from changes in the values of primary assets. There are derivative contracts based on stocks, currencies, commodities, etc. Because of the amount of leverage involved, small price fluctuations on the primary asset cause magnified price fluctuations on the derivative asset. Oversized gains and losses are to be expected when dealing with derivatives.

Finally, the agreed upon portfolio allocation between the client and the financial planner is documented in writing in the investment agreement, and becomes part of the financial planning documents. The agreement includes the client's financial goals, investment horizon, risk preference, as well as other preferences with respect to the choice of investment assets. For instance, the client may not want any tobacco or alcohol assets purchased with his or her funds. If the financial planner will manage the client portfolio, the planner will have to respect the client's social sensitivities, and avoid purchasing any such assets for the client's portfolio, despite their potentially high expected return.

The investment agreement can also include specific performance metrics, like portfolio expected return, maximum risk level, and asset turnover ratio during a year. Such a detailed investment agreement protects both the client and the planner, as it sets formally the framework for client expectations and planner accountability.

7.4.4 Practical application: the milfords' investment portfolio

Ric and Vanessa Milford have scheduled a session with their financial planner to review their investments. They got worried after their financial statement analysis revealed that their investment assets are inadequate for their age and income level (Chapter 4.2.2). Their combined investment assets are $196,000 comprised of $162,000 in retirement accounts, $14,000 in cash value life insurance, and $20,000 in a 529 college fund for Michael, Ric's older son. They also have $27,000 in monetary assets. Given their $150,000 combined income, Ric and Vanessa have an investments-to-income ratio of 1.48 ($223,000/$150,000), which is much less than the 3 to 4 times gross income people in their 40s should have.

The financial planner examines the current asset allocation of the retirement accounts, and determines that while both ric and vanessa split their monthly retirement contributions equally between stock index and bond index funds, due to a stock market downturn, the value of their holdings has tilted towards 30% stocks and 70% bonds. The heavy bond allocation however, protected their portfolio during the stock market downturn, and their portfolio return was 6.33% during the last year.

Given how far behind the Milfords are on their retirement savings, and the fact they want to support their children to go to college, there are no easy solutions. Fortunately, the milfords realize their predicament, and are willing to make the necessary changes to have a realistic chance of achieving their goals.

The financial planner makes the following recommendations:

1. The Milfords need to rebalance the retirement accounts to reflect an "aggressive" portfolio allocation with 80% stocks and 20% bonds. Buying stocks when the stock market has experienced a decline will allow the milfords to purchase more shares with their funds.
2. New retirement contributions should also be allocated 80% to stocks and 20% to bonds. The Milfords are at least 25 years away from retirement, therefore they can afford to be aggressive with their portfolio allocation, to take advantage of the superior long term returns of the stock market.
3. They need to set an expected return for their investment portfolio at a higher level, which will allow them to reach their financial goals. With the long run average annual return of the stock market around 11% to 12% (Table 7-8) it is possible to earn 10% average annual return with a portfolio allocation of 80% stocks and 20% bonds. For example, if the future average annual returns are 11% for the stock market, and 6% for the bond market, the Milfords' expected return should be:

   $$E[R_P]=(w_S * R_S)+(w_B * R_B)=(0.8 * 11\%)+(0.2\% * 6\%)=8.8\%+1.2\%=10\%$$

   An average annual return around 10% would allow them to double their portfolio value approximately every 7 years (rule of 72) excluding new contributions.
4. Additional savings are needed for the children's college expenses, so retirement contributions are not diverted to college funds. Achieving one goal should not be detrimental to the other. (These additional savings were calculated in Chapter 6.) With michael going to college in just 3 years, his college funds need to be reallocated to safe bond index funds. Given the young age of the two daughters however, the savings for their college expenses can be invested in stock index funds, as the investment horizon is 7 to 15 years away.

Like other risk-averse people, the Milfords would prefer less risk and more guarantees for their investments. Unfortunately, to achieve the goals they set for themselves they will have to assume more risk than before. As long as they are comfortable with this choice, rebalancing their holdings and future contributions towards more risk will allow them a realistic chance to achieve their goals.

Life is full of choices. If they are not comfortable assuming more risk, there are other options, but all require immediate and drastic life style changes. They could drastically reduce their current living standard to pay for the children's college expenses and save for retirement. They could sell their house and rent a small apartment. They could look for second jobs or new careers. They could choose not to pay for the children's college costs, or they could choose to downgrade their retirement lifestyle expectations. There are plenty of options, and rebalancing their portfolio towards a heavier stock allocation is just one of them. What would you choose if you were in the Milfords' situation?

Summary

Achieving your financial goals will require you to become an investor. Investors allocate their capital to risky assets in order to realize higher returns than those offered by risk-free assets. Instead of realizing higher gains however, it is entirely possible you could suffer losses any given year. This is the nature of risk. But over long periods of time, riskier assets outperform safer assets, which provide you with a realistic chance of creating wealth for you and your family. Since people have different risk preferences, the investment planning process takes into account your attitude towards risk, your ability to undertake risk, as well as, the size and time frame of your financial goals to suggest a portfolio allocation you are comfortable with. Remember however, the direct relationship between risk and return. You are compensated more for "worrying" and "waiting" than for "waiting" alone. The chapter describes specific metrics of risk and return you can use to monitor your portfolio performance, to ensure you are on track to achieve your financial goals.

Review Questions

1. Brian purchased 500 shares of ABC for $20 per share. He later sold the shares at $25 per share. During this period he received dividends of $5 per share. What is Brian's percentage return on the ABC investment?

2. Brian purchased 2,000 shares of ABC for $20 per share. He later sold the shares at $15 per share. During this period he received dividends of $5 per share. What is Brian's percentage return on the ABC investment?

3. Connie held 1,000 shares of PST for 5 years. The annual returns were 18%, −5%, 14%, 9%, and −2%. What is the arithmetic average on these returns? what is the geometric average of these returns?

4. Julia's portfolio has three assets U, V and W. The values of these assets are $20,000, $40,000 and $40,000 respectively. The assets' returns this year are 16%, 14% and −10% respectively. What is the percentage return on Julia's portfolio?

5. Olivia is looking to invest in the DDDD Mutual Fund. During her research she figured that during booming economic times DDDD gains 18% in value, during years of moderate economic growth DDDD yields 12%, while during economic contractions the fund loses 10% of its value. If olivia believes the odds are 25% to experience a contraction, 50% to experience moderate economic growth, and 25% to have an economic boom during the next 12 months, what is olivia's expected return for the DDDD fund?

6. Corey experienced the following annual returns on the PQR Stock: 17%, 10.5%, −8%, 14%. What is the arithmetic average return and the standard deviation of these returns?

7. Lisa is analyzing the following assets K, L and M, which have average returns of 9%, 11%, and 12% respectively. Their Standard Deviations are 14%, 15% and 18% respectively. If Lisa wants to invest in the least risky asset, which one would you advised her to buy?

8. What is the difference between systematic and non-systematic risk?

9. Eric has a well diversified portfolio of assets and interest rates are rising this year. Does this pose a risk for his portfolio and why?

10. If Amy is risk averse, which of the following three assets do you think she will choose to invest at: E with Expected Return E[R] = 12%, and Standard Deviation SD = 20%, F with E[R] = 12% and SD = 18%, or G with E[R] = 11% and SD = 18%?

11. Steve is a new client of yours, and wants you to manage his investment assets. He states he is conservative by nature and does not like taking risks. What is the first thing you should do with this client?

12. A moderately aggressive client has $500,000 to invest. What dollar amount would you suggest he invests in bonds?

CHAPTER EIGHT

Insurance Planning: Risk Management

8.1. Introduction

A lot of bad things can happen to you on any given day. Some of them cause losses that are small enough to be mainly annoying. For instance, you come out of the grocery store with a cart full of groceries, when you realize you have lost your car keys. You call your boyfriend for help, but he proceeds to break up with you over the phone. Being upset about this turn of events, you release some steam by smashing your cell phone against your car's windshield. So now you have no boyfriend, no phone, no keys, a cracked windshield, a cart full of rotting groceries and it starts raining. While all this may make for an annoying day, all can be replaced with a few hundred dollars, except the boyfriend that is.

Sometimes however, bad things cause serious losses, which can be life altering and catastrophic for your financial life. Maybe you did not lose your car keys, and you call your boyfriend while driving home from the grocery store. He proceeds to break up with you over the phone. This upsets and distracts you so much, that you violate a red light and crash into another vehicle. Now your car is totaled, your broken legs will keep you from working for at least four months, you have to replace the other driver's car, you are responsible for all the passengers' medical bills, and these passengers are also suing you for pain and suffering, and lost wages. This makes for more than an annoying day. Aside from your own injuries preventing you from working and earning income, the damages and liability to other parties can wipe you out financially.

8.1.1 Risk Management

The purpose of risk management is to analyze potential risk exposures, and identify the most appropriate method to deal with each exposure. Some risks can be "retained" because they have low frequency and low severity. In other words, they don't occur often, and when they occur the losses are tolerable—for example, losing your sunglasses or having your favorite pair of jeans destroyed in the laundry. On the other hand, some other risks have to be completely "avoided" because they exhibit high frequency and high severity. They show up often and with catastrophic consequences—for example, drinking and driving. Alcohol is involved in many automobile accidents, and many are fatal.

It is also possible to have some risks "transferred" to others. This typically happens through insurance, and works well for risks that may occur with low frequency but can cause severe losses. Table 8-1 describes the possible risk management strategies per type of risk exposure.

Table 8-1 Risk Management

Frequency/Severity	Low Severity	High Severity
Low Frequency	Retain Risk	Transfer Risk (Insurance)
High Frequency	Retain & Reduce Risk	Avoid Risk

Notice that out of the four types of risk exposures, "transferring" the risk works well only for one of them. For the other types, the recommended strategy is to either "avoid," "retain," or "retain and reduce" the exposure. The last strategy is useful when the losses occur frequently enough to be a nuisance, but are of such small magnitude that "avoiding" or "transferring" the risk does not make good sense.

For example, if you own or manage a retail clothing business, shoplifting is a constant concern. Losing items means you have to absorb the cost of these items, which is a small fraction of their retail price. This is hardly a reason to "avoid" the risk, which can be accomplished only by closing down your business, but you may not want to passively accept the situation ("retain") either, as it may escalate to unsustainable levels. So while you "retain" the exposure, you may try to "reduce" it by installing a surveillance system. The presence of cameras deters some of the shoplifters, but certainly not the most audacious ones.

8.1.2 Insurance

It would be nice to "transfer" all your risks to others. However, such a strategy is costly. No one would voluntarily accept to shoulder your risk exposure without "fair" compensation. Insurance is based on the concept of risk pooling. Each pool participant (called insured) pays into the pool, and the pool resources are used to compensate those participants suffering a loss. Paying into the pool allows you to transfer your risk to the group. To become a member of the group you have to buy an insurance policy, which is a contract between you and the insurance company (called insurer) that organizes and manages the pool. The contract typically describes in detail the type of losses covered, the coverage limits, as well as your contribution to the pool (called premiums).

For the insurance coverage to be real, the pool resources have to be large enough to compensate all who suffer a loss during the year. Insurance premiums therefore, have to be "fair." This means that your annual premiums have to reflect your expected loss for the year, plus additional fees for the administrative expenses of the pool and a nominal profit of the insurance company.

The administrative expenses for an insurance pool are significant. Aside from the sales commissions and ongoing investment expenses of the pool, which include investment analysis, portfolio management, trading costs and regulatory compliance costs, the insurance company has to be able to resolve effectively two problems that threaten to destroy the pool. The first, the adverse selection problem appears when people apply for insurance coverage. Since there is a tendency for people with higher than average probability of suffering a loss to apply for insurance coverage, the insurance company has to be vigilant with its underwriting process or risk going out of business. Underwriting is the process of evaluating the expected loss from the potential insured, and either accept the application and determine the policy premiums or deny the application altogether.

For example, a person applies for a health insurance policy only after he finds out he needs a $500,000 heart transplant treatment. If the insurer's underwriter neglects to discover this nugget of information about the applicant, the insurer may receive a few hundred dollars in monthly premiums before it has to pay half a million dollars for the treatment expenses of the new insured. These funds were in the pool to cover the random losses of other policy owners. If such mistakes are repeated the pool will soon be depleted, and honest people who have been paying their premiums for years will find themselves without coverage.

Insurance works only if the losses are accidental or random, not when they are guaranteed. A lot of resources are spent to ensure the underwriting process is able to stop those who attempt to transfer guaranteed losses to the group, otherwise the group will get hurt. Denying coverage in this case is the equivalent of asking the applicant to pay a "fair" premium, consisting of the expected loss ($500,000) plus the same 30% or so all participants pay for the combined administrative expenses and profits of the insurer ($150,000 = 0.3*$500,000). Since no reasonable applicant would be willing to pay $650,000 for a $500,000 expense, the application is simply declined.

The second problem threatening to destroy the insurance pool appears after the application has been approved, and the insurance policy has been issued. The moral hazard problem refers to the potential for losses imposed on the group from the immoral behavior of some of the insured. If such fraudulent losses are not prevented, the pool will be depleted and the group will lose the coverage it has been paying for.

Consider for example, a homeowner who faces financial problems and cannot pay his mortgage. Instead of letting the loan go into foreclosure, the insured homeowner decides to torch the house, and collect the insurance proceeds. This way he can repay the balance of the mortgage loan and pocket the difference. While the desperate borrower thinks he has discovered an ingenious way out of his mortgage debt, his immoral behavior inflicts a deliberate loss to the pool. Since only accidental or random losses are calculated into the premiums, any fraudulent and deliberate actions causing guaranteed losses will surely deplete the pool and leave the group without insurance coverage. Therefore, significant resources are devoted to investigate all insurance claims, in order to combat insurance fraud.

Because of the administrative expenses, the underwriting costs (to deal with the adverse selection problem), and the claim processing costs (to deal with the moral hazard problem), insurance premiums are not cheap. Therefore, only unavoidable, infrequent, but potentially catastrophic risk exposures are to be insured. These include death, serious illness, disability and some property and liability exposures.

8.1.3 Insurance planning

The first step in the insurance planning process is a compilation of all your exposures. Then it proceeds with a determination of which risks you can afford to retain, which ones you need to completely avoid and which ones it makes sense to transfer based on each risk's probability of occurrence and magnitude of potential loss.

The next step in the process is the examination of all your existing insurance policies. Your financial planner will review all existing policies for the amount and length of coverage they provide, the terms of coverage and their premiums to determine if these policies offer adequate protection at a competitive cost.

New policies may be recommended and additional coverage may be suggested as part of the implementation of a well thought out risk management program that protects your family, dependents and assets.

Periodic reevaluation of your risk management program will be necessary, as life events may change the nature and size of each exposure.

The following sections discuss how different types of insurance policies can help you implement a complete personal risk management program, to protect yourself and your family from the financial hardship that can follow life's unfortunate surprises.

8.2. Life Insurance

A life insurance policy provides coverage against the financial hardship following the premature death of the covered person. Typically, you need a life insurance policy if there are people who would suffer financially, if you were to pass away. These can be your spouse, dependent children or even your parents who may depend on you for their care. In other words, the main purpose for life insurance is to provide income replacement for your dependents, in the event of your untimely demise.

You may also need life insurance even if you have no dependents, but you have significant amounts of debt outstanding. For instance, you may be single with no children, and have loans and credit lines associated with your business. A life insurance can provide your estate with the necessary liquidity to repay the loans and estate expenses, so your heirs (parents, siblings, other relatives, and friends) receive your assets free of liabilities.

For most people life insurance is a weird thing to purchase. You pay your annual premiums for a policy that promises to pay the policy proceeds (called benefit) to your designated beneficiaries, if you die during the year. In other words, life insurance represents a gamble that pays off only if you die. In that respect, this is a gamble you may not want to win. But why would you want to pay for a wager you do not want to win?

You only want to do so when you have reached the level of maturity required to realize you are not immortal, and life for others will continue long after you are gone. When you care about the needs and well-being of your dependents more than your own, you are willing to sacrifice part of your income to ensure the financial needs of your loved ones will be taken care of, when you are not around to provide for them anymore.

It is not unlikely therefore, to find policyholders who did not actively seek to buy life insurance on their own, but were "sold" life insurance after the suggestion of their financial planner or insurance agent. Sometimes, people just need to be educated about their needs and risk exposures. Addressing these needs and exposures forms their new financial goals. This is one of the benefits of seeking the advice of a financial planner.

8.2.1 Practical Application: Who Needs Life Insurance?

A young couple just had a beautiful and healthy baby. They decided that the new mother will quit working and stay home to raise their child. The family would make do with the husband's $50,000 annual income. Within weeks from the baby's arrival, the couple started receiving in the mail life insurance offers for the newborn. They were for small amounts of coverage, around $10,000, but offered guaranteed acceptance and the ability to increase the coverage later on without a medical exam. Since they had never given much thought to life insurance before, they decided to consult a financial planner about the usefulness of these offers and life insurance in general.

Their initial suspicion about these offers was confirmed by the financial planner recommendations:

First, there is little reason for a healthy baby to have life insurance. It is difficult to envision a scenario where a newborn has dependents. Remember, the life insurance is not for the insured. It is for the financial needs of the beneficiaries. These newborn life insurance policies were popular several decades ago, when infant mortality was high. Their small coverage amount reveals their true purpose. They are actually funeral and burial insurance, camouflaged under the more cheerful name of life insurance. In the twenty-first century however, infant mortality in the US is very small, rendering such policies moot.

Second, the guaranteed acceptance, and the ability to increase the coverage later on without a medical exam, are always valuable life insurance policy features. But they are more important to those with impaired health, who may be deemed uninsurable, than to healthy children. So the existence of such features in life insurance policies for newborns does not constitute a compelling reason to buy these policies.

Third, instead of insuring the newborn, the parents should consider insuring themselves. The father, being the sole income earner of this family, definitely needs to have life insurance. If he was to pass away now without such coverage, his surviving spouse and child would suffer enormous financial hardship. Their standard of living would be forever altered.

Fourth, the mother needs to have life insurance too. While the mother is not an income earner, she provides valuable domestic production and child caring services. If she was to pass away now without coverage, her surviving spouse would face serious financial hardship trying to pay for replacement daily child care and housekeeping services.

8.2.2 Amount of Life Insurance Needed

Once the need for life insurance is established, the logical next step is to determine how much coverage you actually need. There are a few methods that can help you reach the appropriate coverage amount. The methods range from a basic rule of thumb, to very detailed estimates of the future needs of your dependents. Two of these methods are presented in this chapter.

Earnings Multiple Method

The earnings multiple method is mainly a rule of thumb estimate of your life insurance coverage need. The method suggests that you need to have coverage equal to 10 to 15 times your gross income. Whether you need to use the lower or the higher multiple of the range depends on personal factors, like the number of your dependents, their age or how many years they will be in the dependency state and the amount of other assets available to support your surviving family members. Obviously, young parents with very little net worth and two or more toddlers should use the higher multiple of the range. The couple from the previous section had one income earner and one at home parent. Given the young age of the couple and their new baby, the father needs life insurance coverage in the amount of $750,000 (15 * $50,000 gross income). Assuming the market value of the mother's child caring and domestic production services is $36,000 per year, she needs life insurance coverage in the amount of $540,000 (15 * $36,000).

Human Life Value Method

Despite its name this method does not attempt to estimate the value of your life. After all, for your parents or children your life is just priceless! What the human life value method does however is to estimate the total amount of income you would have generated, had you had the chance to work a full career, minus your total personal living expenses, which will not be needed if you are not alive.

Your total future earnings are estimated based on your current earnings and the expected average earnings growth rate throughout your career. Incorporating the growth rate of your earnings in the calculation increases the estimated coverage amount. However, because you will not be around anymore, the percentage of your earnings spent on yourself will not be needed by your survivors. This means they can maintain their current lifestyle with less income, if you are not around to consume. This reduces the estimated coverage amount.

The fewer the members in a household, the bigger the percentage of your income spent on yourself. On the other hand, the more the members in a household, the lower the percentage of your income spent on yourself. In other words, your survivors will not need the income you currently spend for your clothing, entertainment, hobbies etc. Furthermore they will need to purchase less food, one less vehicle and probably a smaller house.

The human life value method also takes into account the fact that any life insurance benefit received by your beneficiaries can be invested to generate additional income. This further reduces the estimated coverage amount.

The couple in the previous section had one income earner with $50,000 gross income. Assume he was 27 years old, and he would work until he was 67. His expected average annual pay raises throughout his career would be 3%. If he passed away, his surviving spouse and child could maintain their current lifestyle with 30% less income. The life insurance benefit would be invested in a conservative portfolio generating 6.5% annual return.

Given this information, the amount of life insurance coverage the income earner needs can be calculated as the present value of an annuity generating the required payment for his survivors to maintain the same lifestyle: $35,000 = $50,000 * (1 − 0.30).

Because his income would grow by one rate (3% reflecting the inflation rate and his increased productivity), but the invested life insurance benefit would grow by another rate (6.5%), You need to use the real rate in your calculation:

$$i_R = \left[\frac{(1+i_N)}{(1+\pi)} - 1\right] * 100 = \left[\frac{(1+0.065)}{(1+0.03)} - 1\right] * 100 = 3.3981\%$$

The income earner needs life insurance coverage of around $760,000. Keep in mind that life insurance can be purchased in $1,000 increments.

HP10BII PVA Calculation

1	□ P/YR
40	N
3.3981	I/YR
$35,000	PMT
$0	FV
	PV −759,391.2085

This estimated coverage need, while very close to the $750,000 estimate from the earnings multiple method, is sensitive to the discount rate used in the calculation of the pva. For instance, if the surviving spouse could earn 7% on the invested life insurance benefit, the estimated coverage need would decline to $705,000. If she could earn only 6%, the estimated coverage need would increase to $821,000.

Moreover, this estimated life insurance coverage amount reflects only the need of the survivors to replace their share of the husband's income. This does not reflect any additional funds needed to repay debts or create a college fund for their child. Furthermore, any future additions to the family would require a new evaluation of the needed coverage amount.

8.2.3 Types of Life Insurance

There are several types of life insurance, each with distinct characteristics making them appropriate for specific situations. The main distinction is between term life and whole life. As the names suggest, term life provides coverage for a specific time period or "term," while whole life provides coverage throughout your "whole" lifetime. Whole life in turn can come with features which differentiate it to universal life, variable life and variable universal life.

Term Life

Term life offers pure insurance protection. It pays the policy benefit to your beneficiaries if you (the insured) die within a specific time period (the "term"). Typically, term life is available for 10, 15, 20, 25 and 30 year terms. Once the term expires you are not covered anymore, thus if you still need life insurance you need to shop around for another policy.

The biggest advantage of term life is its low cost. It is the cheapest type of life insurance because there is no guaranteed payoff. After all, you may not die within the specific term, in which case the insurer will not have to pay the policy benefit. The low cost affords you to purchase the most coverage for the money. This makes the term life ideal for younger clients with families, modest income and little net worth whose goal is to purchase the biggest coverage they can afford.

The biggest disadvantage of term life insurance is that it eventually expires, and at that time you may be uninsurable. You will certainly be older and more costly to insure anyway, but if your health has deteriorated too, you may not be able to find another insurer willing to insure you.

While most term life policies are renewable without evidence of insurability (passing a medical exam), the annual premiums increase exponentially, making this option moot. For instance, a 38-year-old non-smoking male can buy a 10-year $500,000 term life policy for $250 per year. At expiration, he has the "opportunity" to renew the policy for another year for a $5,000 premium. Subsequent annual renewals are available at substantially higher premiums.

Whole Life

Whole life provides insurance protection for your entire life, provided you keep paying the premiums, plus a savings component. In other words, whole life is like a bundle of non-expiring term life together with a savings account. The whole life premiums are much higher than those of the term life, because the insurer faces a guaranteed payment of the whole life policy benefit. The benefit will be paid to your beneficiaries when you die, or it will be paid to you if you reach the maturity age. For policies issued until recently the maturity age is 100, but for new policies the maturity age will be 120.

The part of the whole life premium not allocated to the mortality charge or to the administrative expenses and the profit of the insurer is deposited into a savings account earning a guaranteed interest rate. The accumulated balance is called cash value, and it grows tax deferred. The annual premium and the savings account interest rate are calculated to produce a cash value equal to the policy's death benefit by the time the policy matures.

For example, you purchase a $500,000 whole life insurance policy maturing when you reach the age of 120. Your annual premiums of $4,000 buy insurance coverage of $500,000 and build a cash value of $500,000 by the time you reach the age of 120. If you become 120 years old, the cash value will have grown to $500,000 and you will receive this benefit. If you die earlier, say at age 95, the cash value will be less than the death benefit, but your beneficiaries will receive the full death benefit of $500,000 because the insurance coverage kicks in. So as long as you keep making the $4,000 fixed annual premium, you or your beneficiaries will receive the $500,000 policy benefit.

You are allowed to borrow against the policy's cash value, and you are allowed to withdraw the cash value balance in exchange for "surrendering" the death benefit. In other words, if for whatever reason you decide to terminate the whole life insurance policy, you can get the accumulated cash value back. Alternatively, you can choose to receive a paid-up whole life policy with much lower death benefit, or a paid-up term life policy.

The whole life offers two big advantages: first, the coverage lasts throughout your entire life, thus you do not run the risk of needing to buy life insurance and finding out you have become uninsurable. This makes the whole life appropriate for clients who definitely need the death benefit. They may need to provide for the care of a special needs family member, or to provide liquidity to their estate, or to leave a charitable bequest.

Second, the cash value grows tax-deferred, which provides another tax-deferred account to go along with your ira, 401(k), 403(b) or 457 retirement accounts. This makes the whole life also appropriate for high income clients looking for another tax-sheltered account.

However, whole life has two big disadvantages: First, the premiums are very expensive, which means you will be receiving substantially less coverage for the money compared to a term life policy. Second, a significant portion of the premiums goes for sales commissions, other administrative expenses, and the profit of the insurer. Consequently, the cash value accumulates very slowly. Therefore, if you can find a better savings vehicle and you do not necessarily need permanent coverage, perhaps you may not want to bundle insurance and savings into one product.

The following three types of life insurance are variations of the whole life:

Universal Life

Universal life is a more flexible form of the whole life. The biggest advantage of the universal life is that it allows you the flexibility to pay more or less than your assigned annual premium for your policy. When you pay more, the extra funds are added to the cash value balance and earn interest tax-deferred. When you pay less than is needed to cover the mortality charge, the sales commissions, the administrative expenses and the insurer profits, the difference comes out of your cash value. As long as you have sufficient cash value, you may even skip the annual premium payment. The insurer will subtract the needed charges from your cash value, and your policy will be in force. This makes the universal life appropriate for clients with fluctuating income, relying heavily on bonuses and sales commissions.

The biggest disadvantage of universal life is that freedom and flexibility require greater responsibility. While it may be appealing to pay a reduced premium or skip the annual premium entirely, this can devastate the cash value. Since the cash value grows very slowly to begin with, reducing its balance can lower the policy's death benefit. If the cash value is not enough to cover the annual charges the policy will lapse and you will find yourself without insurance coverage.

Variable Life

Variable life has fixed annual premiums like the ordinary whole life, but its big advantage is that it allows you to invest the cash value in stocks, bonds and mutual funds. Instead of settling for the guaranteed interest rate paid on the whole life's cash value, you can opt for potentially higher investment returns, which will accumulate tax-deferred. If your investment choices perform well, it is possible for the cash value and the policy benefit to increase accordingly. This makes the variable life appropriate for clients with investment experience who would like the responsibility of directing their own funds.

The big disadvantage of the variable life is that you are undertaking investment risk with your life insurance, a component of your risk management program aiming to reduce or eliminate the risk exposures from your financial life. If your investment choices do not perform well, the cash value and the death benefit will be adversely affected. If you like to manage your investments and you do not necessarily need permanent life protection, you may not want to bundle your life insurance with your investments.

Variable Universal Life

As the name suggests, this is a combination of a variable life and a universal life. You are allowed to invest the cash value in stocks, bonds and mutual funds of your choice, while at the same time you are also allowed the discretion of paying more, less or no annual premium at all during a year. There are just too many moving parts in this product to make it appropriate for risk management. Since the premium is flexible, and the cash value returns are uncertain, it is difficult to determine what the death benefit will be. This product is more appropriate for high income, high net worth clients interested in another tax-sheltered account.

Table 8-2 summarizes the major features of the life insurance policies described above.

Table 8-2 Life Insurance Policies

Features	Term	Whole	Universal	Variable	Variable Universal
Premiums	Fixed	Fixed	Flexible	Fixed	Flexible
Cash Value	None	Guaranteed	Variable	Variable	Variable
Investment Control/Risk	N/A	Insurer	Insurer	Insured	Insured
Death Benefit	Fixed	Fixed	Variable	Variable	Variable
Appropriate for	Modest Income Large Need	High Income Want Death Benefit	Variable Income	High Income Investment Control	High Income Inv. Control Var. Income

8.2.4 Life Insurance Policy Provisions

There are several possible policy contract clauses that can differentiate one policy from another. However, some of them are fairly standard and can be found in most life insurance policies:

Grace Period Provision

All policies provide you with an automatic extension between 31 and 61 days from the premium due date, to submit your payment without penalty. During this grace period the policy remains in force, so if you happen to die during this time, your beneficiaries will receive the death benefit minus the past-due premium.

Reinstatement Provision

This provision provides you with an opportunity to reinstate a lapsed policy. Typically, you are only allowed to do so within a few years of the policy lapse, and you will have to pay all missed premiums and policy loans back to the cash value. This is a useful provision because it is possible for you to suffer a temporary financial setback, which may prevent you from paying the life insurance premium, even though you still need the coverage. Once you regain the ability to pay premiums, you may try to buy a new policy but discover that the premiums are much higher than with your old policy. Therefore, it may be cheaper for you in the long run to pay back policy loans and missed premiums to reinstate the old policy.

Suicide Provision

This provision states that your death is not a covered loss, if it is due to suicide during the first two years of the policy. Recall that insurance works well only when compensating accidental or random losses. Deliberate losses, like killing yourself, are not figured in the premiums, so the insurer will not pay the death benefit to your beneficiaries.

8.2.5 Life Insurance Policy Riders

Policy riders are special features you can add to your policy to tailor it to your needs. Since riders add benefits to the standard policy benefit, you should expect higher premiums. Popular riders include:

Guaranteed Insurability Rider

This rider grants you the right to add more insurance coverage in the future without having to prove insurability. So if you have more children in the future or acquire more liabilities that you would like to be paid off at your death, you can add more coverage without the challenge of clearing a medical exam.

Disability Waiver of Premium Rider

By adding this rider to your life insurance policy, you ensure the policy will stay in force and your dependents' financial needs covered, even if you become disabled and cannot afford to pay the annual premiums. The rider in effect makes the insurer pay your premiums, thus it can be a pricey rider. The rider is more expensive for whole life type policies, because the insurer may have to absorb more than the mortality charge and the administrative expenses. These types of policies build a cash value too.

Accidental Death Rider

This rider increases the death benefit if your death is caused by an accident rather than from natural causes. The rider typically doubles the death benefit paid to your beneficiaries, and is referred to as double indemnity. Since the chances of dying in an accident are much smaller than dying from natural causes, this rider is not costly to add to your life insurance policy. However, instead of the rider you may also want to check the cost of buying a separate accidental death and dismemberment policy, which may be available without the need of a medical exam, as an employee benefit from your employer.

8.2.6 Buying Life Insurance

While deciding you need life insurance coverage may be easy, particularly if you have dependents and you are not wealthy enough to be able to self-insure, buying a policy is not that simple, because it requires you to make some complicated choices.

First, you have to choose the level of coverage needed. Hopefully section 8.2.2 can help you make this determination.

Second, you have to choose what type of policy is appropriate for your needs. Section 8.2.3 and Table 8-2 should point you to the right policy for your needs.

Third, you have to choose the riders that have the potential to add the most value to your policy. Section 8.2.5 offers some suggestions on this matter.

Fourth, you have to choose the insurer which will issue the life insurance policy. This choice has to take into account the cost of the policy and the financial strength of the issuer. For term life policies there are plenty of online quote services, which can provide you with quotes from hundreds of insurers for free. For instance, you can try select quote (www.Selectquote.Com) or life quote (www .lifequote.Com) to find the lowest cost policy for your particular age, sex, desired coverage amount and length of term.

For whole life type policies you typically need the services of one or more insurance agents to provide you with pricing information and features of policies that may be appropriate for your needs. Unfortunately, every insurer offers multiple policies with different features and assumptions about the investment performance of the cash value, that it is not humanly possible to process and compare all the possible options. This is one of these situations where too many options simply confuse even trained insurance professionals. So you may have to rely on the best judgment of your financial planner to identify for you the best policy at the lowest cost.

Lowest cost however, should not be the only criterion choosing a life insurance policy. The financial strength and claims paying ability of the insurer are of equal importance. You may not feel particularly happy with your choice of policies if a few years down the road you are notified your insurer went out of business and your policy will be honored by another insurer, but only up to a limited coverage amount. It is very important therefore, to choose to buy a policy from an insurer that is highly rated for financial strength by rating agencies. Typically the rating agencies indicate insurers with the best claims paying ability as "AAA" (standard & poor's) or "A++" (A.M best). Any ratings starting with other letters indicate weaker insurers, and you should be very careful buying long-term promises from weak organizations. Unfortunately, the big rating agencies charge a fee to provide you with access to their ratings. However, weiss research offers their ratings for free. You can access insurer and bank ratings for free at www.weissratings.com.

Finally, once you have chosen an insurer and applied for a life insurance policy, the insurer will arrange for a medical professional to come to your home or place of business for a quick physical examination. This information and your medical records will be used during the underwriting process, to determine your insurability and the actual premium for your coverage.

8.2.7 Receiving the Death Benefit

If you keep the life insurance policy in force until your death, your designated beneficiaries will eventually receive the policy's death benefit. They will be presented with two main options: Receive the benefit as a lump sum or as an annuity.

Receiving the benefit as a lump sum may seem the simplest option. Life insurance proceeds are tax free to the beneficiaries, so the whole amount will be available for them to invest and generate income to cover their future needs. The beneficiaries however, will need to have some spending discipline not to exhaust their windfall prematurely.

Choosing to receive the benefit as an annuity can introduce a level of discipline on the spending of your beneficiaries. Still it will be up to them to choose whether they need payments for a certain number of years or a certain amount of money per year for as long as the funds last.

For instance, the couple from the example in sections 8.2.1 And 8.2.2 determined that the husband needed $760,000 in life insurance. If the husband died, his surviving spouse could choose to receive either a 40-year annuity paying $35,028.0589 Per year, adjusting 3% annually for inflation, assuming the insurer could offer a 6.5% rate of return on the life insurance proceeds; or she could choose to receive an annuity paying $50,000 per year, adjusting 3% annually for inflation, but the life insurance proceeds would last only around 22 years. Both scenarios use the real interest rate.

HP10BII Number of Periods Calculation

1	□ P/YR	1	□ P/YR
40	N	3.3981	I/YR
3.3981	I/YR	$760,000	+/- PV
$760,000	+/- PV	$50,000	PMT
$0	FV	$0	FV
	PMT $35,028.0589		**N 21.7475**

While the life insurance benefit is tax free for the beneficiaries, the return earned on the invested death benefit is taxable. If the beneficiaries select the annuity option, their annual payments will be comprised of both a death benefit component and an interest on the invested death benefit component. The death benefit portion of each payment will be tax free, and the interest portion will be taxable.

Notice that even without inflation adjusted payments, the surviving spouse will receive $1,401,122.3560 (40 * $35,028.0589) In payments. Only the $760,000 representing the death benefit is tax free. The rest is taxable because it represents investment income.

8.2.8 Practical Application: The Milfords' Life Insurance Needs

Ric and Vanessa Milford have asked their financial planner to review their life insurance needs. Ric is 42 years old and expects to work until he is 67 (25 years remaining working life expectancy). He has a $200,000 whole life insurance with a $14,000 cash value, and a term life provided by his employer with coverage equal to his $80,000 base salary. Vanessa is 39 years old and expects to work until she is 65 to qualify for Medicare (26 years remaining working life expectancy). She has only a term life policy provided by her employer, with coverage equal to her $50,000 current salary. With limited net worth (primarily retirement accounts) and raising three children, they are concerned that if something was to happen to one of them, the surviving spouse would face significant hardship providing for the family with just one salary.

Utilizing the earnings multiple method first, the financial planner got a quick estimate of the couples' life insurance need. Deciding what multiple to use from the 10-15 range, the planner he considered the two factors reducing the need and the three factors increasing the need for life insurance coverage. Being a two-income family and one child already 15 years old, were factors reducing the need. Having three children, two of them young (7 and 10 years old), and a new big mortgage loan were factors increasing the coverage need. He decided therefore to use a mid-range multiple of 13, and to include Ric's bonus ($20,000) in his calculation since the family used it to cover living expenses.

Ric's life insurance needed coverage is estimated to be $1,300,000 (13 * $100,000), while Vanessa's is $650,000 (13 * $50,000).

Utilizing then the human life value method, the financial planner tried to get a more precise estimate of their coverage need. The planner he assumed the family's share of the deceased's income to be 80% therefore this is what needs to be replaced for the family needs. The planner he also assumed the surviving spouse will be able to earn 7% average annual rate of return on the invested benefit, while at the same time the deceased's income would have grown by an average of 3% per year. Thus the real rate of return would be:

$$i_R = \left[\frac{(1+i_N)}{(1+\pi)} - 1\right] * 100 = \left[\frac{(1+0.07)}{(1+0.03)} - 1\right] * 100 = 3.8835\%$$

HP10BII PVA Calculation

Ric's Life Insurance Need		Vanessa's Life Insurance Need	
1	☐ P/YR	1	☐ P/YR
25	N	26	N
3.8835	I/YR	3.8835	I/YR
$80,000	PMT	$40,000	PMT
$0	FV	$0	FV
	PVA $1,265,299.6654		**PVA $647,504.445**

So Ric and Vanessa's life insurance needs are $1,265,000 and $648,000 respectively. The amounts are rounded because life insurance coverage is purchased in $1,000 increments. Since both of them have some life insurance already, the financial planner subtracted the existing coverage amounts from their needed amounts to determine how much additional coverage they will need to buy.

Ric's additional coverage need is $985,000 ($1,265,000 − $200,000 − $80,000), while

Vanessa's additional coverage need is $598,000 ($648,000 − $50,000).

Notice that these amounts of additional life insurance are the estimated minimum needed funds to maintain the survivors' lifestyle. The estimates do not include additional funds for repaying the mortgage or providing for the children's college expenses.

Given the size of additional coverage needed and the lack of discretionary income (as discussed in chapter 4), the only realistic option for the couple is term life insurance. Ric and Vanessa have limited resources and need the maximum coverage they can get. With the younger child at age 7, 15-year term life policies for both Ric and Vanessa would ensure the children are taken care of throughout their dependency years, if either parent was to die prematurely.

A search on QuickQuote's website for a $1,000,000 15-year Term Life Insurance, for a healthy non-smoker (Preferred Plus) 42-year-old male of average height and weight, yielded 10 quotes from A+ Rated Insurers ranging from $550 to $895 in annual Premiums. A similar search for a $600,000 15-year term life policy, for a healthy non-smoker 39-year-old female of average height and weight, yielded 10 quotes from A+ Rated Insurers ranging from $258 to $403 in annual premiums.

These quotes are only indicative of what perfectly healthy applicants should expect to pay for the requested amounts of coverage. Ric and Vanessa's actual premiums will be determined during the underwriting process, when their medical records and medical exam results are taken into consideration. Using the average quotes for planning purposes, the Milfords need to budget $1,052 annually for their new policies ($722 for Ric and $330 for Vanessa). Reallocating $88 per month ($1,052/12) from other spending to their new policies, will buy them the protection they need for the well-being of their family.

8.3 Disability Insurance

Disability insurance provides you with replacement income, in case you lose the ability to work due to injury or illness. Disability refers to a physical, sensory, cognitive or mental impairment. According to the Council for Disability Awareness (CDA) over 36 million Americans are classified as disabled. That is more than 12% of the total US population. More than 50% of those are between the ages of 18 and 64. In other words, over 18 million Americans are disabled during their income earning years. Table 8-3 lists the leading causes of new disability claims in 2010.

Table 8-3 Leading Causes of New Disability Claims in 2010

Causes	Percentage of New Claims
Musculoskeletal and Connective Tissue Disorders*	27.5%
Cancer	14.6%
Injuries and Poisoning	10.3%
Cardiovascular and Circulatory Disorders	9.1%
Mental Disorders	9.1%

** Includes: Neck and Back Pain, Muscle and Tendon Disorders, Foot-Ankle-Hand Disorders*

Source: Council for Disability Awareness, Long-Term Disability Claims Review, 2011

The interesting and perhaps surprising piece of information from Table 8-3 is that only 10% of new disability claims are caused by accidents (injuries and poisoning). Rather 90% of all new disability claims are caused by illnesses. At the same time, 62% of all personal bankruptcies filed in the US in 2007 were contributed to medical problems, preventing people from working and earning income.

Table 8-4 lists the leading causes of Existing Disability in 2010.

Table 8-4 Leading Causes of Existing Disability in 2010

Causes	Percentage of New Claims
Musculoskeletal and Connective Tissue Disorders	30.1%
Diseases of the Nervous System and Sense Organs	13.4%
Diseases of the Circulatory System	12.7%
Cancer	8.4%

Source: Council for Disability Awareness, Long-Term Disability Claims Review, 2011

The data from Table 8-4 confirm that lingering disability problems are primarily associated with medical problems and disorders, rather than accidents. Advances in medical science and technology may save and prolong the lives of people, but this does not necessarily mean they can continue working and earning income. In other words, illnesses and disorders increase disability cases, because they do not cause as many immediate deaths as before. Therefore, protecting yourself against the effects of disability is now more important than ever.

The more the medical profession becomes capable of saving your life from both terrible accidents and devastating illnesses, the more you are exposed to potentially catastrophic losses from disability. The financial hardship resulting from disability may be more disastrous than that resulting from premature death. While both death and disability will deprive your family from your income stream, with disability you will still be around requiring self-maintenance and medical expenses. Furthermore, most deaths occur after the income earning years are over. Disability on the other hand, is a greater threat during your income earning years.

8.3.1 Who Needs Disability Insurance?

The largest asset most working-age people own may not be their home or retirement plan, but their ability to produce income. This is particularly true for younger workers. In that respect, the most important part of their personal risk management program should be their disability insurance. In fact, anyone who depends on active income from work to cover living expenses needs disability insurance. This is true whether they are married or single, and whether they have dependents or not.

Yet, according to the Council for Disability Awareness (CDA), 67% of workers in the private sector have no long-term disability insurance. There are several reasons american workers do not protect their income against disability, and all of them have to do with lack of education and understanding of disability issues:

First, most workers believe they will not become disabled. The research from CDA shows that 64% of American wage earners believe they have less than 2% chance of being disabled for 90 days or more. Unfortunately, the actual odds of becoming disabled during your lifetime are around 30%. The odds of suffering disability before the age of 65, lasting more than 90 days, are around 12.5%.

Second, a lot of workers suffer from the misconception that disability is caused only by accidents, and they are somehow protected through workers compensation or Social Security. Unfortunately again, Table 8-3 shows only 10% of new disability claims are caused by accidents. Furthermore, less than 5% of accidents causing disability are work related. This means that more than 95% of accidents causing disability are not work related and are not eligible for worker compensation benefits.

As for Social Security, there is Social Security Disability Insurance (SSDI), but the criteria for qualification are strict. For instance, in order for you to be considered for SSDI benefits, your disability must be expected to last at least a year, or result in your death, and you cannot perform the duties of any occupation. Thus, the majority of SSDI applications are denied. For example, 65% of SSDI applications were denied in 2009. And while there were 8.3 million working-age Americans receiving SSDI benefits in 2011, the average benefit was $1,065 per month. Can your support your family on this income?

Third, workers seem to believe disability insurance is expensive. Premiums for disability insurance depend primarily on the hazard level of your occupation. If you are an office worker or a school teacher, you are employed in a less risky occupation than a coal miner or an oil rig operator, thus you will be charged lower premiums. Since disability insurance policies replace a percentage of your income (usually up to 60%), the premiums also depend on your income level. But even if you are employed in a hazardous occupation and are charged high disability insurance premiums, you need to consider the cost (premiums) versus the potential benefit.

For example, suppose that you buy a long-term disability insurance policy, which will pay $3,000 per month until your normal retirement age of 67, in case you become disabled. At age 30 you become disabled and start collecting the policy benefits. By age 67 you will receive $1,332,000 (37 years * 12 months * $3,000). How much would you be willing to pay every year, to have the right to claim this benefit?

8.3.2 Disability Insurance Features

Duration of Benefits

Disability policies are classified into short term and long term according to the duration of benefits they provide. Short-term policies pay benefits for up to 2 years. Typically there is a waiting period (called elimination period) from the day the disability occurs until the benefits begin. The shorter the elimination period is, the more expensive the premiums.

Long-term policies pay benefits until your normal retirement age, when you begin collecting Social Security benefits or until your death. It is also possible to pay benefits for some other specified period of time. The elimination period can last from 1 to 6 months. Having an emergency fund covering 3 to 6 months of your living expenses allows you to select a longer elimination period, which reduces the policy premiums.

Definition of Disability

Your disability insurance policy may define disability as inability to perform the duties of "any occupation" or of your "own occupation." The higher the level of education required by your occupation, the higher the level of your specialization, and the higher the level of your compensation, the more important it is to choose an "own occupation" policy.

For example, a surgeon has a terrible skiing accident suffering permanent debilitating injuries. With an "any occupation" policy, there are no disability benefits if the insured can perform the duties of any occupation he is "reasonably suited" for, even if the compensation is a small fraction of his original compensation. The premiums for an "own occupation" are more expensive, but you do not risk discovering what the insurer thinks you are "reasonably suited" for. A cheaper policy may be available as a compromise between the "any" and "own" definitions. For the first 2 years it uses the "own occupation" definition and after that it converts to the "any occupation" definition. In other words, you have 2 years of benefits to prepare for another career.

Renewable versus Non-Cancellable

Disability insurance policies can be either guaranteed renewable or non-cancellable. With the guaranteed renewable if you want to renew your policy, the insurer is required to renew it. However, the insurer can raise the premiums for your risk group. This may make your right to renew the policy moot, if you cannot afford the premiums anymore. With non-cancellable policies on the other hand, you can always renew the policy, and the insurer cannot raise the premiums. Obviously, non-cancellable polices are better for you, therefore their premiums are more expensive.

Integrated versus Non-Integrated

Disability insurance policies integrated with Social Security reduce your benefits if you begin receiving Social Security Disability Insurance (SSDI) benefits. Policies non-integrated with Social Security on the other hand, do not reduce your disability benefits if you begin receiving SSDI benefits too. Obviously, non-integrated policies are better for you, so their premiums are more expensive.

Taxability

If you receive disability insurance as an employee benefit, and your employer pays the premiums, then when you receive disability benefits the benefits will be taxable income. If you pay for the premiums with pre-tax dollars (cafeteria plan), any disability benefits you receive will be taxable income.

Only if you pay for the premiums with after-tax dollars, you are entitled to receive the disability benefits tax free. Since the disability benefits are only about 60% of your salary, if the benefits are taxable you will be left with less income. Therefore, you may want to buy the disability policy on your own, and pay for your own premiums (after-tax dollars), to ensure your disability benefits will be tax free.

8.4 Health Insurance

Since everyone becomes ill from time to time, with some more often or more seriously than others, an important component of a personal risk management program is a health insurance policy. Much like with the other components of your risk management program, health insurance is meant to protect you from potentially catastrophic losses. Medical costs are certainly capable of inflicting such catastrophic losses to all but the very wealthy. Medical costs have been increasing much faster than the inflation rate, and if you need any treatment requiring surgery or hospitalization you can quickly face medical bills totaling tens of thousands of dollars.

8.4.1 Health Care Costs

Health Care costs have been rising very fast for several reasons:

First, while medical science and technology are advancing quickly and can save lives from conditions that were considered fatal a short while ago, this progress comes at a high monetary cost. You receive more advanced care but at a much higher price. For instance, more than 36% of US hospitals perform robotic surgery, which is more precise, requires smaller incisions and allows for shorter recovery periods, but is more costly. Even the cost of diagnostics keeps increasing. Mris and CTSCANS are an improvement over X-Rays, and new generations of medical technology offer higher resolution, color display and even 3d. Hospitals and medical offices have to keep buying the newer models or risk losing patients to competing facilities using the new equipment. As a result, the life expectancy of costly MRI and CTSCAN devices in the US has been reduced to just over 2 years. Medical facilities have this much time to recover the cost of these devices, by passing the cost to those who need to use them.

Second, the cost of developing new and more effective drugs is enormous. It takes more than a decade and hundreds of millions of dollars to develop a new drug that successfully passes the required Food and Drug Administration (FDA) clinical trials. The cost is passed directly to the US patients. Eventually, the patents expire and generic drugs become available at cheaper prices. For instance, generic drugs account for 80% of the drugs used in the US. However, it takes a long time for patents to expire and for generics to appear in the market. By that time, a newer drug may be promising better results than the available generics. For example, unlike older and perhaps available in generic form chemotherapy medicines, new ones have tumor targeting properties allowing them to attack and destroy the cancerous cells, while leaving the healthy ones intact. The new ones are very expensive, but more effective in saving lives. Which one would you want for yourself?

Third, hospitals and medical facilities are charging you more than the cost of your care, so they can recover the cost of care provided to others. For instance, about 60% of all hospital admissions are Medicare and Medicaid patients. Since these government programs pay the providers a fixed rate which is less than what the providers charge for the services, the providers charge you a higher price to make up the difference. In addition, about 6% of all hospital expenses are spent for the care of patients who cannot pay. Can you guess how the hospitals make up for these uncollectable bills?

Fourth, the existence of private health insurance policies and public (Medicare, Medicaid) health insurance programs pushes medical costs higher. It is a classic case of unintended consequences. The very health insurance that is supposed to help you pay for your medical care makes this care more unaffordable. Insured patients do not pay for most of their care, so they consume more services than they would if they were paying all their medical bills out of pocket. The increased demand for medical services raises the prices. Furthermore, insured patients who do not pay directly for the cost of their care, have little incentive to negotiate the prices they are charged for their care. Do you remember the last time you asked your doctor how much he or she charges for the office visit or how much are the lab tests going to cost you?

8.4.2 Cost of Health Insurance

Since health insurance reimburses you for the medical costs you incur, the more expensive the cost of health care becomes, the more expensive the claims filed on your behalf and the more expensive your health insurance becomes. There has to be a direct and relatively accurate relationship between what goes into the insurance pool (premiums) and what is paid out of the pool (claims), or the pool will be depleted and coverage will be lost for all pool participants.

To protect the viability of the pool, health insurers have to address the adverse selection and moral hazard problems associated with all insurance, as described in section 8.1.2. It is more costly however to address these problems when it comes to health insurance, compared to the other types of insurance. Screening health insurance applicants, to identify their potential for suffering losses and filing claims, is much harder for health insurers than say property and casualty insurers.

A property and casualty insurer can easily determine the size of the exposure the pool undertakes by accepting to insure your house. The location and past claim history of your property are not only good indicators about the future claims from this property, but they are also easy data to acquire. As a result the decision and the premiums are determined within minutes of your application for insurance.

Health insurance applications on the other hand, are difficult to underwrite. Your medical records will have to be retrieved from your physicians and your past health insurance claims will have to be reviewed, to provide an indication of your health condition and the chances of causing new claims. Despite all the time and effort the application review requires, the insurer has just an indication of your health condition. You, on the other hand, have the advantage of knowing exactly how sick you feel. It is entirely possible that while young and healthy, you did not want to waste your money to participate in the pool, but now that you feel sick, you want to transfer the cost of your treatments to the pool. Even if your application looks good on paper, you are still a big risk to the health insurer, and this will be reflected in your premiums. Not surprisingly, individual health insurance policies have higher premiums than group policies.

Addressing the moral hazard problem is also a lot more expensive for health insurers than other type of insurers. There are three reasons for these high administrative costs:

First, it is the sheer volume of health insurance claims that have to be reviewed, processed, and paid according to the coverage provided by each individual policy. A single illness requiring treatment and tests from multiple providers can produce tens of claims. Depending on its severity, a chronic illness can produce hundreds of claims during a year. Other types of insurance do not have to process as many claims per insured. How many times do you crash your car in a year and need to file a claim with your insurer?

Second, before each claim is paid, the insurer has to determine the loss was not due to a "pre-existing" condition. In other words, the insurer has to make sure pool resources are not spent to cover treatments for conditions you acquired before becoming a member of this pool. The Health Insurance Portability and Accountability Act of 1996 (HIPAA) limits the period your pre-existing conditions are not covered by your new insurer to 12 months from enrollment. The Patient Protection and Affordable Care Act of 2010 (PPACA) disallows the exclusion of pre-existing conditions from coverage, effective January 2014. For those younger than the age of 19, this became effective on policies issued after September 2010.

Third, health insurance policies do not cover treatment for all conditions. Furthermore, they do not cover all the possible treatments for the conditions they cover. Typically, only the necessary and established treatments for conditions posing a threat to your life or good health are covered. So no elective or cosmetic procedures and no experimental treatments are covered. Therefore, each claim has to be reviewed to verify that both the condition and the treatment are covered. Only then the claim will be paid, and only up to the policy's covered amount.

All these bureaucratic tasks add to the health insurer administrative expenses, and trickle down to your premiums. Despite the high cost of health insurance, you cannot afford to be without it. Illness and accidents happen without warning, and regardless of your employment situation or ability to pay for treatment.

8.4.3 Types of Health Insurance

Hospital Insurance

Hospital insurance covers the expenses associated with hospitalization, such as room and board charges, nursing fees, operating room charges and drug costs provided by the hospital. The policy may not cover the full cost of the hospital services. Notice that hospital insurance does not cover doctors' fees.

Surgical Insurance

Surgical insurance covers surgeon fees whether the procedure takes place in a hospital or not. Not all procedures are covered and much like with the hospital insurance, the surgical insurance policy may not cover the full fee of the surgeon.

Physician's Expense Insurance

Physician's expense insurance covers all non-surgical doctor fees and expenses, including office visits and lab tests.

Major Medical Insurance

Major medical insurance combines the previous three types of health insurance and covers even more services. It covers hospitalization, surgeon fees, physician fees, lab tests, and adds physical therapy and a drug benefit. Notice, that even major medical does not provide coverage for vision and dental care. Recall that the purpose of risk management is to protect your financial life against catastrophic losses. While dental procedures can be expensive, dental and vision care expenses do not pose a threat for catastrophic losses, therefore they are not covered by major medical.

In an effort to deter frivolous demand for medical services by insured patients, most major medical policies require you to pay an annual "deductible" and "co-insurance" for the services you consume.

The "deductible" is the specific amount of your health care expenses you must pay, before the insurer starts paying. Typical amounts range from $250 to $1,000 per covered person per year, with a maximum of three deductibles per family per year.

The "co-insurance" is the percentage of each claim above the deductible that the insurer will pay. The residual percentage of the claim is your responsibility. Typical co-insurance arrangements include 80/20 and 70/30. An 80/20 policy implies that the insurer will cover 80% of the amount of the approved claim above the deductible.

To limit your exposure to possible expenses, major medical policies come with a "stop loss limit" which limits the amount of each claim you are responsible for. Typical stop loss limits range from $1,000 to $2,500 per claim.

For example, assume that you have a major medical insurance policy with $500 annual deductible, 80/20 co-insurance and $2,000 stop loss limit. A sudden appendectomy, with an overnight stay at a hospital results in a $12,000 medical bill. You will have to pay:

$500	Deductible
$2,000	Stop Loss Limit {20% * ($12,000 − $500) = $2,300 > $2,000}
$2,500	Amount you are responsible for.
	The Insurer will pay the remaining $9,500 ($12,000 − $2,500).

Obviously, if you choose a low deductible, a high co-insurance percentage and a low stop loss limit for your health insurance policy, then you transfer more of your risk exposure to the insurer, who will charge you higher premiums.

8.4.4 Health Insurance Plans

There are two types of arrangements or plans health insurers use to provide benefits: the traditional indemnity plans (or fee for service) and managed care plans.

Traditional Indemnity Plans

Traditional indemnity plans was the way most health insurance benefits were administered in the US until the 1980s. Under this arrangement, medical providers bill you directly and you file claims with your insurer for reimbursement. While you may be responsible for the paperwork, these plans offer you the greatest freedom to choose doctors and hospitals. You are also free to see any specialist you want without the need of a referral or the need to prove the visit was medically necessary in order to get reimbursed. This freedom comes at a cost. You can expect to pay more out-of-pocket expenses in the form of higher deductible, higher stop loss limit and higher premiums for a policy using a traditional indemnity plan. Because of their high cost, most employers have turned to managed care plans to save money.

Managed Care Plans

Managed care plans are arrangements between health insurers and networks of health care providers, which offer you significant financial incentives to use the network providers. Most people with private health insurance have some form of managed care. The two major forms of managed care are health maintenance organizations (HMOs)and preferred provider organizations (PPOs).

> A health maintenance organization is an organization that provides health care through doctors, hospitals and other providers, who have a contractual relationship with the HMO. In exchange for low premiums and no paperwork, the HMO requires you seek care only from the network providers. Flexibility is limited with an HMO. You will have to choose a primary care doctor under contract, who will either treat your illness or refer you to a specialist, who is also under contract with the HMO. This option is often offered by large employers.
>
> A preferred provider organization is an organization of providers under contract with an insurer to furnish medical services to policyholders. Usually you receive discounts negotiated between the insurer and the providers on services rendered. Typically you can go directly to a medical specialist member of the PPO without a referral from a primary care physician. A PPO offers more flexibility than an HMO, but the premiums are higher.

8.5 Social Insurance

Social insurance refers to insurance programs run by the public sector (government). These programs include Medicare, Medicaid, Social Security Disability Insurance (SSDI), and workers' compensation. The latter is an insurance program providing benefits to workers for work-related accidents and illness. Each state runs its own program under its own workers' compensation laws. Recall, Social Security Disability Insurance is discussed in section 8.3.1.

Medicare

Medicare is a federal health insurance plan for individuals 65 years old and older. However, a person who is disabled or who has one or more defined debilitating illnesses can qualify for Medicare at any age. During your working years, a percentage of your salary is deducted and placed into a Medicare trust fund. The withholding percentage is 1.45% of all of your earned income. An additional 0.9% applies to all compensation over $200,000 (single taxpayers), over $250,000 (married filing jointly) or $125,000 (married filing separately). The additional 0.9% Applies only to employee withholding and is not matched by the employer. However, your employer matches the 1.45% Applied to all of your compensation.

Employers are not responsible for knowing whether an employee's combined income with his or her spouse makes the employee subject to the additional 0.9% Tax, so additional tax planning may be necessary to avoid an underpayment penalty.

Medicare requires the payment of premiums, co-payments and deductibles. Coverage comes through two principal ways: original Medicare (Parts A, B and D) or a Medicare Advantage Plan (Part C).

i) Part A covers some of your expenses for inpatient hospital care, skilled nursing facility charges (not custodial or long-term care), hospice and home health care. You are automatically enrolled for Part A coverage at age 65 if you are eligible to receive Social Security retirement benefits. Your Part A coverage does not require a premium. Some individuals will have to initiate and pay a premium for Part A coverage if they are not eligible for Social Security retirement benefits. For those who are automatically enrolled, the amounts deducted from their salary during their working years have paid for this coverage.

   Part A benefits are delivered in benefit periods which begin when a patient first enters a hospital and end after a maximum of 60 days. During that time the patient is required to pay a deductible of $1,132, and Part A coverage pays the balance as long as the services are on an approved list.

   If you continue to be hospitalized after 60 days, a co-insurance payment of $283 per day must be paid for all days up to 90. From the 91st day through the 150th day, you pay $566 per day, and this extended coverage is only available once (lifetime reserve days).

ii) Part B coverage, which is optional, applies to doctor and outpatient care, home health services and durable medical equipment. As is the case with Part A, all expenses are not covered. You are responsible for paying an annual deductible of $162 plus a Co-payment of 20% of the charges on the Medicare approved list. In addition, there is a basic monthly premium for Part B of $115.40 Which is deducted from your monthly Social Security deposit. The premium will gradually increase as your modified adjusted gross income increases.

   Notice, that although Part B pays for physicians' fees, it does not cover routine physical exams, dental care, vision care or hearing aids. In other words, Part B does not cover most of the conditions older people really need care for.

iii) Part D is the third type of coverage under what is called "original Medicare." Part D coverage is optional, and it covers prescription drugs. You can enroll in Part D coverage within the period starting 3 months before the month you turn age 65 and continuing through the 3 months after the month you turn age 65. If you delay enrollment beyond this period, you may have to pay a late enrollment penalty.

This coverage is provided by private Insurers through a variety of plans. Monthly Premiums depend on the range of drugs included, and they average about $25. In addition, most plans require annual Deductibles and Co-payments. It is important to select a plan which covers the drugs you need to purchase.

iv) Part C allows you the choice to access your Medicare benefits through a managed care plan called Medicare Advantage. You will pay an additional premium for Medicare Advantage. However, more services are covered and deductibles and Co-pays on Parts A, B and D may be less. Benefits are usually provided through a Health Maintenance Organization (HMO) or a Preferred Provider Organization (PPO).

Medicaid

Medicaid is a joint federal and state health insurance plan for low income households. The benefits vary by state. It is possible to be eligible for both Medicare and Medicaid benefits, if disabled, 65 years old or older, and low income. In this case, the medicare premiums, deductibles, and Co-payments are paid by medicaid.

8.6 Property and Liability Insurance

No risk management program would be complete without protection against significant losses to your property and against the liability arising from your property causing losses to others. Both types of losses can be catastrophic and wipe you out financially.

Consider for example, being a homeowner with a $300,000 mortgage loan balance. A tornado goes through your neighborhood and completely destroys the house. You are now a former homeowner who is homeless, and still owes the mortgage loan balance to the lender. Without Homeowners (HO) insurance, you would be financially ruined.

Consider also the consequences of lending your automobile to your roommate, who becomes distracted by his relentless wireless communications and causes an accident. The complete loss of your vehicle, while substantial, may be the least of your concerns. You may be surprised to find out that the victims of this accident are suing you for their property losses, medical and rehabilitation costs and pain and suffering. You did not cause the accident, but it was your property that crashed on to them and caused damages and injuries. You are therefore liable for their claims, and without a personal automobile policy (PAP) and some additional liability insurance, you would be financially ruined.

The following two sections provide a brief overview of the Homeowners Insurance, Personal Automobile Policy, and Personal Liability Umbrella Policy.

8.6.1 Homeowners Insurance (HO)

Homeowners policies are either "named peril" or "open peril" policies. Named peril policies cover losses caused only from the specific perils named on the policy. Open peril policies on the other hand cover losses from all perils, except those that are specifically listed on the policy as excluded. Typically, excluded perils are flood, earthquake, war, nuclear hazard, ordinance of law (condemned properties) and neglect (termite damage).

Open peril policies are preferable because they provide you with peace of mind. You are protected against everything, except six perils. You can even purchase additional insurance policies for some of the excluded perils depending on your needs. There is flood insurance if you live in a flood zone, termite insurance is particularly useful if you live in the south and you can add an earthquake rider to your open peril HO policy.

Table 8-5 shows the types of HO policies, and Table 8-6 shows what HO policies cover.

Table 8-5 Types of Homeowner Policies

Policy	Name	Use/Coverage
HO-1	Basic	Named Perils
HO-2	Broad	More Named Perils
HO-3	Special	Open Perils for Dwelling, Named Perils for Personal Property
HO-4	Contents	HO-2 Coverage for Renters' Personal Property
HO-5	Comprehensive	HO-3 with Open Perils for both Dwelling & Personal Property
HO-6	Unit Owners	HO-2 Coverage for Condo Owners' Personal Prop/Appliances
HO-8	Modified	HO-1 Coverage for Older Structures' Repairs/no Replacement

Table 8-6 Homeowner Policy Coverage

Part	Coverage	Coverage Limits
Section I-A	Dwelling: repair/replace house & attached structures	
Section I-B	Other Structures: detached garages, storages	10% of Coverage A
Section I-C	Personal Property: furniture/electronics/clothes	50% of Coverage A
Section I-D	Loss of Use: living expenses/loss of rental Income	20% of Coverage A
Section II-E	Personal Liability: for bodily injury & property damage	$100K – $300K
Section II-F	Medical Payments to Others: for injuries at property	

Notes

i) Parts A through D (Section i) cover losses resulting from property damage, while Parts E and F (Section ii) cover losses caused by liability.

ii) The standard coverage for personal property (Part C) is for actual cash value, which equals the replacement cost of the item minus its depreciation from the day of original purchase. What this means is that standard coverage is inadequate to replace your property items if they are lost from theft or disaster.

For example, suppose your TV set was stolen. You had purchased this large screen high definition TV 3 years ago for $3,600. Naturally, you kept the receipt and you can prove to your insurer you actually owned this nice TV set. If you have standard personal property coverage, the insurer will compensate you for the actual cash value of your TV set. The insurer will shop around for a TV set with the same specifications like yours.

Three years ago, your TV set may have been top of the line, but now the existence of newer models with more advanced features has dropped the price of TV sets similar to yours to $1,500. This is the replacement cost of your TV set. Of course this is for a new set. You did not lose a new set. You lost a 3-year-old set, and to be restored to your pre-theft situation the insurer has to compensate you for a 3-year-old used TV set, with seemingly semi-obsolete features.

Consumer electronics are usually depreciated over a 5-year period. Therefore, your TV set has lost three-fifths of its value, and your insurer will have to pay you:

Actual cash value = Replacement cost – Depreciation = $1,500 – (3/5 * $1,500) = $600

Unfortunately, you have to meet your deductible first. Homeowners policies have a deductible per claim. A typical HO policy deductible is $500 to $1,000. So if the TV set was the only item stolen, and your deductible is $500, you will receive $100 ($600 – $500) from your insurer for the loss of your TV set. This certainly cannot buy you a similar TV set. Therefore, you may want to add a "replacement cost" endorsement to your HO policy. It will increase the HO policy premiums, but you will be able to replace your lost items.

iii) The personal property (Part C) coverage for some items is very limited. For example, losses are limited to: $250 for cash and coin collections, $1,500 for jewelry etc. Therefore, if you have valuable possessions like expensive art, collectibles, jewelry etc, you may want to add "personal articles floater" endorsements to you HO policy to protect against their loss.

iv) It is important to use the HO policy only for serious or catastrophic losses. The HO policy is not meant to be a home maintenance plan, so if you file three or more claims in any 5-year period not only your premiums will skyrocket, but you may be denied coverage.

8.6.2 Personal Automobile Policy (PAP)

According to the National Highway Traffic Administration, there are around 5.25 million automobile accidents per year in the US, killing 43,000 Americans. Most of the victims (63%) are the drivers. Another 2.9 Million people suffer light or severe injuries during these accidents. Contributing factors to automobile accidents include driver impairment, driver error, poor eyesight, bad road conditions and phone distractions. Since the losses resulting from these accidents can be devastating, most states require drivers to be covered by personal automobile policy (PAP) insurance. The handful of states without required pap insurance require instead the drivers to post a bond, to prove they can cover the damages they could cause to others while driving. Table 8-7 shows the different pap parts and what they cover.

Table 8-7 Personal Automobile Policy Coverage

Part	Coverage	Purpose
A	Liability	Bodily and property damage you cause to others
B	Medical expense	For you and your passengers in a covered auto
C	Uninsured motorists	Pays what an uninsured/underinsured should have paid
D	Damage to your auto	Pays for collision & comprehensive damage to your auto

Notes

i) Liability coverage (Part A) is provided for you, your family or any person using your vehicle with your permission. The coverage limits are shown as split limits and indicate thousands of dollars. For example, the minimum recommended PAP split limits are 100/300/100 which indicates that coverage is limited to:

$100,000	for Bodily Damage per person
$300,000	for Bodily Damage per accident
$100,000	for Property Damage per accident

ii) Medical payments (Part B) are covered for you, your family and other occupants of your vehicle, if involved in a car crash; and also for you and your family if you were pedestrians during the accident.

iii) Uninsured motorists (Part C) pays the damages the uninsured or underinsured driver that caused the accident, should have paid but did not. Since your own PAP insurance picks up the difference, or the whole amount, you cannot sue for punitive damages, as you would be suing yourself.

iv) Coverage for damage to your automobile (Part D) covers the damages to your vehicle if you caused the accident or your vehicle was damaged from an object other than another vehicle. Collision coverage protects you when you hit something (other vehicle, tree, sign etc). Comprehensive coverage protects you when your vehicle gets hit by something other than a vehicle (animal, hail, vandalism, etc). Part D is optional coverage, but it is recommended if your vehicle is relatively new, or you cannot afford to repair damages or replace your vehicle out of pocket.

v) PAP coverage excludes losses caused while you participate in racing, use the vehicle for public livery (taxi), other business, without the owner's explicit permission, or the accident occurs in Mexico. Your PAP does cover you in Canada and Puerto Rico.

vi) It is important to remember that the PAP of the vehicle owner is the primary insurance for losses to be recovered. The driver's PAP is secondary. Therefore, allowing others to use your vehicle exposes you to enormous risks.

vii) Your PAP premiums depend on the make and model of your vehicle, your age and sex, your marital status, the location of the vehicle, its use (work or pleasure), your driving record and your credit score. Apparently, if you want to pay low PAP premiums you need to be a middle-aged married female, with perfect credit score and no traffic violations, living in a rural area, driving an unassuming vehicle with little horsepower for pleasure!

8.6.3 Personal Liability Umbrella Policy (PLUP)

With both the homeowners (HO) policy and the personal automobile policy (PAP) imposing coverage limitations, while the liability judgments awarded by juries keep increasing, you may be just an accident away from a catastrophic loss despite having HO and PAP insurance. It is recommended therefore, to protect your assets and your financial future with a personal liability umbrella policy (PLUP).

The PLUP pays for legal judgments due to your negligence. Typical coverage is between $1 million and $10 million depending on the assets you are trying to protect. The PLUP however, is not very expensive because it kicks in only after the HO or PAP liability coverage has been exhausted. The PLUP does not cover liabilities from damages caused intentionally by you, nor does it cover liabilities from operating a business. If you operate a business you need a business or professional insurance to minimize your risk exposures.

Summary

Risk management is an important component of financial planning. Budgeting, saving and investing to create wealth may be moot if you do not take the necessary steps to protect your wealth. Eliminating risk from your life is impossible, but you can plan to minimize your risk exposures. Some risks you will have to avoid, others you can afford to retain. The risks you cannot avoid but it is too dangerous to retain, you need to transfer to others through insurance. Life insurance replaces your future income stream for your dependents, if you die prematurely. Disability insurance replaces your income if you become unable to work due to illness or injury. Health insurance covers part of your medical expenses to reduce the impact of costly medical treatments on your finances. Medicare is a federal health insurance program for people 65 years old and older. Medicaid is a federal and state joint health insurance program for the needy. Homeowners insurance provides protection against both property and liability damages associated with your home. A personal automobile policy protects you against both property and liability damages associated with the use of your vehicle. Additional protection from liability judgments is provided through a personal liability umbrella policy. While no one enjoys paying insurance premiums, you can enjoy peace of mind by creating a well planned risk management program, which protects your family's financial security.

Review Questions

1. A risk has high frequency and low severity. How should you manage this exposure?

2. A risk has low frequency and high severity. How should you manage this exposure?

3. Which type of life insurance allows you to vary the premiums you pay, while paying some minimum return on your cash value?

4. Which type of life insurance allows you to manage the cash value while you pay your fixed annual premium?

5. What type of life policy would you recommend to a young single mother earning $40,000 per year?

6. According to the human life value method, how much life insurance does brian need if he earns $115,000 per year, his remaining working life expectancy is 22 years, he expects to keep growing his income at an average 3% per year, while his surviving spouse will need only 80% of his income and can invest the life insurance benefit to earn 6%?

7. Mira is a very successful and creative architect. She earns $250,000 per year designing commercial venues like museums and convention centers. What type of disability policy would you advise her to buy?

8. Why do health care costs keep increasing?

9. How does the adverse selection problem impact health insurance premiums?

10. An emergency medical procedure produced $18,000 in medical bills for Eric. His major medical health insurance has a $500 deductible, 70/30 co-insurance, and a $2,500 stop loss limit. How much will he have to pay? How much will his insurer have to pay?

11. Beth just became eligible for Medicare and enrolled both in Part A and Part B. She is relieved to have made it into the security of coverage provided by Medicare and believes her health care is paid for the rest of her life. Is she right in her belief?

12. Lisa has insured her home for $320,000. How much coverage does her homeowners policy provide for her personal property?

13. Jason's laptop was stolen from his dorm room. He paid $1,200 to buy it 2 years ago when he was a freshman. Similar laptops now sell for $900. Consumer electronics are depreciated over a 5-year period. Jason's parents have a $500 deductible on their HO policy. How much will the insurer pay on an actual cash value for Jason's laptop?

14. Lisa was driving home on a dark rural road one evening when out of nowhere a cow appeared on the road. Lisa could not avoid the cow. That chance encounter did not end well for the cow or for lisa's car. What coverage does Lisa have to have on her personal automobile policy for the insurer to cover the damages on her car?

15. You are late for a date and you need to borrow your roommate's car. He is at the library and has turned off his cell phone. The car is parked in front of the apartment. He regularly lets you borrow it, so you pick up the keys and go. Unfortunately, you had a car accident. Will your roommate's PAP cover the damages to the other vehicle?

CHAPTER NINE

Retirement Planning: Retirement for Older People, Planning for Young and Old Alike

9.1 Introduction

This chapter provides the framework for understanding retirement and the lifelong process of planning for it. Someday the paychecks will stop, and what happens next depends on how well or how poorly you plan for life during retirement. Most people will want to continue a standard of living similar to what they enjoyed while working. Doing this without a paycheck requires a lot of thought, planning and saving many years before leaving the workforce.

It's a common misconception that Social Security alone will provide enough income for a comfortable retirement. The amount of your Social Security retirement benefit depends on factors such as how long you worked, how much of your income was subject to Social Security withholding taxes and when you start your benefits. But don't expect it to provide enough for retirement financial security. The estimated average monthly benefit in December 2012 is $1,262 ($15,144 annually) according to the Social Security Administration website, barely enough to maintain a subsistence standard of living.

Adding to your retirement income is your responsibility, and the material in this chapter will show you ways to reach your goals.

The illustration below is a three-legged stool, like the ones found in many kitchens. Think about what would happen if the stool only had one leg. It would be unstable, not very comfortable to sit on, and most likely it would dump you on the floor. Adding a second leg would make it better, but it still could topple over. But adding a third leg would make it stable, and you could sit on it with more confidence.

Think of the three-legged stool as the framework for retirement planning with one leg representing Social Security, the second leg as employer-sponsored retirement plans and the last leg as your personal retirement savings plans. How comfortable the seat is depends on how much padding (savings) you put into it during your working years.

9.1.1 When and How to Start

As you start your working career, retirement planning and saving may be low priorities because of other financial obligations like repaying student loans, buying a house or car and starting a family. Your employer may sponsor retirement plans, and you may be eligible to participate soon after you start work. Some employer plans are funded by the employer alone and others provide for funding from both the employer and employee. As an employee you may be given the opportunity to delay receipt of some of your salary and place this money into a retirement account along with money from your employer. Before you say no to salary deferrals, consider all of the circumstances and benefits.

To reach your retirement savings goal, remember three things:

1. Don't start too late.
2. Don't save too little.
3. Don't invest too conservatively.

Too Late

What happens if you decide to postpone saving for retirement until you "can afford it"? Obviously, you will have fewer years to save, therefore you will not benefit as much from the powerful effects of compound interest. Here's what can happen. Assume a retirement age of 65, savings of $500 at the end of each month, and an after-tax return of 5%:

Too Late

HP10BII FVA Calculation

12 □	P/YR	12 □	P/YR	12 □	P/YR
480	N	360	N	240	N
5	I/YR	5	I/YR	5	I/YR
0	PV	0	PV	0	PV
500	+/− PMT	500	+/− PMT	500	+/− PMT
	FV 763,010.0782		**FV 416,129.3177**		**FV 205,516.8343**

Start saving at age 25; 40 years (40*12 = 480 months) later, at age 65 you will have $763,010.0782.

Start saving at age 35; 30 years (30*12 = 360 months) later, at age 65 you will have $416,129.3177.

Start saving at age 45; 20 years (20*12 = 240 months) later, at age 65 you will have $205,516.8343.

Too Little

Continuing with the assumptions above, what would be your balance at age 65 if the monthly amount saved was $250 instead of $500?

Too Little
HP10BII FVA Calculation

12 □	P/YR	12 □	P/YR	12 □	P/YR
480	N	360	N	240	N
5	I/YR	5	I/YR	5	I/YR
0	PV	0	PV	0	PV
250	+/− PMT	250	+/− PMT	250	+/− PMT
	FV 381,505.0391		**FV 208,064.6588**		**FV 102,758.4171**

Start saving at age 25; 40 years (40*12 = 480 months) later, at age 65 you will have $381,505.0391.

Start saving at age 35; 30 years (30*12 = 360 months) later, at age 65 you will have $208,064.6588.

Start saving at age 45; 20 years (20*12 = 240 months) later, at age 65 you will have $102,758.4171.

Too Conservatively

Continuing with the assumptions above, a $250 monthly investment and an after-tax return of 2%, what amount will be available for your retirement?

Too Conservatively
HP10BII FVA Calculation

12 □	P/YR	12 □	P/YR	12 □	P/YR
480	N	360	N	240	N
2	I/YR	2	I/YR	2	I/YR
0	PV	0	PV	0	PV
250	+/− PMT	250	+/− PMT	250	+/− PMT
	FV 183,608.9062		**FV 123,181.3469**		**FV 73,699.2086**

Start saving at age 25; 40 years (40*12 = 480 months) later, at age 65 you will have $183,608.9062.

Start saving at age 35; 30 years (30*12 = 360 months) later, at age 65 you will have $123,181.3469.

Start saving at age 45; 20 years (20*12 = 240 months) later, at age 65 you will have $73,699.2086.

These examples produce a range of future retirement savings from $73,699 to $763,010. Obviously, committing all three mistakes, saving too little, too late, and too conservatively, will yield the worst possible outcome. In this example, the worst case outcome yields an accumulation of retirement savings more than 10 times smaller than the best case outcome. This can make the difference between providing yourself with a comfortable retirement or possibly no retirement at all.

9.1.2 How Much Do You Need to Save for a Comfortable Retirement?

The answer to this question depends on how many years you have until retirement, how long you estimate living after retirement, your desired standard of living, the rate of return on your investments, inflation, income taxes and the availability of other assets which you can use to produce retirement income. Let's look at each of these factors now.

Years until Retirement

In financial planning the period until retirement is often referred to as work life expectancy or WLE. It's common to assume a retirement age of 65, but this will vary depending on individual circumstances. Many employer-sponsored plans are based on a full retirement age of 65, but some may offer retirement benefits as early as 55. According to the Department of Labor, the average retirement age in the US in 2010 was 62.6 years. This implies that on average, even if you start saving right out of college, you cannot reasonably expect to save for retirement for more than four decades. So time is of essence when it comes to building your retirement savings.

Expected Lifespan after Retirement

The period of your life you expect to spend in retirement is often referred to as retirement life expectancy or RLE. None of us knows how long we will live, but there are ways to estimate this based on birth year, current age and status of health and family medical history. The purpose of estimating RLE is to allow planning for enough retirement assets to support you for life and minimize the chances of outliving your assets and income (superannuation). Currently, the average 65 year old female has a 20-year RLE, while the average 65 year old male has a 17 year RLE. Clearly, younger generations should plan for a longer RLE, as medical and technological breakthroughs will improve health care and effectively prolong life expectancy.

Notice that working life expectancy (WLE) and retirement life expectancy (RLE) are interrelated. If you want to retire early in your life (WLE ↓), then you will spend more years in retirement (RLE ↑), which will increase the needed amount of retirement savings. On the other hand, delaying retirement (WLE ↑) implies spending fewer years in retirement (RLE ↓), which will decrease the needed amount of retirement savings. Keep in mind however, that delaying retirement because you have not saved enough may not always be a realistic strategy. Lack of employment opportunities at an advanced age, and/or deteriorating health may deprive you from the option to delay retirement.

Standard of Living

Most retirement planning assumes that a retiree desires to maintain approximately the same standard of living after retirement, as was the case immediately before retirement. What percentage of your pre-retirement income is necessary to do this depends on each individual. If you are approaching retirement soon and have identified the location (state, city, beach) and type of your retirement (house, condo, retirement community), a financial planner could estimate your needed income very accurately based on current cost of living for your selected area and type of retirement choices. If you are decades away from retirement, your needed income can be estimated as a percentage of your current income. Financial planners call this the Wage Replacement Ratio (WRR) and it is usually between 70% and 80% of pre-retirement income. After retirement some expenses decrease or go away, but others will increase.

Expenses that will decrease:

(1) Social Security and Medicare withholding taxes. These taxes are withheld from earned income at a combined rate of 7.65% (15.3% for self-employed individuals), and they do not apply to retirement income.
(2) Saving for retirement.
(3) Some job related expenses such as commuting, parking, clothing and eating out.
(4) Mortgage loan repayment should be completed.

Expenses that will increase:

(1) Health care.
(2) Property taxes.
(3) Travel and entertainment.

Rate of Return on Your Investments

The rate of return on funds in an employer-provided pension plan or your Social Security retirement benefits is controlled by independent trustees who make the investment choices. These plans promise a formula-driven benefit for each retiree. However, you control the rate of return on the balances in individual retirement accounts (IRAs) and some employer-sponsored plans.

A fundamental rule of investing is that greater rewards come from assuming more risk. Choosing conservative investment options, like government bonds and money market products, may help you sleep at night but you may forgo a few percentage points of compound returns for decades. The example in Section 8.1.1 however, clearly indicates that the investment return is a critical factor in your retirement planning success. As a general rule, your investment choices should be more aggressive (risky but with significant gain potential) in your younger years. As you age, you should shift into more conservative investments to reflect the fact that as you near retirement, your tolerance for risk is less. in the event of a market downturn, you have a shorter time to recover. You will have many choices for investment including mutual funds, stocks, bonds, real estate and even precious metals.

All investment choices should be reviewed periodically and adjusted to reflect your individual situation. If you achieve significant gains in the early years of retirement savings, the temptation will be there to continue with an aggressive strategy. Many mature retirement savers failed to adjust their portfolios to a more conservative mix and as result their retirement accounts suffered significant losses during the 2000–2001 and 2008–2009 stock market crashes.

Inflation

Inflation is defined as a continuous increase in the aggregate price level, and it is manifested as an increase in the cost of living over time. Inflation causes a decline in the purchasing power of your money, which means that today's dollar will buy less in the future. For instance, consider the effect of an average 3% decline of the purchasing power of the dollar over a long period of time (resembling a retirement life expectancy). In 10 years the dollar will lose about 26% of its purchasing power ($1-0.7374 = 0.2626$), in 20 years it will lose about 45% ($1-0.5438 = 0.4562$), while in 30 years it will lose almost 60% ($1-0.4010 = 0.5990$) of its purchasing power.

Inflation

HP10BII FV Calculation

1 □ P/YR	1 □ P/YR	1 □ P/YR
10 N	20 N	30 N
3 +/− I/YR	3 +/− I/YR	3 +/− I/YR
1 +/− PV	1 +/− PV	1 +/− PV
FV 0.7374	**FV 0.5438**	**FV 0.4010**

Therefore even having "a million dollars" saved for retirement may not be enough. Assuming annual inflation of 3%, today's $1,000,000 will only have the purchasing power of $543,794.34 in 20 years, so setting a retirement goal has to allow for expected inflation during the WLE and RLE years.

Income Taxes

Investment income such as dividends, interest and capital gains is subject to current income taxes, and this can consume a fourth or more of your gross return. Fortunately, there are some tax breaks for retirement savers to delay or even eliminate these taxes, leaving you with more funds to invest. Employer-sponsored plans may allow for employees to defer some salary into the plans, and the amounts deferred are often deducted from currently taxable income. The amounts put into these plans by the employer on behalf of eligible employees are also not currently taxable, leaving the entire amounts available for investment and growth. Of course, there is a day of reckoning for these funds as they are taxed upon withdrawal at the personal income tax rates in effect at that time.

Remember that the IRS doesn't go away when you retire. "A million dollars" in retirement savings which you have not paid income taxes on will be taxed as you withdraw it, so aim high in your savings goals to allow for income taxes.

One little noticed fact is that the amounts withheld from your salary for Social Security and Medicare are taxable income. Look at your next Form W-2 to verify this. And then, when you begin receiving Social Security retirement benefits, some part of your benefits may be taxable, depending on your income level from other sources.

Income from Other Assets

You may acquire or inherit significant income-producing assets during your lifetime, and these assets are held outside of retirement accounts. These investments can take many forms such as stocks, bonds, mutual funds, life insurance policies, rental real estate or even assets held in a trust account. Usually they produce currently taxable income which is available for consumption or re-investment. Obviously, the more assets you have available to complement your retirement account assets, the lower the needed retirement savings you will have to accumulate, and the easier it will be for you to retire early and/or comfortably. You should be careful however, to monitor the combined risk profile of all assets inside and outside of retirement accounts.

9.1.3 Practical Application: Retirement Need Calculation

The Milfords, Ric 42 years old and Vanessa 39 years old, have a combined gross income of $130,000. They would like to retire once Vanessa becomes 65 years old, so both will be covered by Medicare. They expect to live 25 years in retirement (RLE), and would like to be able to receive 80% of their pre-retirement gross income as retirement income. They expect to receive $38,000 per year from Social Security, in today's dollars. They have accumulated $100,000 in their retirement accounts, and they believe they will be able to earn 8.5% pre-tax return on all their investment assets, while inflation will average 3% per year throughout their life. How much do the Milfords need in retirement savings to achieve their goals?

To estimate the needed retirement savings we can use one of the three methods presented in this section. All three methods use the variables discussed this far in this chapter, and their only difference is how conservatively they estimate the needed savings amount.

A. Annuity Method (less conservative)

Step 1: Estimate the retirement income needed in today's dollars as follows:
(Current Gross Income * Wage Replacement Ratio) − Social Security Benefit = ($130,000 * 0.80) − $38,000 = $104,000 − $38,000 = $66,000 per year.

Step 2: Inflate retirement income needed to dollars reflecting the year of retirement:
Vanessa is 39 years old and the Milfords want to retire when she turns 65.
So WLE = 65 − 39 = 26 years.
With 3% inflation, $66,000 today purchase what $142,335.0237 will purchase in 26 years.

Step 3: Estimate the amount of retirement savings needed at the time of retirement:
This is an annuity due calculation, as annual retirement savings withdrawals will be taking place at the beginning of every year (RLE = 25 years) to allow for living expenses during the year.
Also, while the Milfords are expecting to earn 8.5% nominal annual return on their investments, inflation will be eroding the purchasing power of their retirement assets and the Milfords will need to increase their annual withdrawals by the rate of inflation 3%, to maintain the same standard of living. Therefore, we will need to use the real rate of return for this calculation:
$I_R = [(1+ i_N /1+\pi) - 1] * 100 = [(1.085/1.03) - 1] * 100 = 5.3398\%$.
The required Savings at the time of retirement are $2,043,049.9378.

Step 4: Estimate the monthly savings required during the remaining working life expectancy to reach the retirement savings goal from step 3:
WLE = 26 years, therefore N = 26 years * 12 months/year = 312 months.

Annuity Method

HP10BII Keystrokes

STEP-2		STEP-3		STEP-4	
1 ☐	P/YR	1 ☐	P/YR ☐ BEG/END	12 ☐	P/YR
26	N	25	N	312	N
3	I/YR	5.3398	I/YR	8.5	I/YR
66,000	+/− PV	142,335.0237	PMT	100,000	+/− PV
	FV 142,335.0237	0	FV	2,043,049.9378	FV
			PV −2,043,049.9378		**PMT −1,002.4570**

The Milfords have accumulated already $100,000 in their retirement accounts. Therefore, the required monthly savings amount is $1,002.4570, which is quite doable given their annual income, and the fact that part of this monthly savings can come from the employers' contributions to the Milfords' retirement accounts.

While relatively straightforward, the annuity method's estimate of the required retirement savings ($2.4 million) cannot ensure the Milfords will not outlive their "nest egg." looking at step 3 in the previous table, FV = $0, which means all funds will be exhausted in exactly 25 years. What happens if the Milfords live longer? What happens if inflation is higher or the return on investments is lower than expected? The Milfords' retirement plan will be derailed with unpleasant consequences for the aging couple. Therefore, the annuity method's estimate of the needed retirement savings is best viewed as the bare minimum amount, or the starting point for a household's retirement planning.

B. Capital Preservation Method (more conservative)

One way to ensure the Milfords will not outlive their retirement savings is to plan to accumulate a "nest egg" large enough to provide the desired retirement income throughout the retirement life expectancy (RLE) years but also to provide an inheritance (or legacy) amount. Thus, if some of the model assumptions do not materialize over their lifetime, the Milfords could always rely on the legacy funds for their living expenses.

The capital preservation method plans for the legacy funds at the end of RLE to equal the retirement savings at the beginning of RLE. This is a concept similar to consuming their retirement funds and having them too. For this to happen, the Milfords will need to have at the end of their RLE $2,043,049.9378 (the "nest egg" estimated under the annuity method). A simple time value of money calculation will tell you that the Milfords need to have saved by the time they start their retirement an additional $265,788.0969, bringing their total retirement savings to $2,308,838.0347 ($2,043,049.9378 + $265,788.0969). The monthly savings required during their WLE would be $1,236.4745.

So for an additional $234 ($1002.4570 - $1,236.4745) per month in retirement Savings, the Milfords can reduce the risk of outliving their money, and possibly provide a nice inheritance to their children or to a charity.

Capital Preservation Method
HP10BII Keystrokes

1 ☐	P/YR	12 ☐	P/YR
25	N	312	N
8.5	I/YR	8.5	I/YR
2,043,049.9378	FV	100,000	+/− PV
	PV −265,788.0969	2,308,838.0347	FV
			PMT −1,236.4745

C. Purchasing Power Preservation Method (even more conservative)

This method plans for a legacy fund at the end of RLE, which is equal to the original retirement savings calculated with the annuity method, and adjusted for inflation. In other words, under this method the Milfords could consume their original retirement savings, and at the end of RLE leave a legacy with the same purchasing power as their retirement savings at the beginning of their retirement.

Repeating step 3 of the annuity method but instead of FV = $0 we set the FV = $2,043,049.9378 to equal the retirement savings balance at the date of retirement, we find that the Milfords need to have saved by the beginning of their retirement $2,599,551.1890. To raise this amount, the Milfords will have to save $1,492.4377 per month for the remaining 312 months of their work life expectancy.

While this monthly savings amount is $489.98 ($1,492.4377 - $1,002.4570) higher than the one required according to the annuity method, it will go a long way towards preventing the Milfords from outliving their funds. After all, one of the goals of financial planning is to reduce the uncertainty in clients' lives.

Purchasing Power Preservation Method
HP10BII Keystrokes

1 □ P/YR	□ BEG/END	12 □	P/YR
25	N	312	N
5.3398	I/YR	8.5	I/YR
142,335.0237	PMT	100,000	+/− PV
2,043,049.9378	FV	2,599,551.1890	FV
	PV −2,599,551.1890		**PMT −1,492.4377**

9.2 Sources of Retirement Income

Now that you know how to estimate how much you need to accumulate in retirement savings to provide yourself with the necessary income to retire with your desired lifestyle, let's look at the potential sources of your retirement income.

9.2.1 Social Security (The First Leg of the Retirement Stool)

History

The Social Security Act was signed into law in 1935 as a social insurance program to provide income to retired workers at age 65. Until 1940, payments to retirees were in the form of a lump sum which averaged $58.06. Monthly retirement benefits began in early 1940, and cost-of-living adjustments were added in 1950. Beginning in 1975, the law allowed for benefit adjustments based on the annual increase in consumer prices.

Amendments during the 1950s provided payments for disabled workers aged 50–65 and disabled adult children. During the 1960s, the minimum age for retirement benefits was lowered to 62, and Medicare was enacted into law providing health care coverage to Social Security beneficiaries age 65 and over.

According to the Social Security Administration, in 2013 almost 58 million Americans will receive Social Security benefits totaling $821 billion.

Social Security Retirement Benefits

Qualification: During your working career, Social Security taxes are withheld from your paychecks. At the 2013 percentage of 6.2% of the first $113,700 of annual wages, the maximum amount withheld is $7,049.40. Your employer pays 6.2% of your first $113,700 of annual wages as a matching amount for you. A self-employed individual pays both parts of Social Security and Medicare taxes.

As you pay Social Security taxes, you earn quarters of credit toward retirement benefits. In 2013 you earn one quarter of credit for each $1,160 in compensation up to the maximum of 4 quarters in one year. In other words, if you earned $4,640 in January and nothing for the remainder of the year, you earned 4 quarters of credit. Once you have earned 40 quarters of credit, you have qualified for a retirement benefit. The quarters do not have to be consecutive, allowing for individuals to enter and leave employment without losing their accumulated quarters of credit.

Amount of Your Benefit

The amount of your retirement benefit depends on your level of earnings while you are working and the age at which you decide to retire. The Social Security Administration will use the earnings during your highest 35 years, and each year will be indexed to current dollars to account for inflation. Your benefit, which is called a "primary insurance amount," is converted into a monthly dollar amount which is payable at your full retirement age and for the rest of your life. Importantly, it is up to each individual to decide when to begin Social Security retirement benefits.

Full retirement age depends on your year of birth. For example, if your birth year was 1957, your full retirement age is 66 years and 6 months. If your birth year was 1960 or later, your full retirement age is 67. Age 62 is the minimum age to receive a Social Security retirement benefit. If you begin your retirement benefit early, it will be permanently reduced depending on how many months remain until you reach full retirement age. The formula for calculating reduced benefits is as follows:

5/9 of 1% reduction for each month up to 36 months of early retirement
Plus
5/12 of 1% for each additional month up to 24 months of early retirement

For example, if in the month you turn 64 years old, you begin your benefit and your full retirement age is 67, your benefit will be reduced by 20% (5/9 * 1% * 36 = 20 %). Therefore, a full benefit of $1,200 will be reduced to $960.

If you decide to begin your benefit at age 63 and your full retirement age is 67, your benefit will be reduced even further:

5/9 * 1% * 36 = 20% plus 5/12 * 1%* 12 = 5%, for a total reduction of 25%

Deciding to begin your benefit at age 62 will result in a reduction of 30% using the same formula as above. The reduction for taking an early benefit is permanent. However, all Social Security retirement benefits are subject to annual cost-of-living increases based on changes in the consumer price index.

Earnings Limitation Test

If you begin your benefits early and you are still working, your benefits will be subject to an earnings limitation test. Since the Social Security benefit is designed to replace income received from working, if you earn more than $15,120 in a year before reaching your full retirement age, your Social Security benefit will be reduced by $1 for each $2 above $15,120. For example, if you have working income of:

Earnings	$25,120	
– Limit	($15,120)	
= Excess	$10,000	⇒ Social Security retirement benefits will be reduced by $5,000 in the next tax year.

When the calendar year arrives in which you reach full retirement age, the reduction changes to $1 for each $3 above $15,120, but this only applies until the month before full retirement age is reached. Once you reach full retirement age, the earnings limitation test does not apply and the full benefit is restored.

Taxation of Social Security Retirement Benefits

If you have income from sources other than Social Security retirement benefits, up to 85% of your Social Security retirement benefit may be subject to federal income tax. The threshold number from an income tax return is based on your modified adjusted gross income (MAGI), which is adjusted gross income plus certain deductions for higher education and other expenses. Taxation begins at $25,000 of MAGI (including one-half of your SS benefits) for a single return and $32,000 for a joint return. Taxation of the appropriate amount of SS retirement benefit is at the taxpayer's ordinary income tax rate.

9.2.2 Employer-Provided Retirement Plans (The Second Leg of the Retirement Stool)

Background

Today most individuals who work for an employer have access to some type of employer-sponsored pension or retirement plan. There is no requirement that an employer has to offer a pension or retirement plan, but if a plan is offered, it has to comply with government regulations. Participation in some plans is voluntary, but even with this option, most choose to participate. Regulation of employer-sponsored plans protects the interests of participants from employers and creditors.

The major regulation governing employer-provided plans is the Employee Retirement Income and Security Act of 1974 (ERISA). Enforcement of ERISA is handled by the Internal Revenue Service and the Department of Labor. Protections include requirements that benefits promised are paid and pension asset managers and administrators act always in the best interests of participants. In addition, ERISA established the Pension Benefit Guaranty Corporation (PBGC) to protect benefits promised to employees of failed companies and their retirement plans.

Retirement plans are either "qualified" or "non-qualified." A qualified plan has met the requirements of the IRS for this classification, and this allows employers to deduct current contributions to plans and for plan participants to defer taxation of benefits until funds are withdrawn. A qualified plan also has limitations on benefits for "highly-compensated" and "key employees." Qualified plans are classified as pension plans or profit-sharing plans, and they are further divided into defined benefit and defined contribution plans.

Qualified Plans

<table>
<tr><th></th><th>PENSION PLANS</th><th>PROFIT SHARING PLANS</th></tr>
<tr><td>DEFINED
BENEFIT
PLANS</td><td>Mandatory employer contribution
Less flexible / More expensive to run
Employer bears the risk</td><td rowspan="2">No mandatory contribution by employer
More flexible
Less expensive to run
Employee bears the risk</td></tr>
<tr><td>DEFINED
CONTRIBUTION
PLANS</td><td>Mandatory employer contribution
More flexible / Less Expensive
Employee bears the risk</td></tr>
</table>

i) Pension Plans

There are several types of pension plans, but we will focus only on one, a defined benefit pension plan, due to its prominence among employer-sponsored plans.

Defined Benefit Pension Plans

The name of this type of plan is very descriptive because as a participant you are promised a benefit. That benefit, simply stated, is that if you work for the employer long enough to own the benefit (called vesting) a specific amount will be paid to you during your retirement years. These are the traditional pension plans which have been popular for many decades.

However, the use of defined benefit pension plans has dropped dramatically in recent years due to cost and availability of other types of plans. According to the 2009 Pension Insurance Data Book, in 1980 there were 95,439 single employer programs while in 2009 the number of programs was down to 27,607.

Funding and Administrative Requirements

A pension plan is usually funded solely by the employer. Contributions to a plan are deducted from the employer's income and classified as an employee benefit. The funds are placed into a trust account where they are held for the benefit of all employees in the plan. Each year the plan must use an actuary to compute the amount needed to fund the promised benefits, and the company must fund those benefits without regard to the company's profitability. As years of service accumulate, the promised benefits increase and the amount needed in the plan grows. Many pension plans have seen the value of their investments shrink with recent turmoil in the stock and bond markets, and this produces additional pressure on plan sponsors to return their plans to fully funded status. Costly administration and mandatory contributions have caused many employers to freeze their pension plans and shift to other types of plans.

Eligibility to Participate

You are usually eligible to participate at age 21 and when a year of service has been completed. A year of service is defined as 1,000 hours worked in one 12-month period. An employer can permit eligibility under age 21 or 1,000 hours of service. These are standard requirements, but there are certain exceptions requiring up to 2 years of service.

Vesting

Vesting is the process by which employer-provided retirement funds become the permanent property of a plan participant. Funds placed into a retirement account that come from your salary deferrals are always 100% vested. Vesting takes place over time, and it usually occurs in one of two ways.

Cliff Vesting: Nothing is vested until a 5-year period of service has been achieved. If you leave before 5 years have passed, all funds provided by the employer are forfeited. After the 5-year period, all funds from the employer are 100% vested.

Graded Vesting: Vesting takes place in percentages of the amount provided by the employer. ERISA mandates that graded vesting has to begin after not later than 3 years and complete in not later than 7 years. A frequent schedule is 20% after 3 years and 20% annually until 100% is reached at the end of the seventh year. If you leave during the graded vesting period, you forfeit the unvested percentage of the employer-provided funds.

Defined Benefit Plans – Vesting Schedules

YEAR	5-YEAR CLIFF	7-YEAR GRADED
1	0%	0%
2	0%	0%
3	0%	20%
4	0%	40%
5	100%	60%
6		80%
7		100%

Employers can always be more generous to their employees with respect to the vesting schedules, but cannot be less generous than the vesting schedules in the above table. In addition, vesting increases to 100% if the employee reaches normal retirement age as defined in the plan or if the plan is terminated.

Limitations on Benefits

ERISA places limitations on benefits to certain "highly-compensated" and "key employees." These limits are to ensure that a plan does not discriminate in favor of those at the top and against the interests of the rank and file employees. In 2013 the maximum annual compensation which can be used to calculate pension benefits is $255,000 and the maximum annual pension benefit is $205,000.

Calculation of Benefits

There are several methods by which defined benefit pension plan benefits are calculated. We will discuss the unit credit calculation, which is based on the employee's salary, years of service and an annual percentage credit as defined in the plan documents.

"Employee's salary" is usually the final salary or the average of the highest 3 of the last 5 years.

"Years of service" is the number of years of service.

"Annual percentage credit" is specified in the pension plan document, and will vary from plan to plan.

For example, assume your salary is $80,000, you have completed 30 years of service and the credit for each year of service is 2%. Your annual pension benefit would be calculated as follows:

$80,000 * 30 years * 2% = $48,000 annual pension

Payment of Pension Benefits

Benefits are usually paid monthly for the life of the retiree. Once the payments have started, they are usually fixed and not adjusted for changes in the cost of living. This exposes you to gradual erosion in purchasing power due to inflation. If a married worker is covered by a pension plan, the plan must offer two types of annuities to provide retirement benefits to a surviving spouse. These benefits can be waived in writing by the spouse during the life of the participant. The first type of annuity required is a qualified pre-retirement annuity which provides retirement Income to a surviving spouse if the plan participant dies before retirement. The second type of annuity is a qualified joint and survivor annuity, which continues to pay a retirement benefit to the surviving spouse after the death of a retiree. An unmarried worker will have a slightly larger pension payment since neither of these survivor annuities will apply.

ii) Profit-Sharing Plans

The term "profit-sharing" denotes significant differences between these plans and a defined benefit pension plan. From the point of view of the employer, administrative costs to operate a profit-sharing plan are much lower than for pension plans. Also, in most Profit-Sharing Plans, annual funding by the employer is optional, allowing flexibility for strong earnings years versus weak earnings years or even operating losses. These differences have accelerated the growth of profit-sharing plans over the last few decades while the number of defined-benefit pensions has decreased significantly.

There are many types of profit-sharing plans. We will focus our attention on the two frequently-encountered versions of 401(k) plans, traditional and roth.

Traditional 401(k) Plans

These plans are also referred to as cash or deferred arrangements (CODA). They fall in the qualified plan category, and they can be offered by corporations, partnerships, proprietorships, limited liability corporations and some tax-exempt employers. Since these are qualified plans, they are subject to rules on eligibility to participate, non-discrimination in favor of "highly-compensated" employees, required coverage, vesting, income tax treatments and withdrawals.

The basic operation of a traditional 401(k) Plan is as follows:

(1) Your employer offers a plan to eligible employees who have the option to participate or not participate.
(2) If you agree to participate, you agree to delay receipt of some salary, and the amount deferred (usually a percentage of salary) is placed into a retirement account in your name. These funds are always vested. However, your access to these plan assets is restricted and may require payment of early withdrawal penalties and income taxes.

(3) The employer may agree to place company funds into your account in the form of a match and/or a pre-defined share of company profits. Employer contributions can be in the form of company stock or cash. The amounts from the employer can be changed from time to time to reflect the changing fortunes of the employer. Employer provided funds usually vest (become your permanent property) over a period not to exceed 6 years.

(4) You are given investment options of a variety of mutual funds with differing risks and objectives. If the company match is in the form of company stock, you must have the option of selling the stock and placing the sale proceeds in mutual funds. Periodically you can change your investment choices on both new money going in and funds already in the plan.

(5) Withdrawals of vested balances are permitted. Some plans allow loans of up to $50,000, which must be repaid with payroll deductions. Loans which are repaid are not distributions, and there is no income tax or 10% early withdrawal penalty unless the loan is not repaid.

Hardship withdrawals are also permitted if you can demonstrate an immediate and heavy need, which can only be met with the funds withdrawn. These withdrawals are subject to the 10% early withdrawal penalty and income taxes.

(6) At retirement there is no promised benefit as is the case with a defined benefit pension plan. You just have an account with an accumulated balance, and you have to decide how much to withdraw each year from your account. A rule of thumb used extensively in financial planning, is to limit your annual withdrawals to no more than 4% of your account balance. This conservative withdrawal schedule is consistent with reducing your risk of outliving your funds, even under a modest 4–5 annual investment rate of return. Opting for a higher annual withdrawal rate you will have to earn much higher rates of returns on your retirement assets to avoid superannuation.

(7) The amounts withdrawn are subject to ordinary income taxes, and as long as the withdrawals take place after age 59 ½ there is no early withdrawal penalty. At your death the balance is transferred to a beneficiary or to co-beneficiaries which you have selected.

Eligibility to Participate

The standard qualified plan eligibility requirements of one year of service (1,000 hours in a 12-month period) and age 21 must be met. Employers can allow plan entry in less time of service and at an earlier age. In addition, some plans are "automatic enrollment safe harbor 401(k) plans" which allow immediate employee participation unless you choose not to participate. By choosing an automatic safe harbor 401(k) plan, the employer can avoid costly annual computations with regard to non-discrimination in favor of "highly-compensated" or "key employees."

Non-discrimination in Favor of Highly Compensated Employees

401(K) plans, with the exception of the automatic safe harbor 401(k) plans mentioned above, must meet annual tests comparing the actual deferral percentages and actual contribution percentages of "highly" and "non-highly" compensated employees. These tests may have the effect of limiting the salary deferrals from the "highly-compensated" employees.

Vesting

Employer-provided funds must vest 100% in no more than 3 years if the plan uses "cliff vesting," which means no vesting until 3 years have passed. If the plan offers "graded vesting," 20% of employer funds must vest in no more than 2 years and subsequent vesting must take place at 20% per year until the end of the sixth year. As stated earlier, the employer can always choose to be more generous with the vesting schedule, but not less generous than the vesting schedules of the following table. Keep in mind that the employee salary deferrals are always 100% vested.

Defined Contribution Plans—Vesting Schedules

YEAR	3-YEAR CLIFF	6-YEAR GRADED
1	0%	0%
2	0%	20%
3	100%	40%
4		60%
5		80%
6		100%

Forfeitures

Plan participants who terminate employment before the employer-provided funds are vested will forfeit the unvested amounts. These funds are returned to the plan, and they can be used toward the costs of operating the plan or allocated to the remaining participants according to a pre-determined formula.

Annual Limitations on Plan Contributions

In 2013 the IRS imposes a limit of $51,000 on plan contributions, regardless of the source. Funds can come from you, your employer and forfeitures. Your contribution is limited to $17,500 (up to age 49) and $23,000 (age 50 and above), subject to not exceeding 100% of compensation. Funds from your employer are then limited to the remainder.

Distributions From a Traditional 401(k) Plan

A distribution is a withdrawal which you do not intend to return to the plan. The intent of a 401(k) plan is to allow you to save money for retirement, so plan rules discourage withdrawals prior to age 59 ½ except for death, disability or retirement. A 10% early withdrawal penalty applies to most other withdrawals. Since income taxes have not been paid on salary deferrals and employer contributions to traditional 401(k) balances, all distributions are taxable. Examples of distributions include:

An unpaid loan balance, hardship withdrawals, balances not rolled over into another plan, and periodic withdrawals for retirement.

If you terminate employment but you don't retire, you will have an option to withdraw the vested balance in your 401(k) plan, and pay income taxes and possibly the 10% early withdrawal penalty (if you are under age 59 ½). But you also have the option of rolling the balance into another tax-deferred account which will delay taxation and the 10% penalty. There are two types of rollovers—direct and indirect; one is easy and the other is complicated.

A direct rollover is the easy choice. You establish another tax-deferred account, probably a traditional IRA, and you instruct the trustee of the 401(k) plan to transfer the entire balance to your new account.

An indirect rollover will happen when you tell your soon-to-be former employer to send you the balance while you decide what you want to do with it. The check you will receive will only be for 80% of the balance because the 401(k) account trustee has to withhold 20% and remit that to the IRS. If you then decide to roll your balance into a new tax-deferred account, you have a maximum of 60 days and you have to find the 20% that was sent to the IRS from other sources so that the totals coming out of your 401(k) account and going into your IRA are the same. Since you ended up avoiding a taxable distribution, you can apply for a refund of the 20% previously withheld by your former employer, on your next income tax return.

As you begin retirement, you may choose to delay distributions from your traditional 401(k), and you can do this until the year in which you turn age 70 ½. At that age your balance will be subject to IRS imposed required minimum distributions. Each year thereafter your balance at the end of the prior year will be divided by a factor from an irs table, and you will be required to withdraw that minimum amount and pay income taxes on the funds withdrawn. Failure to withdraw at least the minimum amount will result in a penalty of 50% of the amount that should have been withdrawn but was not.

One option for the balance in your account is to purchase a life annuity from an insurance company. This will make sure that you have a regular income for as long as you live, and it will relieve you of the responsibility of making investment decisions.

Another choice is for you to make periodic withdrawals at a rate you will determine based on your investment results, need for funds, expectations for life expectancy, but always subject to the required minimum distribution rule. Remember, the IRS will be eagerly waiting for your retirement to collect income taxes on all salary deferrals and investment earnings accumulating over decades in your retirement account.

Roth 401(k) Plans

Roth 401(k) plans have been available since 2006. They have many common features with traditional 401(k) plans, but there is a major difference in taxation. In a roth 401(k), your contributions as an employee are after tax, in contrast to the before-tax treatment of a traditional 401(k). At distribution, you have paid taxes on all of your contributions and you will pay no income taxes on the accumulated earnings in the account. In other words, you have created a tax-free source of retirement income.

If an employer offers a Roth 401(k), it must also offer a traditional 401(k). There is no employer matching contribution for a Roth 401(k), and this requires you to evaluate carefully your decision on whether to participate in one or both types of plans. You can divide your $17,500 annual limit ($23,000 if age 50 or older) between the two plans any way you choose, but it makes sense to put enough in the traditional to qualify for the full employer match and then put additional salary deferrals into the Roth.

A withdrawal from a Roth is income tax and penalty free if it meets the requirements of a qualified distribution. To fulfill these requirements the account must have been open for five tax years and the distribution must be due to the account owner's death, disability or reaching the age of 59 ½.

A distribution which is not a qualified distribution may be subject to taxes and early withdrawal penalties, depending on your age and the nature of the funds withdrawn.

Required minimum distributions also apply to Roth 401(k) accounts starting in the year you reach 70 ½. The computations are the same as for a traditional 401(k).

9.2.3 Individual Retirement Arrangements (The Third Leg of the Retirement Stool)

IRAs

IRAs have been offered since 1974, and they share many of the same benefits and characteristics of qualified plans. We will focus on the two main types of IRAs:

Traditional, which offer the possibility of tax deductible contributions in the accumulation phase, but have taxable distributions during the retirement years, and Roth, which can be funded only with after tax contributions, but offer tax free distributions. Note that while these are individual accounts, meaning they have only one owner, that owner can name one or more beneficiaries to receive the balance in the account at the death of the account owner.

IRAs are held by a custodian, usually a mutual fund company, bank, credit union or a securities brokerage firm. An annual custodian's fee is charged and the amount will depend on the complexity of the account.

Eligibility to Invest in a Traditional IRA

Your annual eligibility to place funds in a traditional IRA requires only that you have earned income (salary, bonus, commission, alimony) during the year. The IRS rules allow you to invest up to $5,500 ($6,500 if you are age 50 or older), but not exceeding the amount of your earned income. You can make your investment during the calendar year but not later than the date on which you file your tax returns for that year.

These annual $5,500 contributions can compound tax-deferred into a significant amount during your working years. For example, $5,500 invested at the end of each year for 40 years at a 9% return will produce a balance of $1,858,353.45. Therefore, you will be well advised to take advantage of the availability of this account and your eligibility to participate in one, to build additional retirement assets to complement your employer retirement account assets.

HP10BII FVA Calculation

1 ☐	P/YR
40	N
9	I/YR
0	PV
5,500	+/− PMT
	FV 1,858,353.4477

There is one exception to the earned income requirement and it is called a spousal IRA. When only one spouse has earned income, that spouse can transfer funds to the other spouse for investment in a second IRA. As an example, if one spouse earns $11,000 that spouse can contribute $5,500 to each of two accounts. If the individuals are age 50 or older, the contributions can be $6,500 each, subject to an earned income requirement of at least $13,000.

Eligibility to Deduct Contributions to a Traditional IRA

Being able to deduct your annual IRA contribution depends on several factors. The first test is whether or not you are an "active participant" in a qualified or other retirement plan. If you are not an active participant, you can deduct the full amount of your contribution without any income restrictions.

On the other hand, if you are an active participant (defined as one who has received or accrued a benefit from a qualified Plan, SIMPLE, SEP, 403(b) plan or annuity plan), your deductibility will depend on the level of adjusted gross income on your income tax return.

Different AGI limits are imposed depending on your tax filing status. An active participant filing a single return has a limit of $59,000 in 2013, and an active participant using married filing jointly status has a limit of $95,000. Incomes above these limits are subject to phase out ranges of $10,000 and $20,000 respectively beginning at the lower limits. When the lower limit plus the range is reached, you cannot deduct any of your IRA contribution. AGI within the range limits deductibility proportionately to the percentage above the lower limit. For example:

Filling Status	Lower Limit	Upper Limit	AGI	% Deductible	% Not Deductible
Single	$59,000	$69,000	$60,000	90%	10%
Single	$59,000	$69,000	$64,000	50%	50%
Single	$59,000	$69,000	$68,000	10%	90%

Contributions cannot be made to a traditional IRA after the account owner reaches age 70 ½, and the required minimum distributions begin.

Investing Your IRA Contributions

The IRS allows a wide variety of permitted investments for funds in traditional and Roth IRAs. Mutual funds, stocks, bonds, limited partnership interests, options, bank certificates of deposit and rental properties are often used. Life insurance and collectibles are prohibited investments.

Prohibited Transactions

It is important to understand that contributions to an IRA are only in cash. Consequently, an IRA owner can use cash in the account to purchase permitted investments only from third parties. An IRA cannot borrow money, lend money or be used as collateral for a loan. Purchasing property for present or future personal use is also prohibited. If the account owner makes a prohibited transaction, the account is no longer an IRA and the entire balance is a distribution subject to income taxes and possibly a 10% early withdrawal penalty.

Traditional IRA Distributions

As a general rule, withdrawals from a traditional IRA are subject to taxation as ordinary income in the year of withdrawal. The exception is non-deductible contributions, which of course have already been taxed. An IRA is a retirement savings account, and to discourage withdrawals prior to age 59 ½, the IRS enforces a 10% early withdrawal penalty in addition to taxation.

Some exceptions to the 10% penalty are death, disability, higher education expenses, up to $10,000 for a first-time home purchase and taking substantially equal periodic payments over the expected lifespan of the IRA holder.

The balance in a traditional IRA is subject to the required minimum distributions (RMD) rule in the year the account owner reaches age 70 ½. The same IRS formula used for traditional 401(k) accounts is applied to the balance in the IRA at the end of the calendar year before the taxpayer reaches age

70 ½, and the first required distribution must be taken by April 1 of the next calendar year. The IRS penalty for failure to take a timely RMD is 50% of the amount not taken.

Eligibility to Invest in Roth IRAs

Roth IRAs, available since 1997, share many of the characteristics of traditional IRAs. Annual contribution limits, investment choices and prohibited transactions are the same, but contributions can be made to a Roth IRA even after age 70 ½, as long as you have earned income.

Unlike traditional IRAs, contributions to a Roth IRA are not tax deductible and qualified distributions are not taxable. Individuals face an income limitation which restricts higher income earners from making Roth IRA contributions. Computations are similar to the phase-out ranges used by individuals who receive or accrue benefits from qualified plans and want to invest in a traditional IRA. The Roth phase-out ranges begin at AGI of $112,000 for single tax filers and $178,000 for those who are married and file jointly. These limits have prevented many high-income taxpayers from using Roth IRAs.

Conversions from Traditional to Roth

If you are a higher income taxpayer, you may decide to convert your traditional IRA to a Roth. You should consider present income tax rates and anticipated tax rates in the future. If you conclude that marginal tax rates will be higher when you need your distributions, a conversion may be beneficial. At conversion time the amount of the distribution is taxable at ordinary income tax rates. The amount of the tax can be paid over two tax years at your option. However, any possible early withdrawal penalty is waived as long as the conversion is a timely rollover into the Roth account. The amount going into the Roth IRA will be net of applicable taxes, and all future qualified distributions will be income tax free.

Summary

This chapter has focused on the financial aspects of retirement planning with emphasis on the need for multiple sources of lasting retirement income. When you think of your retirement, you should consider additional factors such as how you will spend your time, where you will live and the needs of other members of your family. Every person has a unique situation, and working through this major life-changing event takes extensive long-range planning and preparation. Back to our three earlier admonitions: Don't delay your planning and saving–start now. As you plan for when your paychecks stop, put aside enough in your working years to continue your lifestyle and remain financially independent for life. Make smart and aggressive investment decisions appropriate for your age, and lastly, take advantage of the tax protected retirement accounts described in this chapter to help you grow more retirement savings faster.

Review Questions

1. Assume you can only do one of the following: Save for your children's college education or save for your retirement. Which would you choose and why?

2. What are the factors that you should take into account during your retirement planning?

3. What changes would you make to the Social Security retirement program to accommodate the needs of future retirees?

4. What two factors determine the amount of a person's Social Security retirement benefit?

5. Ric Milford's wife, Vanessa, is 3 years younger than Ric, and she intends to retire from her job as a school teacher at the same time Ric retires at age 67. If she begins her Social Security retirement benefits when she retires, what percentage of her full retirement benefit will she receive?

6. How much will an individual have withheld from his or her paycheck for (a) Social Security and (b) Medicare in 2013 if the annual salary is $145,000?

7. You own a 2-year-old business supplying paper and plastic products to restaurants. The business is new and the cash flows have been erratic. You want to start a retirement plan at your business for yourself, but also as a tool to attract and retain employees. You don't want to spend too much money or time administering the plan. Would you prefer a defined benefit or a defined contribution plan?

8. Your employer's defined benefit pension plan promises to pay you a monthly pension of $2,500 when you retire. What is the good news and what is the not-so-good news about the payments you will receive?

9. Using the unit credit formula and 2013 IRS rules, calculate the annual pension benefit for a person with average annual final compensation of $300,000, 30 years of service and a pension accrual rate of 1.50%.

10. You leave your job after 4 years. You had contributed $20,000 to your 401(k) plan account, and your former employer had contributed another $20,000. What will be the available amount you can rollover to an IRA after you leave your job, if your 401(k) plan followed a 6-year graduated vesting schedule?

11. When you use the indirect rollover method of transferring a balance in your former employer's traditional 401(k) plan to an IRA, what are the consequences?

12. Explain the differences between eligibility to invest contributions and eligibility to deduct contributions to a traditional IRA.

13. Michael Milford (now age 18) worked as a lifeguard at the local swimming pool and his earnings for the season were $4,200. He has agreed to put half of his earnings in an IRA account. Would you recommend a Roth IRA or a traditional IRA?

14. Ric Milford currently earns an annual base salary of $80,000. He is 42 years old and anticipates retiring in 25 years at age 67. If inflation averages 3.5% per year and his base salary increases at the inflation rate, what will his base salary be at the time he retires?

15. At age 42 Ric has $300,000 in retirement savings. He wants to retire at age 67 and have $1,500,000 for retirement. If he can earn an annual after-tax rate of return of 7%, how much will he need to save at the end of each month?

16. Sabrina earns $70,000 a year, pays $5,355 in payroll taxes, saves $8,400 for retirement, and spends $17,500 on a mortgage which intends to pay off completely before retiring at age 65. What will be Sabrina's wage replacement ratio at retirement?

For the following seven questions use the following facts:

Jason is 25 years old this year and wants to plan for his retirement. He thinks he needs to work until he is 65 years old, and then retire. His family history indicates longevity, therefore he believes he will live to be 95 years old. Currently he earns $65,000 a year, and he would like to replace 80% of his salary during retirement. Social Security will provide him with an annual benefit of $18,000 in today's dollars. He has no savings at this point in time, but he is committed to saving for retirement from now on. He believes he can earn an average 10% pre-tax return on his investments, while inflation will average 3.5% A year throughout his life.

17. What is Jason's wage replacement income need at today's prices?

18. According to the annuity method, what should Jason's retirement savings be at the age of 65, to be able to retire as he desires?

19. How much will Jason have to save at the end of every month until the age of 65, to be able to reach his retirement goal?

20. Using the capital preservation method, what should Jason's retirement savings be at the age of 65, to be able to retire as he desires?

21. How much more will Jason need to save at the end of every month until retirement, to be able to reach his retirement goal under the capital preservation method instead of the annuity method?

22. Using the purchasing power preservation method, what should Jason's retirement savings be at the age of 65, to be able to retire as he desires?

23. How much more will Jason need to save at the end of every month until retirement, to be able to reach his retirement goal under the purchasing power preservation method instead of the annuity method?

CHAPTER TEN

Estate Planning: Closing the Book and Leaving a Legacy

10.1 Introduction

This chapter covers an important part of personal financial planning, a topic that many people are uncomfortable with, estate planning. Admitting that we are mortal and that, sooner or later, each of us will have to deal with the deaths of friends, family members and ourselves is difficult. But the consequences of ignoring planning for what is inevitable can be costly, both in monetary ways and also in the emotional toll it may take on your survivors.

How do you want to be remembered by your survivors? If you don't prepare and execute the necessary documents while you are alive, how will your survivors know what you want to do with your estate (the assets you own at death) and how you want your ongoing responsibilities (guardianship for your minor children, care for aging parents or arrangements for children of any age with special needs) to be carried out? Specific instructions from you can head off confusion about your intentions and help your survivors through a transition period with minimal difficulty and emotional turmoil.

It's your choice. Will you be remembered as one who planned carefully for the benefit of your survivors or will they argue and fight over your estate, not knowing what your intentions were?

10.1.1 The Estate Planning Process

You might think of estate planning only in the context of preparing for infirmity, old age and death. It's actually a lifelong process of accumulating, preserving and distributing assets. Your distributions may start during your lifetime and continue after your death therefore, it takes special planning to navigate the details of the gift, estate and generation-skipping transfer taxes.

The process for all estates, small and large, begins with your commitment to seek professional advice from a trusted expert. **Step 1** is to select this person, who may be an attorney, Certified Financial Planner™, certified public accountant or some other skilled professional. An important part of selecting a competent advisor is to choose someone you can trust he or she will put your interests first. In your initial meeting, you should discuss what the advisor will charge and what each party's duties are.

In **step 2** your advisor will ask you for complete and comprehensive financial information. This will include current lists of your assets and debts, recent income tax returns, bank, brokerage, and retirement account statements, life insurance policies, how your assets are actually titled (single ownership or joint with other parties) and benefit summary statements from employer-provided benefit plans.

Step 3 consists of your advisor's analysis of this information to develop a full picture of your financial position.

In **step 4** your advisor will create a plan to fulfill your wishes. You and your advisor will discuss the plan, make adjustments as necessary and then agree on a timetable and responsibilities for implementation.

Logically, **step 5** is to implement all aspects of the plan. This may include document preparation and execution, changing ownership of some assets, consolidating investment accounts, changing beneficiaries on insurance policies and other actions to make the plan both efficient and effective. In this sense, "efficient" means your transfers incur the lowest possible cost, while "effective" means your transfers actually happen as you intend.

Step 6 in this process is a periodic review of the plan to see if your evolving circumstances over time call for plan modifications. Major life events such as marriage, divorce, births of children, deaths of family members and retirement are among the changes which may call for plan revisions.

10.1.2 Estate Planning Documents

Comprehensive estate planning covers not only planning for transfers at death but also providing lifelong goals for accumulating and protecting wealth. To accomplish this, several fundamental documents are necessary.

Wills

A "will," sometimes called a "last will and testament," is a legal document you execute to direct the transfer of your estate at your death to recipients of your choosing and to appoint individuals to handle your on-going responsibilities, such as guardianship for minor children or others. In addition, you get to choose a person or persons to handle your estate. This person formerly had the title of executor (male) or executrix (female), but today's terminology is most often personal representative.

To execute a valid will, you must be of legal age (18 or older in most states), you must be competent and understand the consequences of your instructions and you must not be under any undue outside pressure from other parties regarding your instructions.

Wills prepared by an attorney are called statutory wills, and they are usually typewritten. Many states permit handwritten wills, referred to as holographic wills. Oral wills can be accepted in some states, but the intentions of the person can often be misinterpreted.

Statutory wills usually have to be signed with witnesses present. These witnesses cannot be recipients of any benefits from the decedent's estate. A self-proving will has the witnesses' signatures notarized, and this expedites the process of validating that the document bears the signature of the decedent. Otherwise, the witnesses may have to testify in court that they actually saw the execution of the document.

Once you execute a will, you can revoke it or change it at any time. A will is an inactive document until the death of the will maker. You can revoke it by destroying all copies with original signatures or you can include wording in your new will stating that "this is my last Will and I hereby revoke all prior Wills." In some cases, you may want to make only a minor change, such as deleting a paragraph and substituting a new paragraph in its place. In that case, you and your attorney would either prepare a new will or a codicil, which leaves your existing will in place and defines the change you want to make. The codicil must also be witnessed, and it should be kept with the original will.

Typical wills include clauses that appoint a personal representative, identify the place of residence of the will maker, direct the distribution of the decedent's estate assets, provide for payment of debts and taxes owed by the decedent at death and by the estate while it is under administration, appoint guardians for legal dependents and/or minor children and a disclaimer clause allowing an heir to refuse a bequest.

Wills also may include a no contest clause to deter heirs who do not feel they have been fairly treated from overturning the wishes of the decedent in court. This clause will reinforce the decedent's intentions by reducing or denying any distribution to the heir in the event of a contest.

It is interesting to know that you already have a will, whether or not you have actually executed a valid document. That may come as a shock to you, but each state has a will for residents who die without an executed, valid document. A person who dies (called a "decedent") with a valid will is said to have died "testate," while a person who dies without a will is "intestate." Your state has intestacy laws that provide for distribution of an intestate decedent's assets according to a formula. Usually, intestate distribution is only to blood relatives with your surviving spouse as first priority. However, if you have surviving minor children, the arbitrary formula may also distribute a percentage of your estate assets to them. If you have no surviving spouse or minor children, the formula may assign assets to other blood relatives such as parents and siblings. In addition, a guardian and, if necessary a trustee, for your minor children will be court-appointed. State laws govern the process of estate administration through special probate courts, which are located in the county in which the decedent lived.

Having a valid will is a key part of estate planning, but you should also prepare and execute other important documents during the implementation phase. These documents will include your instructions on how to handle major life events and circumstances when you are unable to handle them for yourself.

Power of Attorney

A power of attorney is a legal document in which you, the principal, grant authority to someone else, your agent or attorney-in-fact, to act on your behalf. To execute a power of attorney, you must have attained the legal age of majority (18 in most states) and you must be legally competent. A power of attorney can be general or limited to specific actions, and it can be cancelled by the principal at any time. At the death of the principal, a power of attorney ends.

A power of attorney may be "durable," in which case the powers granted survive the incapacity of the principal and only end at the death of the principal. This is often used by aging parents who grant their child or children the authority to handle their affairs when they are no longer able to do so on their own.

Power of Appointment

A power of appointment is another legal document involving a principal and an agent or attorney-in-fact. The authority granted is to transfer ownership of the principal's assets. A power of appointment can be general or limited, and it can survive the death of the principal. It can also be revoked at any time, including by instructions in the principal's will.

A general power of appointment can allow the agent to transfer the principal's property to anyone, including to the agent. If the agent has a general power of appointment and the agent dies first, the property of the principal will be included in the agent's gross estate. Since a general power of appointment grants such wide authority, its use should be infrequent and only with a trusted agent.

A limited power of appointment on the other hand, can allow the agent to transfer the principal's property to anyone, including to the agent, but the power is limited by a measurable (ascertainable) standard like providing support for medical expenses, tuition costs, etc. When the power of appointment is limited by such a measure, then if the agent dies first, the property of the principal subject to the power will not be included in the agent's gross estate. For example, you want your sibling to take care of your aging parents while you are living and working in another state. You grant a limited power of appointment to your sibling over some assets (house, bank accounts) by specifying on the document that the assets are to be used only for the support of your parents. This way, you don't run the risk of your assets being inherited by your sibling's spouse if your sibling was to pass away unexpectedly.

Durable Health Care Power of Attorney

This is another type of power of attorney which deals with healthcare decisions. You can authorize a trusted person to make decisions regarding your medical treatment when you are unable to make these decisions, like under anesthesia or in a coma. Generally, it doesn't grant authority to terminate artificial life support, although in some states it does. Without this document, your health care decisions might have to be made through the legal process.

Living Will

A living will or advanced medical directive allows you to define your wishes on how much medical treatment you want when you are terminally ill, and under what circumstances to terminate artificial life support. Many states have natural death acts which permit you to make these choices on your own. Having a living will is a tremendous benefit to your friends and family because your wishes are known, thereby avoiding disputes at a stressful time.

Do Not Resuscitate Order

A do not resuscitate order indicates your wishes regarding usage of cardiopulmonary resuscitation (CPR) in the event your heart stops beating. It has nothing to do with other forms of medical treatment. This document is not usually executed until you are terminally ill. It should be located with your other medical records. Many states have DNR registries for quick access by medical professionals.

10.1.3 Property Titling

The ownership type of assets is a very important issue in estate planning because some assets can transfer automatically either through contract law (life insurance benefits, annuities, pension benefits), titling law (joint accounts), or trust law (trust assets), while other assets can only transfer through a will or the intestacy transfer process. Assets that only transfer by will or intestacy make up the probate estate. The total of the probate estate and all of the other decedent's ownership interests transferred by contract law, titling law, or trust law comprise the gross estate, which is used to determine whether or not the estate will be subject to federal and/or state estate taxes.

Assets owned only by you are classified as being held fee simple, and they will not transfer at death without going through probate. They are a part of the probate estate. Assets owned by you and one or more others fall into one of three categories of joint ownership. The method of ownership can be indicated in the title of the account, e.g. "Owner A and Owner B, Tenants in Common" or "Owner A and Owner B, Joint Tenants with Rights of Survivorship." However, a jointly owned bank account will have the method of ownership defined on the signature card.

The first joint ownership category is tenancy in common, which involves two or more joint owners, related or unrelated, of an asset. During life each owner can transfer his or her interest without permission of the others, and at the death of an owner, that owner's interest will only transfer through probate, thus becoming part of the decedent's probate estate.

A second joint ownership category is joint tenancy with right of survivorship (JTWROS). This also includes ownership interests by two or more persons, related or unrelated. The terms of the ownership contract are governed by state law and provide that at the death of an owner, that owner's interest is automatically transferred to the other owner(s). Property owned JTWROS does not transfer by will or intestacy, so it is not included in the probate estate. However, it will be included in the decedent's gross estate.

The final category of joint ownership applies to married couples. For common law states, tenancy by the entirety involves only two married individuals, neither of whom can transfer their interest to a third party without permission of the other. At the death of one spouse, the property automatically transfers to the survivor without going through probate. The value of these transfers however, will be included in the decedent's gross estate. For community property states (mainly in the southwest US) community property of married couples includes all assets acquired during the marriage. These assets cannot be transferred without permission by both spouses. In the event of a death of the first spouse however, unlike the tenancy by the entirety assets, community property assets do not transfer automatically to the surviving spouse. These assets will be distributed according to the will of the decedent by going through probate. Half the value of these assets will be included in the decedent's gross estate.

Keep in mind that in community property states, assets acquired by a spouse before the marriage, or by gift or inheritance are not considered community property assets, as long as, they are not commingled with other community property assets. For example, if Ric and Vanessa Milford lived in a community property state, and while married Vanessa inherited a townhome from her mother, the townhome will not be a community property asset. If vanessa rents the apartment and deposits the rents in her own bank account, the rents are community property because they represent income produced during the marriage.

Property interests can also be partial. For example, you can have legal title to an asset (legal ownership) and you can agree to allow another person to have full use and enjoyment of the property at the same time. The other person's interest is called beneficial ownership. If the period of beneficial ownership is for the life of the other person, their interest is called a life estate. If the period of beneficial ownership is defined as a period of time, e.g. 10 years, that is a term estate. At the end of either a life estate or a term estate, the property is transferred to another person who is called a remainder beneficiary.

For example, a trust (discussed in Section 10.3) holds the legal ownership of trust assets while the beneficiaries of the trust have the beneficial ownership of the assets.

10.1.4 The Probate Process

Recall from Section 10.1.2, that administration of estates is under the supervision of a special probate court. The probate process begins when the appointed personal representative locates the decedent's will and takes it to the probate court, where it will be accepted if the format, execution signature and witnesses' affirmations are in order. The personal representative will then be sworn in with a pledge to execute the instructions in the will honestly and fairly, and to submit to the court an inventory and accurate valuation of the estate's assets, to provide evidence of protection of the assets from harm, to pay legitimate debts and taxes owed by the decedent and the estate and to submit a final plan prior to distributing the estate's assets.

Advantages of Probate

The probate process protects the interested parties in an estate. First, it enforces the intentions of the decedent by insuring that the instructions in a will (or the intestacy laws) are followed. Secondly, it protects the creditors of the decedent because their legitimate claims will be paid from the estate's assets. Thirdly, assets transferred through probate are transferred to the recipients with clear title.

Disadvantages of Probate

The biggest disadvantage to the probate process is lack of privacy. Once a will is accepted for probate, the contents of the will are available to the public. You can go to a probate court anywhere in the US and obtain a copy of a probated will.

A second disadvantage of probate is the cost. Many states base their probate court fees on the size of the probate estate, and this can mean fees well in excess of $10,000. A third disadvantage is the amount of time it takes to transfer assets through probate. Assets transferring through contract law can be completed in short periods of time, but assets transferring through the probate process can take many months.

Individuals can minimize the disadvantages of the probate process by having their assets properly titled, which will make the transfers take place effectively but without the disadvantages of the probate asset transfer process. For example, using payable on death (POD for bank accounts) or transfer on death (TOD for investment accounts) designations retains single ownership of the asset during life, and only at death does the asset transfer by contract and outside of probate to the designated beneficiary(ies).

A significant estate planning technique involving creation of a trust during your lifetime is also an effective and efficient way to transfer assets outside of probate. This is a living trust which can be revoked during the life of the trust creator. Most of the individual's assets are transferred to the trust, which becomes irrevocable at death, and they are then transferred according to the beneficiary designation in the trust. Importantly, at death the assets belong to the trust and not to the decedent, so they transfer outside of probate. Trusts are discussed in Section 10.3.

Administering a Probate Estate

A probate estate includes the assets owned at death which have to transfer through the probate process. This is where the category of ownership is important. Assets owned fee simple and by tenancy in common are included because they have no transfer provision other than through probate. These assets must be valued by your personal representative either at date of death or six months later (the alternative valuation date). Assets which transfer through contract law are not part of the probate estate, but they have to be valued and included along with the probate estate assets in the gross estate. The gross estate is used to determine the estate tax.

Valuing estate assets can be a challenge for a personal representative. Bank, retirement and brokerage accounts, publically traded stocks, bonds and mutual funds and insurance proceeds are relatively easy to value. Hard to value assets include privately owned businesses, real estate, jewelry, antiques and collectibles. These typically require an independent appraisal.

One of the protections provided by probate is that the decedent's debts will be paid before assets are distributed. It is the duty of a personal representative to determine what the decedent owed and to validate claims from creditors. To accomplish this, the personal representative will post several weekly notices in a newspaper with general circulation in the city/county of the decedent's residence. The notice will identify the decedent and the personal representative and notify creditors to submit claims to the personal representative within a specified time (usually 90 days). Creditors will be informed that claims not submitted in time will be denied.

While an estate is open and under administration, the personal representative is responsible for collecting and protecting the decedent's assets. Collecting means locating the assets and transferring them into the name of the estate when possible. This would include taking title to assets such as vehicles, real estate, bank, retirement and brokerage accounts, mutual funds, stocks and bonds and collecting the death benefit from any insurance policies on the life of the decedent. Personal property such as jewelry and furniture should be secured and under control of the personal representative. Homeowner's policies protecting real estate and personal property must remain in force. During the period of the estate, income may be earned from the assets of the decedent. Examples would be interest, dividends or rent.

The personal representative is responsible for filing federal, state and/or local income tax returns on behalf of the decedent from the end of the last tax year filed by the decedent until the date of death. Any unpaid taxes must be paid and any income tax refunds due must be collected and included in the estate's assets. Prior to closing an estate, the probate court will require that appropriate estate income tax returns have been filed.

A third tax responsibility for the personal representative is to determine whether or not the estate is large enough to be subject to the estate tax at the federal and state level. Less than 1% of estates in the US are subject to the federal estate tax, but there may be an advantage to a surviving spouse to file an estate tax return even if no tax is due. Estate taxes are discussed in more detail in Section 10.2.

The final step in the probate process is to submit a report of the estate's assets, debts, expenses, taxes and distribution instructions to the probate court. When the report is approved, the personal representative will distribute the assets and close the estate.

10.2 The Federal Estate Tax (Transfers at Death)

The estate tax is a federal tax on the right to transfer assets. It applies to all US citizens and residents and to all assets owned at death regardless of where the assets are located. Non-US citizens and non- US residents are only subject to the US estate tax to the extent that their property is located in the US.

Gross Estate

The estate tax is based on the gross estate, which includes the assets in the probate estate, plus any other assets owned by or were under the control of the decedent. Assets transferring through contract (or state) law such as beneficiary designations on life insurance policies, retirement accounts, and assets transferring through titling law such as jointly owned property are included in the gross estate.

Assets transferring through titling law such as revocable living trusts (discussed in Section 10.3) are deemed to have been owned by the decedent, and must be included in the gross estate.

Gifts made and gift taxes paid within 3 years of death have to be considered in the estate tax computations. Life insurance proceeds may also have to be included. To remove life insurance proceeds from the gross estate total, the policy ownership must have been completely transferred more than 3 years before the individual died. A complete transfer means that the decedent had no retained right to cancel the policy, change the beneficiary, borrow or pledge the cash surrender value. Any revocable transfer or retained interest in property is included in the gross estate.

A single life annuity ends at the death of the annuitant, so no value is included in the gross estate. However, the present value of a survivor annuity which came from the decedent must be included.

Gross Estate

Asset and Type of Ownership	What Is Included in Gross Estate
Fee Simple Assets Revocable Living Trust Assets	100% of asset Fair Market Value (FMV)
Joint Tenancy JTWROS	Decedent's Actual share of ownership = contribution %
Tenancy by Entirety Community Property	Decedent's Deemed share of ownership = 50% of Asset FMV
Life Insurance Policy	100% of benefit, if decedent owned the policy within 3 years of death
Gifts	Gift Taxes paid within 3 years of death

The personal representative is responsible for valuing the assets in an estate. Some assets are easy to value and others are more difficult, requiring the services of independent appraisers. Assets in an estate are always valued at date of death. However, if the estate is large enough to be subject to the estate tax, the personal representative has the option of valuing the assets either at date of death or six months later (the alternative valuation date). The alternative valuation date allows the personal representative to choose the lower of the two totals for inclusion in the gross estate. However, even if the estate is valued as of the alternative valuation date, annuities must be valued at date of death, and property disposed of during the estate administration must be valued as of the date of disposition.

10.2.1 Calculating the Estate Tax

A personal representative is responsible for completing an estate tax return (Form 706) and submitting it to the IRS within 9 months of the decedent's date of death. The return may not be necessary for small gross estates where there is no estate tax liability, but a personal representative should consider filing to accomplish transferring the decedent's unused exemption amount to the surviving spouse.

Expenses of the Estate

While an estate is under administration, a personal representative will incur necessary expenses such as the probate court fee, asset transfer fees, appraisals, attorney and accounting fees, insurance to protect the estate's assets, final medical expenses for the decedent, funeral expenses, taxes, payments to the personal representative, debts of the decedent and any casualty losses to the property of the estate. These expenses are deductions on the estate tax return, thereby reducing the value of the gross estate.

Deductions

There are two categories of deductions available to the personal representative based on instructions in the will of the decedent. The first one is an unlimited charitable deduction. If the decedent's will provides for a mandatory and specific bequest to a qualified charity, that amount will qualify as a deduction. This can allow the decedent to direct estate assets to a favorite charitable cause instead of having the assets go to pay estate taxes. The second deduction is called the unlimited marital deduction, which includes all of the property in the estate passing to the surviving spouse. This can have the beneficial effect of eliminating the estate tax on the estate of the first spouse to die, and postponing any tax until the death of the second spouse.

Taxable Estate

To calculate the estate taxes it is required that lifetime taxable gifts made since 1976 be added to the taxable estate. This is where the estate and gift taxes join into one unified taxable amount. If there had been taxable gifts, the estate will deduct the amounts of taxes paid on these gifts.

Applicable Estate Tax Credit

Currently each person has a $5,250,000 lifetime exemption from estate and gift taxes combined. This allows tax free transfers during life and at death to total $5,250,000 before a transfer tax is incurred. The tax would amount to $2,045,800, but the applicable estate tax credit is used to offset this. Looking at the following chart, which applies to gift, estate and generation-skipping transfer tax computations, the estate tax for the first $1,000,000 of a taxable estate is $345,800. For any taxable estate amount above $1,000,000, the applicable tax rate is 40%. Therefore, the estate tax on a $5,250,000 taxable estate is calculated this way.

Taxable Estate	$5,250,000
Less first $1,000,000	($1,000,000)
	$4,250,000
Tax on first $1,000,000	$345,800
Tax on $4,250,000	$1,700,000
Total Tax	$2,045,800

For estates larger than $5,250,000, the estate tax rate is 40%. So for a taxable estate of $6,250,000, the applicable estate tax credit would eliminate the tax on $5,250,000, and the estate tax would be $400,000 (40% of the amount over $5,250,000).

Since 2010, the law allows for lifetime exemption portability. This means that if the decedent had an estate smaller than the $5,250,000 lifetime exemption amount, some of the applicable estate tax credit will not be used. Therefore, the surviving spouse could file an estate tax return, even though no estate tax is due, and transfer the other spouse's unused applicable estate tax credit for use when the second spouse dies. This results in a larger lifetime exemption and applicable estate tax credit for the second spouse's estate.

Unified Rate Schedule

Taxable Amount	Tax
Over $0 but not over $10,000	18% of such amount
Over $10,000 but not over $20,000	$1,800 plus 20% of the amount over $10,000
Over $20,000 but not over $40,000	$3,800 plus 22% of the amount over $20,000
Over $40,000 but not over $60,000	$8,200 plus 24% of the amount over $40,000
Over $60,000 but not over $80,000	$13,000 plus 26% of the amount over $60,000
Over $80,000 but not over $100,000	$18,200 plus 28% of the amount over $80,000
Over $100,000 but not over $150,000	$23,800 plus 30% of the amount over $100,000
Over $150,000 but not over $250,000	$38,800 plus 32% of the amount over $150,000
Over $250,000 but not over $500,000	$70,800 plus 34% of the amount over $250,000
Over $500,000 but not over $750,000	$155,800 plus 37% of the amount over $500,000
Over $750,000 but not over $1,000,000	$248,300 plus 39% of the amount over $750,000
Over $1,000,000	$345,800 plus 40% of the amount over $1,000,000

Adjusted Cost Basis and Holding Period for Estate Beneficiaries

The term "basis" is used in accounting to denote the cost of acquiring an asset. Comparing the cost of acquiring an asset (basis) with the price it is sold for later on, allows you to determine whether the sale resulted in a capital gain or loss. For most assets transferred from an estate to an heir, the heir receives a "step up" in basis to the fair market value (FMV) of that asset in the estate. In other words, the asset's FMV at the death of the decedent becomes the cost basis for the heir. What the decedent originally paid for the asset is no longer relevant. The heir's holding period of the asset is considered long term, no matter the decedent's holding period of the asset. So, when the heir sells the asset, any capital gain or loss is long term.

For example, Ric Milford inherited from his Aunt Jessica 100 shares of Apple, Inc. Aunt Jessica had purchased the shares 8 months before her unfortunate demise at $300 per share. At the time of her death the shares were trading at $500 per share. Ric sold the shares 3 months later for $600 per share. Ric receives a "step up" in basis to the FMV of the shares at the time of Aunt Jessica's death.

Ric's basis = 100 shares * $500/share = $50,000
Ric's capital gain = ($600 − $500) * 100 shares = $100 * 100 shares = $10,000
Ric's holding period of the Apple shares is long term because he inherited the shares, despite the fact that both Aunt Jessica and Ric each held the shares for less than one year.
Ric is facing a maximum LTCG tax rate of 20%, and a $2,000 maximum tax bill from the sale of the shares.

Some estate assets however, do not qualify for this "step up" in basis. If the estate contains assets on which income tax was deferred during the decedent's life, such as a traditional IRA, 401(k) account or an annuity, that asset is called an income in respect of a decedent (ird) asset and the new owner has the same basis in that asset as did the decedent.

10.2.2 Practical Application: Estate Tax Calculation

Motivated by Aunt Jessica's recent death, Ric Milford decided to talk to a Certified Financial Planner™ about starting his estate planning. Ric asked the financial planner to estimate the size of his estate and the possible estate taxes due if he was to die this year. The financial planner collected a lot of information from Ric and after careful analysis he estimated the following figures:

Gross Estate = $6,000,000, Expenses of the Estate = $400,000, Charitable Bequest = $100,000
Lifetime Taxable Gifts = $0, property passing to his spouse Vanessa = $2,000,000

Estate Tax Calculation for Ric Milford (Short Form)

Gross Estate	$6,000,000	
Expenses	($400,000)	
Adjusted Gross Estate	$5,600,000	
Charitable Deduction (Unlimited)	($100,000)	
Marital Deduction (Unlimited)	($2,000,000)	
Taxable Estate	$3,500,000	
Taxable Gifts	+ $0	
Tentative Tax Base	$3,500,000	
Tentative Tax	$1,345,800	[$345,800 + (0.40 * $2,500,000)]
Applicable Estate Tax Credit	$2,045,800	
Estate Tax	$0	

Because Ric wants to transfer $2,000,000 from his estate to Vanessa, utilizing the unlimited marital deduction to ensure Vanessa's well-being after his death, the size of his taxable estate ($3,500,000) is $1,750,000 less than the $5,250,000 lifetime exemption amount. Therefore, the estimated tentative tax is less than the applicable estate tax credit by $700,000, and Ric's estate would have $0 estate tax liability. It would be advisable however, for Vanessa to take advantage of the exemption portability provision in the law to claim Ric's unused $1,750,000 lifetime exemption, and add it to her $5,250,000 for a total of $7,000,000 exemption from estate taxes. At the estate tax rate of 40%, this transfer of $1,750,000 has a value of $700,000 as an extra applicable estate tax credit.

10.3 Trusts and Estate Planning

A trust is a legal entity created by a written agreement involving three parties. A trust is created to own property provided by a grantor(s), and managed by a trustee(s) for the benefit of a beneficiary(ies). The trust has legal ownership of the property and the beneficiaries have equitable or beneficial ownership interests. The trustee has a fiduciary level of responsibility to manage the trust assets for the exclusive benefit of the beneficiaries. This is a legal duty requiring utmost confidence, care and loyalty.

A trust can be created during the grantor's lifetime (called an *inter vivos* or living trust) or it can be created after the grantor's death, usually from instructions in the grantor's will. In this case, it falls in the broad category of testamentary trusts.

Trusts have many different characteristics. A trust can be revocable at any time by the grantor prior to incapacity or death, or a trust can be irrevocable meaning the grantor cannot take back the assets placed into the trust. Both revocable and irrevocable trusts transfer their assets under trust law, therefore these assets are not included in the probate estate of the grantor. Only the irrevocable trust transfers the grantor's assets permanently out of his/her control, thereby reducing the future size of the grantor's estate, and the corresponding estate tax.

10.3.1 Estate Planning Strategies Utilizing Trusts

Asset Management

One of the main reasons to create a trust is to manage assets. Some individuals do not have the ability, disposition, experience, or interest in managing sizeable portfolios of assets. Professional management in the form of a carefully-selected trustee can protect the trust's assets and ensure that they are used to carry out the intentions of the grantor.

Credit Protection

Another reason to create a trust is to protect the beneficiaries from having assets seized by creditors. The beneficiary does not have legal title to the trust's assets, so they are not available to satisfy creditors' claims. In addition, to protect from creditors the trust income payments to the beneficiaries, the grantor can include the spendthrift clause in the trust documents, which does not allow beneficiaries to pledge their trust income payments as collateral for their loans. Typically, the trustee is given discretionary authority not to distribute payments to beneficiaries if the payments are to be seized by creditors. The payments are to be distributed to an alternate beneficiary. For example, Ric Milford may want to transfer some assets to his son Michael as part of his estate plan implementation. Unfortunately, Michael has a known gambling problem, he is always behind in his bills, and creditors are always after him. Clearly, transferring assets directly to Michael makes no sense, as they will be soon seized by creditors. Ric however, can transfer the assets to a trust with a spendthrift clause for the benefit of Michael, and designate Michael's children as alternate beneficiaries. As long as Michael stays out of credit troubles, the trustee will be distributing payments from the trust to Michael. If Michael gets in to trouble again, the trustee will redirect the payments to Michael's children. This way, Ric can help his son, and at the same time ensure that his hard earned assets will not be completely wasted paying off gambling debts.

Avoiding Probate

Another very important use of a trust is to minimize assets transferring through probate, thereby avoiding the cost and public access to the nature and extent of a decedent's property passing through probate. You can create a revocable living trust and transfer virtually all of your assets to the legal ownership of the trust. You can appoint yourself as the trustee and the beneficiary, and at your death the trust will become irrevocable. Your assets will then transfer according to your instructions in the trust agreement, not through the probate process. This will not reduce or avoid estate taxes however, because you had control of the assets in the trust, thus these assets will have to be included in your gross estate.

Reducing Estate Taxes

When you transfer assets to an irrevocable trust, you give up control of these assets permanently therefore these assets will not be included in your gross estate. By transferring into an irrevocable trust income producing and/or fast appreciating assets, you can also reduce both income and transfer taxes, because both your assets and the future increases in the value of your assets will not end up in your estate. However, a transfer to an irrevocable living trust may be subject to gift taxes (Section 10.4). For example, ownership of an insurance policy on your life will cause the life insurance benefit to be included in your gross estate. However, you can transfer ownership of the life insurance policy to an irrevocable life insurance trust (ILIT), excluding the life insurance benefit from your gross estate and reducing your exposure to estate taxes, while the benefit going to the trust's beneficiary. Keep in mind however, that the cash value of the policy when transferred could be subject to a gift tax.

Dividing Asset Interests

A trust can be used to divide property into an income interest, which allows distributions to beneficiaries during the term of the trust, and a remainder interest, which determines who receives the trust's assets when it is terminated.

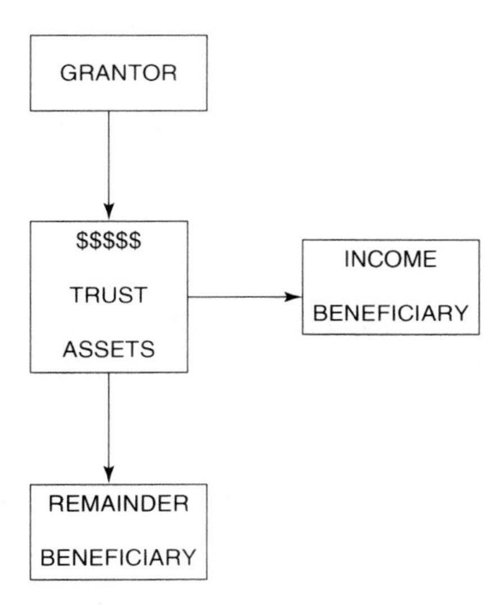

A frequently-used trust in estate planning is called a bypass or credit shelter trust. This can be created from instructions in your will and funded with up to $5,250,000 in estate assets. This amount would be subject to the estate tax but the tax would be offset by the applicable estate tax credit. The trust agreement can allow your surviving spouse to receive all of the income from the trust and to withdraw principal as needed. After the death of the surviving spouse, the trust's assets are distributed to others, usually children. These distributions are not subject to the estate tax. This trust is useful when you want to utilize your lifetime exemption (up to $5,250,000) from transfer taxes, control where your assets will go after your death, and provide income for your surviving spouse.

Another popular trust in estate planning is called a qualified terminable interest trust (QTIP). You can place assets into a QTIP trust instead of transferring them directly to your surviving spouse. The assets transferred to the QTIP qualify for the unlimited marital deduction therefore, the QTIP assets will not be subject to the estate tax until the death of your surviving spouse. While alive, your surviving spouse will be receiving all of the trust's income. You, the trust grantor will get to specify how the trust's assets are to be distributed after the death of your spouse. This can be very useful when you have a child or children from a prior marriage and want to protect their inheritance, while also providing lifetime income to your surviving spouse. You can use the QTIP trust if you have exhausted the lifetime exemption, which eliminates the option of using the bypass trust.

10.4 Gifts (Transfers during Life)

You don't have to pass away to transfer some or all of your assets to others. You may want to do so while you are still alive and around to enjoy seeing your assets improving the lives of others, like helping your children live a more comfortable life, or young students pay their tuition at your Alma Mater. For a transfer to be a gift, the transfer has to be voluntary and the donor has to intend to make the transfer. Also, the donor must be competent and the recipient or donee must be able to receive the gift. Finally the donor must fully part with the gift—no strings attached. If there is any remaining string attached to the gift, it is an incomplete gift.

Sometimes a gift may involve a partial transfer of value back to the donor. This is called "consideration," and the net difference between the value of the asset and the consideration is the value of the gift. As an example, you transfer a vacant lot worth $25,000 to a friend, but you require that friend to sign a promissory note payable to you for $15,000. The amount of your gift is the difference, $10,000.

A gift is always valued at the time of the transfer, and as is the case of valuing assets in an estate, some gifts are easy to value, e.g. cash, shares of stock, bonds, mutual funds, while others may require an independent appraisal.

10.4.1 The Federal Gift Tax

The federal government has imposed a transfer tax on gifts since 1932. Generally, the party liable for the gift tax is the donor. The gift tax only applies to gifts to other individuals. It does not apply to transfers to charities. Furthermore, transfers between spouses are not taxable, although there is a $136,000 annual limit on the amount which can be transferred to a non-US citizen spouse without gift tax consequences. Funds transferred for the support of minor children are also not subject to gift taxes.

Qualified Transfers

Transfers to others to pay for their medical costs or college tuition costs are not considered taxable gifts and they are called "qualified transfers." Therefore, if you want to help someone with medical bills not covered by insurance, you can do so by making payments directly to their medical service providers. The amount you can transfer is unlimited, and you will owe no gift tax as long as you make the payment directly to the doctor or hospital. A payment to the individual, so he/she could pay medical bills, will not be a qualified transfer, and it will be a taxable gift. The same rule applies to the other type of qualified transfer as well. You can pay an unlimited amount for others' college tuition, and as long as you pay directly to the educational institutions, the transfers will not be subjected to gift taxes.

The Annual Exclusion

For gift tax purposes, you can give up to $14,000 to another individual every year with no gift tax consequences. The nature of the gift must be such that the recipient can use it immediately. Note that this amount is adjusted each year to account for inflation. If you are so inclined, you can give up to $14,000 to any number of individuals during a year with no gift tax consequence. You and your spouse can combine to give $28,000 to any one or any number of individuals. This is called "gift splitting" and it also does not create a taxable gift. The annual exclusion is not cumulative, so if unused at the end of a year, the amount does not carry over.

The Lifetime Exemption

Recall from Section 10.2.1, That currently each individual has a $5,250,000 lifetime exemption from the gift and estate tax combined. This allows tax free transfers during life and at death to total $5,250,000 before a transfer tax is incurred. Amounts under the gift tax annual exclusion do not count toward the $5,250,000 lifetime exemption. Gifts which cannot be used immediately are called future interest gifts, and they do not qualify for the $14,000 annual exclusion. For example, suppose you choose to make an immediately usable gift of $100,000 to another person this year. The first $14,000 would fall under your annual exclusion and the remaining $86,000 would be part of your lifetime exemption, reducing it to $5,164,000. You would report the $86,000 on an annual gift tax return (Form 709), but no tax would be payable until you have used up the rest of your lifetime exemption. Cumulative gifts over $5,250,000 would incur gift tax at the current rate of 40%.

Each individual is entitled to the $5,250,000 lifetime exemption, so you and your spouse can combine your exemptions to make gift tax free substantial transfers of wealth during your lifetimes. Use of your lifetime gift tax exemptions however, reduces the amount of your estate tax exemptions.

10.4.2 Practical Application: Gift Tax Calculation

Ric Milford won $20,000,000 in the powerball lottery, and wants to share some of his good fortune with his beloved sister Teresa. Ric has made no previously taxable gifts, so he decides to gift Teresa $5,264,000 this year. The first $14,000 donated to Teresa fall under the annual exclusion per donee, so this amount is not taxable. The remaining $5,250,000 of the gift equals Ric's lifetime exemption and the gift tax is offset completely by the applicable credit amount, resulting in no gift tax for this very generous gift to his sister. By making this gift however, Ric will exhaust his lifetime exemption and his estate will be taxable.

Gift Tax Calculation for Ric Milford

Amount of the Gift	$5,264,000	
Annual Exclusion	($14,000)	
Taxable Amount	$5,250,000	
Tentative Tax	$2,045,800	[$345,800 + (0.40 * $4,250,000)]
Applicable Credit Amount	($2,045,800)	
Gift Tax	$0	

10.4.3 Adjusted Cost Basis and Holding Period for Gift Recipients

If at the date of the gift, the fair market value (FMV) of the gifted asset is greater than the donor's basis, then the donee basis equals the donor basis, and the holding period of the donor is "tacked on" the holding period of the donee for determining capital gains/losses when the donee sells the gifted asset. For example, Vanessa Milford's father had purchased a townhome 20 years ago for $40,000. He gifts the townhome to Vanessa this month, when its fair market value is $120,000.

Since FMV > Donor's basis ⇒
- Donee (Vanessa) basis = the Donor (father) basis = $40,000
- Donee (Vanessa) holding period includes the Donor's 20 years

If Vanessa was to sell the townhome 6 months later for $125,000 net of expenses, she would realize a long term capital gain of $85,000 ($125,000 − $40,000).

The situation is more complicated if at the date of the gift the fair market value of the gifted asset is smaller than the donor's basis. Then the donee basis and holding period are determined according to the double basis rule. For example, if Vanessa's father had purchased the townhome 20 years ago for $100,000, but at the date of the gift its value is only $70,000, then Vanessa's basis and holding period of the townhome will not be determined until she sells it 6 months later.

If Sale Price = $130,000 **Donor Basis = $100,000**	⇒ Donee Basis = Donor Basis = $100,000 Donor's Holding Period "Tacks On"	Long Term Capital Gain ⇒ LTCG = $30,000
If sale Price = $80,000	⇒ Donee Basis = Sale Price	⇒ No Gain or Loss
At gift FMV = $70,000 If Sale Price = $50,000	⇒ Donee Basis = FMV = $70,000 Donee's Holding Period starts at Gift date	Short Term Capital Loss ⇒ STCL = $20,000

When a gifted asset is sold and the donee does not know the donor's cost basis, the income tax treatment is to assume the basis is zero, thereby making the entire sales proceeds taxable income. Often, a better alternative to selling such gifted asset is to use it to make a charitable contribution, which allows the current fair market value to be used as an income tax deduction.

10.4.4 Gifting Strategies

If you have assets which are expected to appreciate a lot, you may want to gift them early on. This way you will not have to pay income taxes that would result from selling the assets on a later date. Furthermore, by gifting these assets early, they will grow in value out of your estate, reducing your estate taxes.

If you have assets that have already appreciated a lot since you acquired them, you may want to gift them to a charity, since there is no gift tax for charity donations. Furthermore, you may get an income tax deduction to offset taxable income.

If you have income producing assets, you may want to gift them to donees that are in the lowest marginal tax rate (MTR) for income taxation. They will get the most after tax benefit out of your gift.

You rarely want to gift assets at a loss. In other words, if you have investment assets with a smaller fair market value than your basis, you can sell them to realize the loss and get an income tax deduction. There is no loss deduction in the gift tax.

10.5 The Federal Generation-Skipping Transfer Tax

Yes, there's one more transfer tax system to be aware of if you want to skip the next younger generation and transfer assets directly to someone two generations younger than you are. Appropriately, this is called the generation-skipping transfer tax (GSTT), and it is designed to ensure that wealth transfers can't skip generations to avoid gift and/or estate taxation at each level. The tax rate for GSTT is currently fixed at 40%.

A "skip person" is a recipient who is two or more generations younger than the transferor. For non-family members the IRS defines a generation as 25 years. The transferor is placed at the middle of a 25-year generation based on age. In other words, a 75-year-old transferor's generation is assumed to be from age 62 ½ to 87 ½. The next younger generation is from age 62 ½ to 37 ½, and the first skip generation begins at age 37 ½ and extends to age 12 ½. A transfer to someone aged 12 ½ to 37 ½ would be potentially taxable under GSTT.

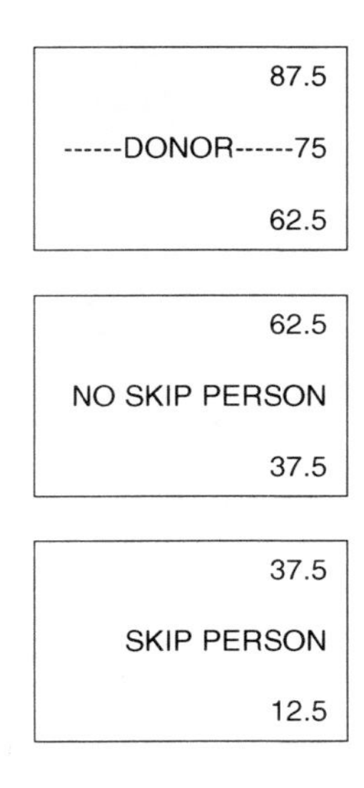

Age is not considered when determining whether or not a lineal family member is a skip person. The easiest example is grandparent (donor or transferor), child (no skip person) and grandchild (skip person). If the child dies before the grandchild, the grandchild moves up a generation and is not considered a skip person anymore. Any spouse, current or former, of the transferor is considered to be in the same generation as the transferor, no matter how young the spouse may be. A trust benefitting only a skip person or persons is also a skip person.

A direct skip is a transfer directly to a skip person, and the transferor is responsible for paying any GSTT. If the transfer is to terminate a trust which benefits a skip person, the trust is responsible for paying any GSTT. If the transfer is a distribution from a trust to a skip person, the recipient is responsible for the GSTT.

Similar to the gift tax, the GSTT has an annual exclusion of $14,000 for each skip person recipient as long as the asset transferred qualifies for present use. Gift splitting, as was discussed with the gift tax, is also available. Spouses can combine for an annual total exclusion of $28,000 to each skip person. Each individual also has a $5,250,000 lifetime and at death exemption from the gstt which results in the same estate tax credit equivalency. This is the same amount as the exemptions from the gift and estate taxes, but it is not in addition to the other exemptions. In other words, each person has $5,250,000 to be used for any combination of the three transfer tax systems.

The tax credit equivalency on all generation skipping transfers is automatically allocated in the order of the transfers unless the transferor or personal representative chooses another method.

10.5.1 Practical Application: Calculating the GSTT for the Milford Farm

Ric Milford's father is contemplating transferring the family farm to Ric. The family farm has been in the Milford family for many generations, and Ric will probably pass the farm to his son Michael. Grandpa Milford is thinking to go ahead and transfer the farm directly to his grandson Michael, to save Ric the trouble of having to transfer the farm to Michael in the future. The Milfords visited a Certified Financial Planner™ to help them estimate the amount of the generation-skipping transfer tax. The farm has a fair market value of $6,264,000 and Grandpa Milford has the entire $5,250,000 lifetime exemption available.

In order to calculate the GSTT, the financial planner has to deduct the transferor's $14,000 annual exclusion from the amount of the transfer. Therefore the remaining $6,250,000 transfer minus the $5,250,000 exemption leaves $1,000,000 taxable, which at a 40% tax rate produces a $400,000 GSTT.

GSTT Calculation for the Milfords

Transfer Amount	$6,264,000
Annual Exclusion	($14,000)
	$6,250,000
Exemption	($5,250,000)
GST Taxable Amount	$1,000,000
	* 40%
GSTT	$400,000

There is a second step in calculating the GSTT which involves the amount of the GSTT. Since that amount is paid by the transferor, it must also be subject to the gift tax. More taxes!

Gift Tax Calculation for Milfords' GSTT

Transfer Amount	$6,264,000	
GSTT	+ $400,000	
	$6,664,000	
Annual Exclusion	($14,000)	
Tentative Tax Base	$6,650,000	
Tentative Tax	$2,605,800	[$345,800 + (0.40 * $5,650,000)]
Gift Tax Applicable Credit	($2,045,800)	[$345,000 + (0.40 * $4,250,000)]
Gift Tax	$560,000	

In order to net the $6,264,000 farm to his grandson Michael, Grandpa Milford will need to pay $960,000 in transfer taxes ($400,000 GSTT + $560,000 Gift Tax).

Summary

As you now know, life-long estate planning is an important part of personal financial planning. The material in this chapter can help you preserve your assets and use them during your lifetime for the financial security and well-being of your family. The issues discussed are complex, involving multiple tax systems and estate-related laws enacted by each individual state. As you develop and refine your estate plan, it is vitally important for you to select a competent financial advisor who can involve other estate planning professionals as needed. The up-front costs of their advice are minor compared to the peace of mind and cost savings which can be achieved.

Review Questions

1. Ric Milford does not have a will. What are some of the potential consequences for his family if he dies intestate?

2. Ric has executed a power of attorney which grants Vanessa the authority to transact business on his behalf. He is under the impression that this replaces the need for a will. Is he correct or not?

3. One of the reasons Ric has avoided execution of a will is that he has heard that wills go through the probate process, which is not a good thing. What are the advantages and disadvantages of the probate process?

4. Ric and Vanessa own their home as joint tenants with right of survivorship. What will happen to ownership of the home upon Ric's death?

5. When Ric and Vanessa decide to meet with a Certified Financial Planner™ to begin their estate planning process, what will take place in the first step of the process?

6. What events in Ric and Vanessa's lives would call for a review of their estate plan?

7. Vanessa has fee simple ownership of a vehicle. How will this ownership transfer at her death?

8. What are the three parties to a trust and what are their respective duties and functions?

9. What does the term "irrevocable" indicate in a trust document?

10. Using the gift tax rules in effect for 2013, how can an individual avoid all gift tax consequences for paying a grandchild's college tuition expense of $22,000?

11. Ric wants to make sure that his son from his first marriage, Michael, receives an inheritance. He also wants to provide income for Vanessa during her lifetime. If Ric dies first and Vanessa remarries, how can Ric ensure that both of his intentions are carried out?

12. Vanessa has just received a $1,000,000 inheritance from the estate of her late grandmother. She wants to use $60,000 of her inheritance for a gift to her alma mater to repay the scholarship she received for her undergraduate education. What are the tax consequences of her gift if (a) she makes it during her lifetime, and (b) she designates it in her will?

13. How does the $5,250,000 lifetime exemption from estate and gift taxes relate to the applicable tax credit of $2,045,800?

14. Calculate the capital gain tax on the following assset, which was received from an estate and later sold. The long-term capital gains tax rate is 20%.

Value of asset when purchased by decedent:	$12,500
Value of asset on date of death	$20,000
Value of asset on date of sale	$24,000

15. An elderly lady (age 78) is considering a gift to the son of a close friend. The son is 39 years old. Is the son of her close friend a "skip person"? How did you determine your answer?

CHAPTER ELEVEN

The Legal and Regulatory Environment of Financial Planning

11.1 Introduction

There are thousands of rules and regulations applicable to financial planning and all of them, in one way or another, can be summarized in the Golden Rule: "Do unto others as you would have them do unto you." All aspects of the financial planning process are extensively regulated at the federal and state levels. This chapter introduces some of the laws, regulations, and regulatory agencies and the areas they govern, with particular emphasis at the federal level. Each of the individual states also imposes regulatory requirements, and some of these are noted too. Furthermore, each of the laws and acts mentioned are briefly summarized.

11.1.1 Consumer Protection Laws

The financial services industry includes products like securities, mutual funds, banking, insurance and pension funds, each of which is heavily regulated. Many of the rules and regulations were enacted in response to investment practices in the 1920s and 1930s which had eroded the public's confidence in the industry.

The Banking Act of 1933 (Glass Steagall Act) was enacted to separate investment banking from commercial banking. The motivation behind this act was to separate the risks of investment banking from insured, deposit-taking commercial banks. Prominent signage in bank lobbies and advertisements now contains words such as "investments are not bank deposits, not FDIC insured and may lose value." This is to alert and remind depositors that investment products are separate from bank deposits.

To address the failure of more than 9,000 commercial banks between 1930 and 1933, and the resulting losses to depositors prompted the Banking Act of 1933 to create the Federal Deposit Insurance Corporation (FDIC) as a temporary body. Its success in reducing bank failures and depositor losses prompted the Banking Act of 1935 to make the FDIC a permanent body. The FDIC protects bank depositors, but not the bank's shareholders, from loss when a bank fails. Each depositor is insured up to a maximum of $250,000 per type of account (individual, joint, trust) per bank. The FDIC covers the insured depositors in one of two ways: The first alternative is "purchase and assumption," in which the depositor's funds are transferred under FDIC supervision to another insured institution upon the failure of the depositor's original institution. The second method is for the FDIC to pay claims up to the insured limit to the depositors of the failed bank. Most often a bank failure results from problems on the asset side of the bank's balance sheet, principally from excessive losses in the loan and/or investment portfolios. The FDIC will take control of these assets and eventually sell them or transfer them to other parties to minimize its losses.

The FDIC uses regulator-provided risk-based assessments to assign risk categories to each insured bank based on bank capitalization and periodic bank examinations, which results in higher deposit insurance premiums for riskier institutions. The FDIC has the authority to adjust the premium percentages based on its funding requirements.

According to the FDIC, there have been 414 bank failures between 2008 and the end of 2011. The states with the most failures are Georgia, Florida, Illinois, California and Minnesota. The largest banking companies to fail were Washington Mutual, Inc. ($307 billion in assets) and IndyMac Bank ($32 billion in assets).

The Securities Act of 1933 regulates the issuance of new securities in the "primary market." The act requires firms that are about to issue securities to the public to provide investors with financial information (prospectus) about their securities, and it prohibits fraud in securities trading. This act defines an "accredited investor" as one who is financially sophisticated, has a substantial net worth and is experienced in financial matters. Clients who are qualified as accredited investors can make transactions in securities which are not subject to SEC registration (see below).

The Securities Exchange Act of 1934 regulates the "secondary market" where securities are traded. The act created the Securities and Exchange Commission (SEC), which has extensive authority to regulate the securities industry. Securities firms and self-regulatory organizations such as FINRA, NASAA and the major securities exchanges are also governed by the SEC. Securities firms are frequently referred to as "broker-dealers." Brokerage refers to handling securities transactions for clients, while the term "dealer" applies to transactions on behalf of the firm itself. Companies with publically-traded securities are required to file timely reports of financial information and significant events (such as a merger or the departure of a key executive).

The Investment Company Act of 1940 authorized the SEC to regulate mutual funds and other types of investment companies with required disclosure of investment policies, securities holdings and financial condition. Significantly, mutual funds contain a substantial portion of publically-held securities. Purchases of shares in funds must be preceded by a prospectus, which describes the fund's objectives, history, management, fees and securities holdings.

The Investment Advisers Act of 1940 required investment advisors to register with the SEC or a state. Notice the different spelling of advisers in the title of the act. See more about this act in section 11.1.2.

The Securities Investor Protection Act of 1970 established the Securities Investor Corporation (SIPC) to protect investors from the loss of their securities due to broker theft or the failure of a securities firm. Importantly, the physical possession of the securities is insured against loss, not the value of the securities. In other words, the SPIC does not insure investors against bad investment choices.

The Employee Retirement Income Security Act of 1974 (ERISA) was landmark legislation in the area of employer-provided retirement plans. ERISA involved the Internal Revenue Service and the Department of Labor in the administration of private plans. The basic purposes of the act were to protect covered workers with defined vesting schedules, require the plan sponsors to fund promised benefits and prevent discrimination in favor of "highly-compensated" employees. An important component of ERISA is the Pension Benefit Guaranty Corporation (PBGC), a federal agency empowered to take over the assets and liabilities of a failed pension plan and pay the plan's vested benefits to participants at retirement. Plan sponsors pay an annual premium to the PBGC, based on the number of plan participants and the level of funding each plan has in relation to promised benefits. Maximum benefit payments from the PBGC however, are limited to $4,653 per month in 2012.

The Insider Trading and Securities Fraud Enforcement Act of 1988 prohibited "insiders" from trading their "inside" information. Insider is anyone possessing information which is not available to the general public. For example, it is illegal for a corporate executive to purchase shares of the company he or she manages, just before the company announces an unexpected increase in quarterly profitability.

The Financial Services Modernization Act of 1999 (Gramm-Leach-Bliley Act) repealed the Banking Act of 1933 (Glass Steagall Act) by allowing financial holding companies to acquire investment and insurance companies, while at the same time owning commercial banks as separate subsidiaries.

In 2002 Congress passed the Sarbanes-Oxley Act (SOX) to improve standards for financial disclosures and internal controls in public companies. SOX established the Public Company Accounting Oversight Board (PCAOB) to oversee accounting firms in their roles as auditors. Senior executives, usually the CEO and the CFO, are assigned personal responsibility for the accuracy of financial reports with civil and criminal penalties for non-compliance. Additional public disclosures include off-balance sheet transactions and stock purchases/sales by senior company officers.

In 2010 the US Congress passed the Wall Street Reform and Consumer Protection Act (Dodd-Frank), a massive piece of legislation containing 849 pages, 16 titles and over 1,500 sections. The stated purpose of Dodd-Frank is "to promote the financial stability of the United States by improving accountability and transparency in the financial system, to end "too big to fail," to protect the American taxpayer by ending bailouts, to protect consumers from abusive financial services practices, and for other purposes."

Full implementation of the requirements of Dodd-Frank will take place over the next several years, and many of the provisions will affect the regulatory environment within which a financial planner works. Dodd-Frank creates many new regulatory agencies while it eliminates or combines existing agencies. The following sections apply to the financial planning process.

> Title IV, Regulation of Advisers to Hedge Funds and Others: Many provisions of the Investment Advisers Act of 1940 have been modified or are being studied for possible revision. Reporting requirements for investment advisor have been increased, and the definition of an "accredited investor" has been changed by excluding the value of a residence. The new definition applies to an individual (or married couple with joint ownership) who has an average net worth over the last four years of more than $1,000,000.
>
> Title V, Insurance: This section establishes a Federal Insurance Office within the Department of the Treasury. Its purpose is to monitor the insurance industry (except for health insurance) to identify potential problems which might contribute to an industry-wide crisis. Insurance has traditionally been regulated only at the state level.
>
> Title IX, Investor Protections and Improvements to the Regulation of Securities: The role of the Securities and Exchange Commission (SEC) and the relationships between broker dealers, investment advisors and customers have been revised. An Office of the Investor Advocate, an Investor Advisory Committee and an investor ombudsman are created within the SEC. In addition, the SEC is required to publish and enforce point-of-sale disclosure rules applicable to retail customers when they purchase investment securities.
>
> The SEC is also granted the authority to require a fiduciary level of care by broker-dealers to their customers. This provision is still under study, and full implementation will take place in the future.
>
> Other sections of Title IX deal with increased oversight of credit rating agencies, the asset-backed securitization process, public corporation accountability and executive compensation,

corporate governance, municipal securities and creation of a new Public Company Accounting Oversight Board.

Title X, Bureau of Consumer Financial Protection: This Section applies to consumer financial services and products as regulated by federal law through a newly established Bureau of Consumer Financial Protection (CFPB). A consumer advisory board has been established with a minimum of six members recommended by regional Federal Reserve Bank presidents. However, the bureau operates independently from the fed. The CFPB has rulemaking, supervisory, enforcement and other authorities, which transferred from seven other federal agencies. Inherited regulations include, among others, Federal Reserve Regulations B (Equal Credit Opportunity), C (Home Mortgage Disclosure), F (Fair Debt Collection Practices Act), M (Consumer Leasing), V (Fair Credit Reporting, X (Real Estate Settlement Procedures Act), Z (Truth in Lending) and DD (Truth in Savings). An initial goal of the CFPB is to review these and other regulations to find opportunities to update, modify or eliminate some of their provisions, consistent with its goal of protecting consumers and creating a fairer marketplace.

Title XIV, Mortgage Reform and Anti-Predatory Lending Act: This section defines the term "residential mortgage originator," establishes national underwriting standards for home loans, sets mortgage servicing procedures, and amends the Real Estate Settlement Procedures Act of 1974 (RESPA). Another provision deals with written property appraisals by certified or licensed appraisers. The secretary of the treasury has new duties under the Home Affordable Modification Program, which specifies procedures to assist homeowners in modifying the terms of existing home mortgage debt.

The Dodd-Frank Act will have a significant impact on the legal and regulatory framework in which a Financial Planner works. Various provisions of Dodd-Frank will be gradually implemented after required studies are completed and the final rules are developed. Accordingly, the responsible agencies and rules described in this section and the next are subject to changes which will become effective in the next couple of years.

11.1.2 Legal and Regulatory Requirements for Financial Planners

A financial planner already works in an intensely regulated environment which involves supervision and rules from both federal and state agencies. The principal federal regulator is the Securities and Exchange Commission (SEC), which supervises advisors under the Investment Advisers Act of 1940 (Act). Again notice the different spelling of advisers in the title of the act.

Traditionally, the term *securities* is reserved for stocks and bonds. But the act has a broad definition of securities which also includes, among others, notes, bank certificates of deposit, limited partnerships, some life insurance and annuity contracts, options and rights to purchase any of the above.

Also, the act defines an advisor as someone who (1) provides advice or issues reports on securities, and (2) is in the business of providing advice and/or reports on securities, and (3) provides these services for compensation. A person who meets these three definitions must register with the SEC if they have more than $100,000,000 in assets under management. Advisors with less than $100,000,000 in assets under management must register with state securities regulators.

Exception to SEC registration is granted to the following:

i) Banks which are not investment companies
ii) Broker-dealers/accountants/lawyers/teachers/engineers whose advice is only incidental to their profession
iii) Publishers of newspaper or magazine of regular circulation, and
iv) Advisors who only deal with US government securities.

Exemption to SEC registration is granted to the following Advisors if they:

i) had fewer than 15 clients the previous year
ii) advise only insurance companies
iii) do not deal with securities listed on national exchanges
iv) deal with clients from their state only.

Some provisions of the SEC regulations apply to state-registered advisors. For example, Section 206 of the act prevents illegal activities such as fraudulent or deceptive practices, insider trading, fee arrangements based on investment performance, assignment of advisory contracts without the client's permission and direct buying and selling transactions of securities between the advisor and client without disclosure in writing.

11.1.3 Registering with the SEC

A financial advisor who registers with the SEC becomes a registered investment advisor (RIA) upon initial electronic submission and approval of Form ADV, which has two parts. Part I requires the applicant to provide general background information, whether or not he or she has been convicted of any crimes and a description of the types of clients to which the advisor will provide account management services. Part II asks for more detailed information on specific services to be provided, fees to be charged, the applicant's experience in securities transactions, names of the applicant's associates in the securities business and in some instances a personal financial statement.

After initial registration as an RIA, there are six categories of on-going compliance responsibilities:

i) There are 17 record-keeping requirements ranging from journals and ledgers, record retention, disclosure brochures, operating policies and procedures, to a code of ethics with violations and penalties.
ii) The RIA must maintain a schedule of fees for services rendered and retain prior fee schedules. Except for managing client Assets in excess of $750,000 or where the RIA believes the client has a Net Worth in excess of $1,500,000, fees cannot be based on appreciation in the value of the client's assets.
iii) The RIA cannot transfer a client's contract to another advisor or practitioner without the express written consent of the client.
iv) The RIA cannot claim to be an "investment counsel" unless (1) his or her principal business is investment advising and (2) delivering investment supervision is a major part of that business. An advisor can claim to be a "registered investment financial advisor" but cannot use the letters RIA after his or her name on business cards or stationery, as it may provide the false impression of a certification.

v) The RIA is required to deliver a disclosure statement to all clients within 48 hours of executing a new investment agreement. This can be accomplished by providing the client a copy of Section II of Form ADV or by preparing a narrative statement covering 14 categories of information. Most RIAs will use Section II of Form ADV since the SEC recognizes this as adequate disclosure.
vi) The RIA must comply with the anti-fraud portion of the act. This makes it unlawful to deceive or defraud a client or potential client, prohibits the advisor from selling a security to or purchasing a security from a client without written disclosure.

SEC registration and compliance with its regulations imposes a fiduciary duty on the RIA to act in good faith and always put the interest of the client first. This also is part of the code of ethics under which a Certified Financial Planner™ must practice.

11.1.4 Required Licenses

In addition to professional certification and registration, one more important step is required. You must have a license to advise and offer securities and insurance products for sale. Insurance regulations are handled by each individual state and not by the federal government. Accordingly, a financial planner will have to meet the licensing requirements of a state insurance department or commissioner when any part of his/her financial planning practice involves recommendations or the sale of insurance products.

The National Association of Securities Dealers (formerly NASD, but now known as the Financial Industry Regulatory Authority, FINRA) handles all procedures for granting the various types of securities licenses. This includes licensing examinations, record-keeping and disciplinary actions. There are three general licenses held by most advisors and representatives.

A <u>Series 7 License (General Securities Representative</u>) allows the licensee to handle transactions in all types of securities. All registered representatives of broker-dealer firms must hold this license. The license is awarded to individuals who complete a six hour examination on a wide array of investment products including bonds, stocks, options, open and closed-end mutual funds and limited partnerships.

A <u>Series 6 is a Limited Investment Securities License</u>. It permits the licensee to handle mutual funds, unit investment trusts and variable annuities, often referred to as "packaged products."

A <u>Series 63 License, known as the Uniform Securities Agent License</u> is required by each state, and this is administered by the North American Securities Administrators Association (NASAA).

When securities licenses have been issued, they must be registered with and held by a broker-dealer. The broker-dealer will then supervise the activities of the licensee and receive a portion of the commission income generated. However, a registered investment advisor is not required to affiliate with a broker-dealer.

11.2 Business Law

The Principal-Agent-Client Relationship

One of your earliest personal finance encounters may have taken place when you decided to purchase vehicle insurance, which is often sold through agents who represent one or more insurance companies. That <u>agent</u> was empowered to represent an insurance company, which is the <u>principal</u>. You, as the purchaser of the policy issued by the principal, are the client. An agent acts for the principal and establishes a legal relationship between the principal and client.

The principal and agent form a mutual relationship which is supported by an agreement or written contract. The agency contract defines the authority granted to the agent, and it specifies the agent's duties to the principal, among which are diligence, loyalty, accountability and confidentiality. An agent can be held responsible for losses incurred by the principal for not upholding these duties.

An agent also has a duty to keep the principal informed of significant changes in the affairs of the client, particularly when the changes could harm the principal. An agent's knowledge of a client's personal or business bankruptcy is an example of information that the principal needs to know. An agent must avoid conflicts of interest by acting solely in the interest of the principal, which elevates the principal-agent relationship to the fiduciary level.

The principal has responsibilities to the agent which include compensation for services rendered, reimbursement to the agent for payments the agent makes on behalf of the principal and indemnification of the agent for losses incurred when the agent was acting under directions from the principal.

An agency agreement can be terminated at any time by mutual agreement of the parties. The principal can, with proper notice, cancel the authority given to the agent. The agent can also cancel the agency relationship by notifying the principal and renouncing the authority conveyed by the principal. Some negative events in the affairs of the agent will terminate the relationship. Examples are death, bankruptcy, incapacity or disloyalty.

Contracts

A contract is a legally enforceable exchange of promises between two or more parties that is legally enforceable. The promises are for the parties to perform or not to perform specified acts. There are several requirements which define a contract. Absence of these requirements can void a contract or make it unenforceable.

- Agreement: The parties mutually agree as evidenced by a clearly-stated offer by one party which is accepted by the other party. This offer and acceptance can be in writing or oral.
- Consideration: This is the exchange of value received for value given. The values exchanged do not have to be equal when the parties have executed the agreement freely. A contract is bilateral when each party promises value to the other. For example, you agree to sell my house and I agree to pay you a commission. A contract can also be unilateral as would be the case if I offered you a reward for finding my lost watch. You have no obligation to find the watch.
- Legal capacity: The parties must have legal standing to execute the agreement. A minor, mentally incompetent or intoxicated person cannot execute a legally binding agreement.
- Legality: An agreement to perform something that violates a statute or injures the public is not enforceable. An agreement to obstruct commerce or reduce competition will also not be enforceable. As an example, when an owner sells a business and the buyer seeks to prevent the former owner from becoming a competitor, often a non-compete agreement will be part of the transaction. That agreement cannot be so extensive as to prevent the former owner from earning a living. It may have a time and/or geographic limit and incorporate severance payments to the former owner, which would be enforceable.

- Genuine consent: Compliance with the terms in a contract must be voluntary and genuine. Issues such as mistakes, fraud, unintended misrepresentation, undue influence (where one of the parties has an unfair advantage over the other) or duress (threat of or forcing a party to agree) may void a contract.
- Form of the agreement: Some types of agreements must be in writing to be binding. For example, a contract to sell real estate must be in writing.
- Breach of contract: This occurs when one of the parties fails to perform their agreed-upon duties and the other party is injured. Frequent legal remedies are monetary damages, equitable remedies requiring the breaching party to perform, an injunction (a court order requiring the breaching party to perform or cease to perform an specific activity) or restitution (returning the consideration or comparable value to the injured party).

Dispute Resolution

When the parties to a contract cannot settle their differences on their own, a third party will need to be brought in to resolve the dispute. This can take the form of litigation, mediation or arbitration.

- Litigation involves the use of the civil court system, which is costly and takes an extensive amount of time. All other avenues of resolution should be exhausted before resorting to litigation.
- Mediation is a process in which the disputing parties agree to bring in an impartial third party (the "mediator") who will encourage communication between the parties and manage the process. Importantly, the mediator does not participate in the decisions made by the parties. If successful, this could resolve the problem and avoid litigation.
- Arbitration is a process in which the disputing parties agree to make their arguments to a disinterested person or persons who will then make a decision. Arbitration can be either binding or non-binding. Usually, the arbitration agreement is binding with limited appeal rights. A non-binding arbitration decision can then be taken to the courts for litigation.

Negotiable Instruments

You have used a Negotiable Instrument whenever you have written or received a check, since a check is the most prevalent form of negotiable instrument. Negotiable instruments are governed by Article 3 of the Uniform Commercial Code, which has been adopted by all states, with some modifications. A negotiable instrument is a written, unconditional promise or order to pay an amount of money which can be transferred by endorsement or delivery. Timing of the payment can be on demand or at a specific date, and the person or entity to receive payment can either be identified or described as "bearer."

An order to pay is a check or draft. There are three parties, you (the drawer of the check), your bank (the drawee, where your money is in an account) and the payee (the person or entity intended to receive payment). Remember the words on your check "Pay to the order of ...." A draft is similar, but the drawee may be an entity other than a bank.

After receipt of your check, the payee will either cash it, or transfer it to another party, or deposit it into an account. In any of these cases, the payee will endorse the check, indicating receipt or transfer of value. Endorsements can be "blank," which would allow another party to possess and negotiate the check, or "restrictive," such as "For deposit only" or "Pay to the order" of another person.

Another type of negotiable instrument is a promise to pay, such as a promissory note you would sign when you borrow money or acquire a bank certificate of deposit. You are promising to repay your loan according to the terms in the note. The bank which issued the certificate of deposit has promised to repay the funds at the maturity of the certificate.

Note the requirements for a negotiable instrument in the examples given: In writing, signed, order or promise to pay, specified amount of money, no conditions attached or other instructions, payable at a defined time or on demand and payable to the bearer or a specific payee.

11.3 Types of Business Entities

The three main forms of business organizations are sole proprietorships, partnerships and corporations. Other types include limited liability companies and joint ventures. All types have certain advantages and disadvantages, and the choice of a particular type of business organization depends on the individual owner needs. Factors to consider are difficulty and expense of formation, income tax treatments, liability to third parties, ability to transfer ownership, and ownership/management succession.

A sole proprietorship is unincorporated and it is owned and controlled by one person. For income taxation, a sole proprietorship is not a separate taxable entity, and operating results are reported on Schedule C of IRS Form 1040. The sole proprietor receives "self employment" active (or ordinary) Income, requiring payroll taxes (FICA) for both the employee and the employer's share. The sole proprietor is personally responsible for all of the proprietorship's debts, and ownership can be transferred easily. At death a sole proprietorship is dissolved.

Partnerships are unincorporated associations owned by two or more individuals. A partnership can be created informally with no required filing of documents. The partners can choose to be either a separate taxed entity or the partnership net income can be divided and reported by each partner. Each partner is personally liable for all of the partnership's debts. Ownership interests can be reassigned but a new owner can become a partner only with the consent of the other partners. When each of the partners has equal ownership status, this type of organization is a general partnership. Partnerships which have multiple levels of ownership are called limited partnerships. Creation of a limited partnership requires registration with the state. A general partner is personally responsible for the partnership's debts, and a limited partner has no liability. The general partner manages and controls the organization while the limited partners have no management role. As such, the general partner will have "self employment" active (or ordinary) income , requiring payroll taxes (FICA), while the limited partners will receive passive income, requiring no payroll taxes. As with a general partnership, an election can be made either to be taxed as a business entity or for the partners to report their shares of income on individual tax returns.

A limited liability company (LLC) is an unincorporated business form that limits the personal liability of its owners (called members). It also permits all the members to be involved in management and control of the business. The LLC is very versatile therefore it has a few advantages over a partnership. First, it can elect to be taxed as a sole proprietorship, partnership, C-corporation, or S-corporation, although typically LLCs tend to elect to be treated as partnerships for federal income tax purposes. Second, all members receive passive income, requiring no payroll taxes, unless they perform services for the business, in which case they receive "self employment" active income requiring payroll taxes (FICA). And third, all members have limited personal liability for the debts of the business. LLCs are governed by state laws which define the ways ownership interests can be transferred at the bankruptcy, death or withdrawal of a member.

Joint ventures are usually formed for short-term business ventures, while partnerships are long term in nature. Basic partnership principles govern the operation of joint ventures.

The third major category of business organization is a corporation. A corporation is an independent legal entity which is separate from its owners and employees. One can be created by filing articles of incorporation with the state government. Taxation is as a separate entity if the corporation is a "C-corporation." This results in double taxation as the business income is taxed first at the business level, and the dividends to shareholders are then taxed again at the individual level. However, the dividend income tax rate is currently lower than active (or ordinary) income tax rates. Owners (shareholders) who are employees of the entity receive also active (or ordinary) income, subject to payroll tax (FICA) withholding. Ownership shares can be freely exchanged. A board of directors elected by the shareholders governs the corporation.

Some corporations may elect to be treated as S-corporations for Income tax purposes if they have no more than 100 shareholders, who are US citizens, residents, or estates and trusts. In this case, the earnings of the corporation are passed through to the shareholders and each shareholder reports that passive income (no payroll taxes) individually. Owners (shareholders) who are employees of the entity receive also active (or ordinary) income, subject to payroll tax (FICA) withholding. The legal liability of the owners for the corporation's debts is limited, as is also the case for C-corporations.

Summary

The material in this chapter provides only a brief description of the legal and regulatory complexities affecting the financial planning profession. An individual who has earned the Certified Financial Planner™ designation is aware of the laws and rules, all of which are designed to promote the fiduciary standard of interaction between a financial planner or advisor and the client. A CFP certificant has continuing education course requirements, and much of the material covered in these courses is devoted to changes in the rules.

The changes mandated by the Dodd-Frank Act are extensive, and as they are enacted they will modify the terms of many of the existing rules and regulations.

Review Questions

1. What are the requirements to qualify someone as an "accredited investor," and what does this qualification mean to an investment advisor?

2. What is a "broker-dealer"?

3. What are the three requirements, according to the Investment Advisers Act of 1940, for someone being classified as an investment advisor?

4. What is the purpose of Form ADV?

5. In what types of transactions can a person holding a Series 7 securities license engage?

6. What two federal agencies are involved in regulating private retirement plans?

7. What are the advantages and disadvantages of operating a small business as a sole proprietorship?

8. What are the differences between a general partner and a limited partner?

9. Compare a limited partnership with a limited liability company.

10. What are the responsibilities of an agent to a principal?

11. What is consideration in the context of a contract?

12. What are the differences between mediation and arbitration?

13. What is a "negotiable instrument"?

CPSIA information can be obtained
at www.ICGtesting.com
Printed in the USA
FFOW04n1632250717
38145FF

9 781465 231376